Rubicon

Transition Year **English**

Hugh Holmes

MENTOR
BOOKS

1 Exploring Language

'Think of an essay as a collection of tweets, only joined together.'

2 Speaking Out: Speeches & Debating

Gerald sensed that more than just his reputation was riding on the success of the presentation.

3 Poetry: The Packsack of Invisible Keepsakes

" I hope you'll dump me . . I want to start writing poetry."

4 Short Fiction: The Truth that Didn't Happen

5 Drama: Life with the Dull Bits Cut Out

6 Film: The Most Beautiful Fraud in the World

At last, the movie goers were finally settled and relaxed. However, seconds later, Larry would realize the error of sitting between spooked buffalo and the exit door.

Mentor Books Ltd.,
43 Furze Road
Sandyford Industrial Estate
Dublin 18
Tel: +353 1 295 2112/2
Fax: +353 1 295 2114
e-mail: admin@mentorbooks.ie
www.mentorbooks.ie

A catalogue record for this book is available from the British Library

ISBN: 978-1-906623-79-1

Editor: Treasa O'Mahony
Cover, typesetting and design: Mary Byrne

Acknowledgements

The Publishers would like to thank the following for kind permission to reproduce material:
CartoonStock.com; Random House for 'Hotel Room 12th Floor' by Norman MacCaig, 'Leaning into the
Afternoons' by Pablo Neruda, *Muscles, Bicycles, Cigarettes* by Raymond Carver, and an extract from
The Lost Continent by Bill Bryson published by Secker & Warburg; The *Irish Independent* for 'Diary of
a Demented Mum'; New Island Publishing for 'The Boy Soprano' by Bernard Farrell and 'The Enamel
Jug' by Peter Jankwosky from *A Treasury of Sunday Miscellany* and an extract from *The Irish Male: His
Greatest Hits* by Joseph O'Connor; The *Irish Sunday Mirror* for 'Abused and Humiliated in the name of
Tourism' by Nick Owens; *The Sunday Times* for 'Who's Deprived Now' by India Knight and 'A Pioneering
New Way to Face up to Dyslexia' by AA Gill; The *Irish Daily Mail* for 'I am a Paddy: Ergo I Drink' by Peter
Cunningham; *Irish Times* for 'Seaside Society' by Conor Goodman; Faber & Faber for 'Mother of the
Groom' and 'Death of a Naturalist' by Seamus Heaney, 'I Am Very Bothered' by Simon Armitage,
'Lovebirds' by Jo Shapcott, 'Mushrooms' by Sylvia Plath and an extract from *Lord of the Flies* by William
Golding; Anvil Press for 'Stealing' by Carol Ann Duffy and 'The One Twenty Pub' by Wisława
Szymborska; the author and The Gallery Press, Oldcastle, County Meath for 'Lipstick' by Rosita Boland
from *Dissecting the Heart;* Bloodaxe Books for 'The Back Seat of My Mother's Car by Julia Copus,
'Weakness' by Aiden Nowlan and 'Blankets' by Ruth Fainlight; David Higham Associates for 'Prayer
Before Birth' by Louis MacNeice *The Destructers* by Graham Green and an extract from *Eats, Shoots
and Leaves* by Lynne Truss; Rogers, Coleridge & White Literary Agency for *The Trout* by Seán Ó Faoláin
(Copyright © Seán Ó Faoláin); Willy Russell and Casarotto Ramsay & Associates Ltd (© 1973 W.R. Ltd)
for Terraces by Willy Russell; Hodder UK for *The Conger Eel* and an extract from *The Wave* both by
Liam O'Flaherty; the Estate of Michael Hartnett c/o The Gallery Press for 'Death of an Irishwoman'.

The Publishers have made every effort to trace and acknowledge the holders of copyright for material
used in the book. In the event of a copyright holder having been omitted, the Publishers will come to a
suitable arrangement at the first opportunity.

All rights whatsoever in this play (Terraces by Willy Russell) are strictly reserved and application for
performance etc, must be made before rehearsal to Casarotto Ramsay & Associates Ltd., 7-12 Noel
Street, London W1F 8GQ. No performance may be given unless a licence has been obtained.

1 Exploring Language

> The limits of my language mean the limits of my world.
>
> Ludwig Wittgenstein, Austrian philosopher

'Think of an essay as a collection of tweets, only joined together.'

www.CartoonStock.com

Humorous Writing

Growing Up in Des Moines by Bill Bryson

In his travel book, *The Lost Continent*, Bill Bryson describes his journey around small towns in the United States in search of the 'real America'. This extract is taken from the opening of the book where the writer recalls his hometown: Des Moines, Iowa.

I come from Des Moines. Somebody had to.

When you come from Des Moines you either accept the fact without question and settle down with a local girl named Bobbi and get a job at the Firestone factory and live there for ever and ever, or you spend your adolescence moaning at length about what a dump it is and how you can't wait to get out, and then you settle down with a local girl named Bobbi and get a job at the Firestone factory and live there for ever and ever.

Hardly anyone ever leaves. This is because Des Moines is the most powerful hypnotic known to man. Outside town there is a big sign that says WELCOME TO DES MOINES. THIS IS WHAT DEATH IS LIKE. There isn't really. I just made that up. But the place does get a grip on you. People who have nothing to do with Des Moines drive in off the interstate, looking for gas or hamburgers, and stay for ever. There's a New Jersey couple up the street from my parents' house whom you see wandering around from time to time looking faintly puzzled but strangely serene. Everybody in Des Moines is strangely serene . . .

. . . When I was growing up I used to think that the best thing about coming from Des Moines was that it meant you didn't come from anywhere else in Iowa. By Iowa standards, Des Moines is a Mecca of cosmopolitanism, a dynamic hub of wealth and education, where people wear three piece suits and dark socks, often simultaneously. During the annual state high school basketball tournament, when the hayseeds from out in the state would flood into the city for a week, we used to accost them downtown and snidely offer to show them how to ride an escalator or negotiate a revolving door. This wasn't always so far from reality. My friend Stan, when he was about sixteen, had to go and stay with his cousin in some remote, dusty hamlet called Dog Water or Dunceville or some such improbable spot – the kind of place where if a dog gets run over by a truck everybody goes out to have a look at it. By the second week, delirious with boredom, Stan insisted that he and his cousin drive the fifty miles into the county town, Hooterville, and find something to do. They went bowling at an alley with warped lanes and chipped balls and afterwards had a chocolate soda and looked at a *Playboy* in a drugstore, and on the way home the cousin sighed with immense satisfaction and said, 'Gee thanks, Stan. That was the best time I ever had in my whole life!' It's true.

I had to drive to Minneapolis once, and I went on a back road just to see the country. But there was nothing to see. It's just flat and hot, and full of corn and soya beans and hogs. Every once in a while you come across a farm or some dead little town where the liveliest thing is the flies. I remember one long, shimmering stretch where I could see a couple of miles down the highway and there was a brown dot beside the road. As I got closer I saw it was a man sitting on a box by his front yard, in some six-house town with a name like Spigot or Urinal, watching my approach with inordinate interest. He watched me zip past and in the rear-view mirror I could see him still watching me going on down the road until at last I disappeared into a heat haze. The whole thing must have taken about five minutes. I wouldn't be surprised if even now he thinks of me from time to time.

- From *The Lost Continent* (adapted)

Questions

Exploring *Growing Up in Des Moines*

1. What do you think Bill Bryson is suggesting when he writes, 'I come from Des Moines. Somebody had to.'?

2. According to Bill Bryson, what is the most positive thing about growing up in Des Moines?

3. What is your impression of Des Moines from this extract?

4. Explain what the author means when he writes, 'By Iowa standards, Des Moines is a Mecca of cosmopolitanism, a dynamic hub of wealth and education.'

5. **(a)** Bill Bryson often exaggerates in this extract. In your copybook write down two examples of exaggeration you found in this text.
   (b) Why do you think Bryson uses exaggeration in this extract?
   (c) Apart from Bryson's use of exaggeration, do you find this extract amusing? Refer to the text in your answer.

Writers' Workshop

1. Write a composition entitled 'Where I'm From'. This could be an amusing piece, like *Growing Up in Des Moines*, or a more serious description of your area.

2. Imagine you are from Des Moines and you have just read this extract. Write a letter to Bill Bryson commenting on his portrayal of Des Moines.

Language Lesson: Anecdote

An anecdote is a brief account of an incident or event, often only a few lines long. Anecdotes are used to entertain a reader, create interest in an idea or to illustrate a point. Many authors use anecdotes to add colour and variety to a piece of writing.

In *Growing Up in Des Moines*, Bill Bryson includes a number of anecdotes to entertain the reader and to support his comments about Iowa. For example, Bryson recalls the time his friend Stan visited a relative in the country. Stan and his cousin went bowling and had a milkshake: nothing out of the ordinary happened. However, Stan's cousin declared, 'That was the best time I ever had in my whole life!' The story illustrates the idea that there was little to do in the area and provides a vision of a very dull place. It's also very amusing.

Using an anecdote is an excellent way to make a piece of writing lively, entertaining and more convincing.

Diary of a Demented Mum

The Wolverine is busy destroying her hair before school begins.

'Diary of a Demented Mum' is a regular column in the *Irish Independent* in which an unnamed mother describes her relationship with her teenage daughter – often with hilarious results.

Of late you've noticed a scorched odour hanging around the upstairs hallway as you dash out to work. The source, however, remains a mystery.

Then one morning you wake up with a stinking 'flu and pull a sickie. As you lie there snuffling and listening to *Morning Ireland*, the unmistakable odour of singed hair wafts through the open door of your bedroom.

Despite your high temperature, your peeling, blocked and streaming nose; despite the aches surging up and down your body you struggle from your bed of pain and set off to investigate. The Wolverine, you discover, is neither packing her schoolbag nor straightening her uniform prior to hurrying downstairs for a healthy bowl of porridge.

Far from it.

The uniform is still on the floor in a heap while the Wolverine is busy destroying her hair. The reason for the pungent scorched odour and the recent, puzzling deterioration of her mane of silky golden hair into a dry, straw-like tangle of frizzy split ends is now clear. She has invested in a hair-straightener.

She has wielded this rod of torture, secretly purchased with a Christmas voucher, against her increasingly exhausted tresses every single morning since the holidays, she reveals with pride. And some evenings. And prior to going out. And, eh, when she thought her hair looked a bit frizzy.

The temperature of some hair-straighteners can exceed 220°C, you lecture. This can significantly damage hair. Excessive heat can make the hair frizzy and when the Wolverine tries to control the new frizz by straightening the hair even more, she only damages it further, causing yet more frizzing, thus requiring further straightening. 'Oh God,' she cries, dramatically clutching her temples, 'Too much information.'

'Stop burning your hair to a crisp and go down for your breakfast,' you order.

'Oh,' she says insouciantly, she's given up breakfast. 'Breakfast makes you fat.'

'No it doesn't,' you argue, panicked. 'Pfft, yes it does,' says the Wolverine dismissively.

Anyway, she's tired of the hair-straightener. It takes forever. She's decided to start back-combing her hair instead. It boosts volume, she says in a professional tone.

'But back-combing is terrible for your hair' you protest.

'Too bad,' she says. 'And Ma, please don't print out loads of newspaper articles about back-combing. No offence, like, but it's too much trouble to read them.'

You stagger off feeling an overwhelming surge of home-sickness for the days when you were the daughter and Mum was the Mum. For the days when you didn't have to be responsible for everyone and everything. Bring me home, Mum, you think hopelessly. I swear I'll be good.

- From the *Irish Independent*, 2011

Glossary

insouciantly: acting in a light-hearted, carefree or breezy manner.

Questions

Exploring *Diary of a Demented Mum*

1. What does the mother 'lecture' her daughter about in this article?
2. Why does the daughter decide to backcomb her hair?
3. Why do you think the writer refers to her daughter as 'the Wolverine'?
4. Do you think the article suggests a typical mother-daughter relationship? Explain your answer.
5. What does the final paragraph reveal about the writer?
6. Describe the tone of this article. Support your answer by referring to the text.
7. Do you find *Diary of a Demented Mum* amusing? Explain your answer.
8. The article is written in the second person ('you'). Why do you think the writer chose to avoid the first person ('I')?

Writers' Workshop

Write an article entitled *Diary of a Demented Teen*, in which you give a snapshot of life as a teenager.

Language Lesson: Mock-serious tone

In *Diary of a Demented Mum*, the writer uses a mock-serious tone. This means that the writer treats a ridiculous situation as if it was very serious. In this article, a moody teenager's use of a hair-straightener is discussed as if it was something grave, almost life threatening. For example: 'She has wielded this rod of torture, … every single morning since the holidays.' The writer continues this tone throughout: 'You stagger off feeling an overwhelming surge of home-sickness for the days when you were the daughter and Mum was the Mum.' The reader understands that the incident is not really that serious, but the mock-serious tone allows the writer to poke fun at her daughter and laugh at herself.

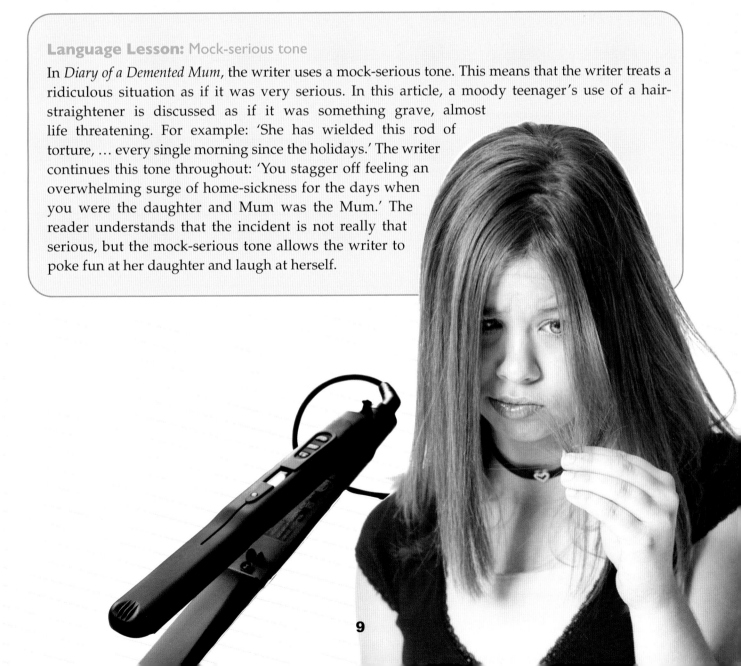

Cowboys and Engines by Joseph O'Connor

Joseph O'Connor is the author of novels, plays, short stories and travel articles. This extract is taken from his collection of comic writings: *The Irish Male: His Greatest Hits*.

Reader, there are some weeks you will never forget in your life and late last year I had one of those. I am talking about the week I finally did my driving test! Although I had attained the age of thirty-two, I had never attempted the test before, even though I did have some lessons once as a student, in an establishment that I seem to recall was called the Saddam Hussein School of Motoring ('Death Before Yielding').

This time around I went to a better school. My teacher, Eamon from the Irish School of Motoring, was a pleasant man with the patience of Sisyphus, the courage of Hercules and the wisdom of Solomon. Through many hours together we studied the intricacies of the three-point turn, the hill start and the smooth right-lane manoeuvre, all of which, three months ago, I would have thought were line-dancing steps. The man's persistence in the face of utter frustration was nothing short of heroic. Again and again, he would repeat the order 'mirror, signal, manoeuvre', like a maharishi chanting a mantra, until even I got the message. Mirror, signal, manoeuvre. I am starting to say it in my sleep.

Another problem was keeping my distance. I don't know why, but this was a problem for me. Youarenotsupposedtodrivelikethis. You are supposed to drive in a nicely spaced-out manner. That's 'nicely spaced out' in terms of your proximity to the next vehicle, by the way, not nicely spaced out on drugs or cheap drink . . .

. . . Despite Eamon's many valiant efforts, the Friday before the test I was still in serious need of improvement. So The Brother, who has been driving since he was a gossoon, admirably stepped into the breach and gave me a few last-minute lessons. He is feeling much better now the blood pressure has returned to normal and the waking up in the middle of the night screaming in abject terror has subsided a little. His last piece of advice to me, as he stepped gibbering out of the car the day before the test, was the following, 'Would you not get out the clippers and do your nasal hair, no? You don't want Yer Man the tester to punt his lunch all over yeh.'

Thus, fully prepared, I turned up to take my test on Monday afternoon. Part One was an oral exam on the rules of the road.

'How would you know a zebra crossing at night?' the instructor enquired. At first I thought this was a joke. I frantically search my subconscious for the punch line. Is it: because he wanted to get to the other side? No. What is it again? Oh, yes. Flashing amber lights. A few more easy-peasy questions followed to which I knew most of the answers. Himself then produced a list of road signs and invited me to identify them. No problem.

Out to the car park, where we leapt into the motor and off we went. The first thing that happened was a pothole so big I got a large number of air miles for successfully negotiating it. Then onwards. A deft right, a couple of lively lefts, the gear changes as smooth as a politician's lies. So far, so good, as the optimist said plummeting past the fifteenth-storey of a sixteen-storey building.

The most disconcerting thing about the driving test is not the actual driving itself, but the fact that the tester does not talk to you, except to tell you what to do. There is no chitchat, no light laughter, no commenting on the beauty of passing a town or the desirability of the indigenous peoples of that parish. . . . . . . Nothing. Zilch. Your tester, actually, is not *allowed* to talk to you. You are thus driving along for over half an hour with a person who is staring intensely at you without ever uttering one single social syllable. It is like being married, I suppose.

Anyway, twenty minutes in and things were going fine. I had reversed around the corner with the grace of … something very graceful. I had demonstrated the hand signals you use to other motorists – or, at least, the polite ones. Everything was groovy and I was definitely in with a fighting chance of passing this test. And then … we were just about to turn off the main road and into an estate when, suddenly, I saw this drunken hairy-looking gom come bounding and staggering out into the road, where, having reached the exact centre, he stopped and gawped at me. Just stopped. He started to beckon. Sheer terror wrapped its cold hand around my heart. I ignored him. He stared at me and beckoned harder. After some moments he sashayed to the side of the road where he stood and watched as I completed my right-hand turn. I couldn't help feeling he was an actor employed by the Department of the Environment for this purpose.

Back to the test centre, where I was invited to park the car. Then, I was requested to follow the tester into the building, where he would tell me the result of my examination. . . . I was so nervous I would cheerfully take a chomp out of a teacup. He sat at a desk. He scribbled a note. He turned. He looked up at me. He didn't smile. Then he said I passed! I couldn't believe it. I sprang out into the crisp winter evening, a new man, a grown-up, a driver, waving my certificate of competency in the air, a banner of self-fulfilment! Mirror, signal, manoeuvre. Mirror, signal, manoeuvre. I will never be the same again.

- From *The Irish Male: His Greatest Hits* (adapted)

Glossary

Sisyphus: a Greek mythological figure who was condemned to continually push a boulder to the top of a hill for eternity

Hercules: a Greek mythological figure famed for his incredible strength

Solomon: a biblical King of Israel famed for his great wisdom

maharishi: a Hindu holy man or religious teacher

mantra: a repeated phrase characteristic of Buddhism or Hinduism

gossoon: a young boy

Exploring *Cowboys and Engines*

1. **(a)** What age was Joseph O'Connor when he finally sat his driving test?
   (b) Describe his early experiences of driving during his student years.
2. What phrase did Eamon from the Irish School of Motoring continually repeat?
3. According to Joseph O'Connor, how was his brother affected after giving him driving lessons?
4. **(a)** Other than the example in Question 3, find two examples where the writer uses exaggeration.
   (b) Why do you think the writer exaggerates in each case?
   (c) Find two other examples of humorous phrases in the text and explain why you found these phrases amusing.
5. **(a)** What was the most disconcerting aspect of the driving test for Joseph O'Connor?
   (b) Do you think he describes this well? Explain your viewpoint.
6. Describe the writer's tone in this piece.

In *Cowboys and Engines* Joseph O'Connor describes overcoming a challenge in life. Write about a memory you have of facing a difficult obstacle. Your piece may be light-hearted and/or serious.

Language Lesson: Hyperbole (exaggeration)

Hyperbole is another word for exaggeration. Writers often exaggerate intentionally to emphasise an idea, e.g. **We had to wait an eternity in the queue.** This is not literally true, but it stresses the idea that it was a long wait. Hyperbole is also used for comic effect, as in *Cowboys and Engines*.

Joseph O'Connor uses hyperbole throughout this extract. For example he describes his first driving school as the 'Saddam Hussein School of Motoring ('Death Before Yielding').' This is clearly untrue and exaggerates how poor the driving school actually was. However, it is very amusing for the reader.

O'Connor again uses hyperbole when he describes the effect his driving had on his brother: 'He is feeling much better now the blood pressure has returned to normal and the waking up in the middle of the night screaming in abject terror has subsided a little.' Although this is a wild exaggeration, the idea is hilarious and allows the writer to poke fun at himself.

Language Lesson: Comic subject matter

Humorous writing usually involves writers laughing at themselves, poking fun at others or describing amusing situations. Joseph O'Connor does all three in *Cowboy and Engines*.

- **Laughs at himself:** O'Connor is keen to show that he is a terrible driver and also jokes about his physical appearance: '"Would you not get out the clippers and do your nasal hair, no? You don't want Yer Man the tester to punt his lunch all over yeh."'
- **Pokes fun at others:** The writer refers to his first driving school as the 'Saddam Hussein School of Motoring ('Death Before Yielding').' The joke is harmless as he doesn't actually name the driving school.
- **Amusing situation:** The driving tester's first question, 'How would you know a zebra crossing at night?', leads to a funny misunderstanding that sees O'Connor treating the question like a joke: 'Is it: because he wanted to get to the other side?'

Who's Deprived Now? by India Knight

India Knight is a journalist for The Sunday Times. *She often writes about current social issues facing society. In this article she explores the modern-day problem of violent crime.*

In the week when the word 'yob' was banned by Scotland Yard because it might 'alienate' teenagers and injure their tender feelings (oh boo hoo), Stevens Nyembo-Ya-Muteba, 40, was murdered by a gang of 'youths' outside his flat in East London.

Stevens, a married father of two little girls, was an immigrant from the Democratic Republic of Congo to Britain, where he held down two jobs – delivering food for Tesco during the day, night portering at a restaurant in the evenings – to pay for his education. He was in the third year of a maths and finance degree at a local university having turned down a place at Cambridge so as to stay closer to home. A 17-year-old 'youth' has been charged with his murder.

Stevens lost his life because he had had the temerity to ask the gang to keep the noise down after they broke into the communal area of the council estate where he lived. It was about 10pm. 'Some of us have work in the morning,' he'd reportedly said which, as rebukes go, is both polite and mild. He was stabbed for his pains and left to bleed to death on a stairwell.

It has since emerged that Stevens and other residents had repeatedly urged the police and the council to do something about the appalling goings-on at the estate. 'Prostitutes, smackheads, people having sex on the stairs,' one resident said. Another mentioned gangs of youths congregating in stairwells, taking drugs, urinating and trying to start fires. 'The police and the council had been aware of it all for some time,' a relative of Stevens said last week.

I used to live in this part of London. There were needles in the local park and crack-smoking paraphernalia littered the pavements. We were once woken in the night by two dozen armed police who explained that there had been a burglary and that the burglars, who had guns, had taken refuge on our roof.

This in an area, by the way, which was last week described by a London newspaper as up-and-coming and made to sound rather charming and cosmopolitan, with bars and cafes open until 5am. (I rather wonder who the paper thinks goes drinking at 5am. Schoolteachers? Yummy mummies? Or – here's a thought – a feral underclass celebrating the night's pickings?) It made no mention of the gun crime, the stabbings, the drugs or the desperation.

What is especially depressing about this whole depressing story, which took place in a depressed area full of depressed people doing depressing things, is that I imagine Stevens himself knew a thing or two about deprivation; and that what he knew would put his assailants' poxy little gripes to shame. Originally from Kinshasa, which is a horrible city in a grim country, I don't expect the offer of a place at Cambridge exactly fell into his lap. 'I believed in myself and got what I wanted,' he once told his college newsletter.

There are unsettling moments when I feel myself turning very conservative, and this is one of them. What's with the pathetic, weedy nonsense from Scotland Yard about hurting yobs' feelings, when stories such as Stevens' have, shamefully, become commonplace? Who cares about their feelings? I don't. I couldn't care less. I don't care how hard their lives are: I don't expect Stevens' life in Kinshasa was much of a picnic either but at least he was doing his best to better himself to make a new life for his family. And I am so tired of the stupid notion (held by me for decades) that gangs of hoodies are all gigantically deprived and thus need our pity, love and support, rather than our approbation. What they need, actually, is to be locked up.

Deprivation is relative: none of them is starving, all of them are clothed and all of them have access to free education. Besides, one of the yobs arrested in connection with Stevens' murder is, if you please, the son of a social worker, which doesn't quite constitute the frontline of ghettohood.

The gangs that periodically terrorise my new extremely salubrious, picture-postcard corner of north London aren't 'deprived' in any material sense that I can understand, either – not when they are wearing several hundred pounds' worth of designer clothing. They are certainly emotionally deprived to which the only solution is first-rate education – starting with nursery and, in some cases, psychotherapy from the age of five.

That is a political point. The broader social point is that the killing in East London is the merest tip of a deformed, monstrous iceberg. We are all, wherever we live, at the mercy of marauding gangs of underclass yobs, intent on damage, and there seems to be little that anyone can do about it (which is why I'm sounding so cross. I'd have been less cross 10 years ago, and hardly cross at all 20 years ago, but the crossness escalates with every year that passes because the problem gets worse and nothing happens).

I was recently told by a representative from my local Safer Neighbourhood Team that its powers were somewhat limited: it could ask gangs of boys what they were doing lurking in residential areas at 2am, but since it was not legally allowed to make physical contact with them, it could not actually remove them if vocal persuasion failed.

Besides, the representative said mournfully, they're often on bikes, which means they move too fast. As for Asbos: not terribly helpful when in some circles an Asbo is a badge of honour. I mean, really: someone's having a laugh and it's not you or me.

Being frightened in the street and even in our own homes – feeling scared to intervene when yobs are behaving badly for fear of one's own safety – has become the norm in this country. We moan about it in the same way that we moan about leaves on the line or automated telephone systems: it's just everyday life.

You have to prepare yourself for the worst before opening the local newspaper, because its tally of crimes makes you come over all agoraphobic. I used to be absolutely appalled by gated communities – the super-rich making themselves safe because they can afford to. These days I grudgingly see the point. And that feels profoundly demoralising.   - From *The Sunday Times*, 2006 (adapted)

Questions

Exploring *Who's Deprived Now?*

1. Describe what happened to Stevens Nyembo-Ya-Muteba.
2. **(a)** What is the overall point India Knight is making in this article?
   (b) Do you agree with her point of view? Why/why not?
3. Describe the tone of the opening sentence.
4. How does India Knight encourage us to sympathise with the victim and his family?
5. **(a)** Find an example of repetition in this article.
   (b) What effect does her use of repetition have on the reader?
6. The writer uses rhetorical questions successfully in this article. Find two examples of this.
7. Read the article's concluding paragraph again. What does Knight find 'profoundly demoralising'?
8. India Knight's opinions are strongly expressed in this article. Find two phrases in it that you feel are particularly powerful and explain why you find theses phrases striking.
9. This article explores the problem of criminality in London. Do you feel the issues raised here are relevant in an Irish context? Explain your answer.
10. This article uses a number of interesting words. Using a dictionary, find the meanings of the following words: temerity, rebuke, deprivation, approbation, salubrious, marauding.

Writers' Workshop

Write an article for a newspaper giving your views on how society should deal with the problem of violent crime.

Language Lesson: Illustration (examples)

An illustration is an example offered by a writer to support an idea. Writers may illustrate their points using a variety of evidence such as: facts, statistics, the views of experts or personal anecdotes.

In *Who's Deprived Now?* India Knight draws on her own experiences throughout the article to support her viewpoint: 'I used to live in East London…We were once woken in the night by two dozen armed police who explained that there had been a burglary and that the burglars, who had guns, had taken refuge on our roof.' This example strengthens Knight's assertion that violence touches many of our lives.

She also uses the sad case of Stevens Nyembo-Ya-Muteba's murder and information from a local community worker, as evidence of a violent society.

India Knight's views on the violence of modern society are strengthened by her use of illustration. The examples she gives make this a compelling piece of writing.

Abused and Humiliated ... in the Name of Tourism by Nick Owens

This article from the Irish Sunday Mirror discusses the mistreatment of performing monkeys in Jakarta, Indonesia. The writer makes a strong case against the practice.

Fear and pain etched across his face, a little monkey cries out as he grabs helplessly at a metal chain biting into his neck. As he lets out a high-pitched scream, a gang of men force him to stand up straight, laughing as they tighten the chain.

It is just one of a series of shocking images of the hell the monkeys endure in the slums of Jakarta in Indonesia, where they are forced to walk upright and wear costumes ... all in the name of entertainment.

An *Irish Sunday Mirror* investigation discovered the monkeys are also made to wear masks, hats and glasses to catch the eye of passing tourists. If a visitor stops, the monkey is ordered by its owner to walk on his hands, sit on toy rocking horses or ride bicycles in the hope the tourist will hand over some loose change.

Other creatures are forced to simply beg. On one Jakarta street, a monkey was found wearing a doll's head mask, her suckling infant clinging to her as she begged for money at the side of a busy road. Disturbing images were passed to us by the Jakarta Animal Aid Network (JAAN), which went undercover to expose the cruelty the monkeys endure.

Their torment starts deep in the forests of Sumatra where the macaques, an endangered species of monkey, live. Teams of poachers use sickening methods to trap them. The most popular one is to shoot the mother and then prise the clinging baby off her. Baby macaques are preferred as they have a longer life as performers. The poachers are paid €2 for each monkey by dealers, who sell them on to street 'entertainers' in Jakarta for €5 each.

It's here the torture really begins. The monkeys are hung upside down so they learn how to walk upright. Chains are then clamped around their necks and they have to stand up straight or be punished.

The monkeys are starved and only fed when they obey to make sure they learn quickly. The highly-social primates are forced to live inside cramped wooden crates and can't interact with each other, leading them to become deeply disturbed.

After being 'trained' they are taken to tourist spots to 'work'. Our revelations will put pressure on the Indonesian authorities to take action. But the illegal animal trade is a multi-million-dollar business. Femke Den Haas of JAAN said: 'It is pitiful to watch how these monkeys dragged from the wild are tortured and condemned to a life of hell.' Sarah Kite, of the Union for the Abolition of Vivisection, said: 'Indonesia must act now.'

- Irish Sunday Mirror, 2011

Questions

Exploring *Abused and Humiliated … in the Name of Tourism*

1. How do the monkeys beg from tourists?
2. How much are the poachers paid for each monkey they capture?
3. Describe the torturous training methods the monkey handlers use.
4. **(a)** The journalist, Nick Owens, quotes experts or authoritative sources in this article. Write down two examples of this.
   (b) Why do you think the journalist includes these quotations?
5. **(a)** Emotive language stirs the reader's emotions or sensationalises a topic (see Language Lesson below). Find three sentences from this article that contain emotive language.
   (b) Rewrite these sentences, replacing the emotive words with less sensational or neutral phrases.
   (c) In what way do the changes you made in (b) alter the effect of the sentences?
6. What effect does the image accompanying the article have on the reader?

Writers' Workshop

Imagine you work for the Jakarta Animal Aid Network. Write an information brochure for tourists providing advice about this issue.

Language Lesson: Emotive Language

Language that stirs the emotions is known as **emotive language**. Look at the following examples of neutral language and the emotive equivalent:

Neutral	Emotive
A group of youths waited outside the school	A delinquent mob was seen loitering outside the school
Community groups express concern over cutbacks	Savage cuts threaten community groups
Gardaí arrested the men last night	The gardaí rounded up the thugs last night

Emotive language is a common feature of tabloid newspapers. The article on the previous page is taken from a tabloid, the *Irish Sunday Mirror*.

This type of language often sensationalises an idea. This means it adds drama and excitement to a topic. The treatment of the monkeys in Nick Owens' article is made more dramatic by his choice of words.

Emotive language also reveals the attitude of the writer. If an article is seen to represent one side of a debate it is often called **biased**. Emotive language often adds bias to a piece of writing. From the way he writes, it is clear how Nick Owens feels about the treatment of the monkeys in Jakarta.

The Noble Art

In this article, the writer uses a variety of strategies to condemn the sport of boxing.

They call it the noble art. But what is noble about two men slugging away at each other until one of them is unconscious on the canvas while hundreds of people, safe in their seats, roar and shriek for blood, and a few others, without lifting a fist, can pour money into their bank deposits?

If you have ever seen a boxer after a bout, you would never call boxing noble. You must have seen the close-ups on television, those bleary half-shut eyes, those bruised thickened lips, that puffy battered flesh, the blood pouring from cuts around the eyes. It is degrading to think that a man has been prepared to put up with that kind of punishment in the name of sport and as a means of making a living. It is degrading to think that it was another man who inflicted that pain and punishment on him for the same reasons.

But it goes beyond a battered face and a loss of dignity. Recently [in 1986], the boxer Steve Watt died in the ring, and pressure rose again for the sport to be banned. And rightly so. What kind of sport is it that ends in a man's death? The chief medical officer for the British Boxing Board of Control has pointed out, that since 1948, there have only been twelve deaths within the game and has said, 'If only every sport could be as safe as that.'

It is true that people die in motor racing or climbing mountains. But there is a difference. In those sports, people are pitting themselves against speed or natural hazards. They are not being pounded to death by their fellow men for the entertainment of the masses. In any case, it's not simply a case of deaths. How many boxers have had to retire into a premature senile old age because of brain damage? A recent televised film on Muhammad Ali was shocking. Someone who had once been a vital quip-a-minute young man became a bewildered inarticulate zombie. Constantly being beaten around the head by men determined to knock you out is bound to have some effect.

And there is evidence to prove it. The British Medical Association Working Party on boxing has stated that x-ray brain scanning shows beyond doubt that permanent brain damage commonly occurs in men who box. Doctors may differ in their opinion, but the fact that the BMA has this kind of evidence and is campaigning to have boxing banned must carry a lot of weight.

It's not just the dangers of boxing itself that cause concern. It is also the whole atmosphere that surrounds it. That crowds of people – men and women – can cheer and get excited at the sight of two men doing their best to hurt and damage each other, is sickening. It is uncivilised. It is little better than the Roman gladiatorial fights to the death which history and society condemned long ago.

It has been argued in favour of boxing that it is one of the few ways in which 'a working-class lad' can achieve fame and fortune. But for how many is this true? One in a million? More typical is the case of Randy Turpin, once a world champion, who ended up a drunk and practically destitute, and finally committed suicide.

No, it's not the boxers who make the money, it's the promoters. With their betting and big deals, and Mafia organisations, they're the ones who go laughing all the way to the bank. When one of their boxers is finished, his brains beaten to a pulp, they drop him without a backward glance and seize on someone else to exploit.

'What a piece of work is man!' says Shakespeare in *Hamlet*, 'How noble in reason! how infinite in faculty! in form, in moving, how express and admirable! in action how like an angel! in apprehension how like a god! the beauty of the world! the paragon of animals!'

The next time you see a boxing match on television, with two exhausted men, faces bruised and bloodied, hanging on to each other because their legs are giving way, being jeered at by the crowd and urged on to show them some action, think of that. Do boxers live up to this view of what man is or ought to be? There is more dignity in sweeping roads.

Anonymous

Questions

Exploring *The Noble Art*

1. In your own words, summarise the author's view on boxing.
2. How is boxing portrayed in the second paragraph?
3. According to the author, what does the story of Muhammad Ali tell us about boxing?
4. (a) The author refers to the chief medical officer of the British Boxing Board of Control. What is the chief medical officer's view of the dangers of boxing?
   (b) How does the author respond to this viewpoint?
5. What scientific evidence is offered in this article to suggest that boxing is dangerous?
6. (a) Why do you think the author makes a comparison between boxing and Roman gladiatorial fights?
   (b) Do you feel that this is a fair comparison? Explain your viewpoint.
7. Aside from the physical dangers, what else is wrong with boxing according to the article?
8. (a) The writer makes use of emotive language. Find two examples of this.
   (b) Why do you think the writer uses this type of language?
9. Do you feel the quotation from *Hamlet* helps to persuade the reader. Explain your answer.
10. Do you agree with the writer's viewpoint? Why/Why not?

Writers' Workshop

Write an article in which you praise a sport, pastime or hobby that you feel is worthwhile.

Language Lesson: Rhetorical Questions

A rhetorical question is one in which the answer is implied. It is used:
- to persuade readers that a particular point of view is correct
- to emphasise a point
- to wrap up an argument.

In *The Noble Art*, rhetorical questions are used to great effect. For example the author writes, 'What kind of sport is it that ends in a man's death?' Here the writer wants to stress the dangerous nature of boxing and encourages the reader to dismiss the sport. The statement is framed as a question to add emphasis.

Rhetorical questions imply the answer and reflect the viewpoint of the author. In *The Noble Art*, Hamlet's view of humanity is quoted; the point is then wrapped up using a rhetorical question: 'Do boxers live up to this view of what man is or ought to be?' The implied answer to this question is a resounding 'No!'

Punctuation: Two

(1) The Punctuation Vigilante by Lynne Truss

Lynne Truss is a self-described 'punctuation vigilante'. The following extract is taken from the introduction to her best-selling book *Eats, Shoots & Leaves*.

Either this will ring bells for you, or it won't. A printed banner has appeared on the concourse of a petrol station near to where I live. 'Come inside,' it says, 'for CD's, VIDEO's, DVD's, and BOOK's.'

If this satanic sprinkling of redundant apostrophes causes no little gasp of horror or quickening of the pulse, you should probably put down this book at once. By all means congratulate yourself that you are not a stickler; that you are happily equipped to live in a world of plummeting punctuation standards; but just don't bother to go any further. For any true stickler, you see, the sight of the plural word 'Book's' with an apostrophe in it will trigger a ghastly private emotional process similar to the stages of bereavement, though greatly accelerated. First there is shock. Within seconds, shock gives way to disbelief, disbelief to pain, and pain to anger. Finally (and this is where the analogy breaks down), anger gives way to a righteous urge to perpetrate an act of criminal damage with the aid of a permanent marker.

It's tough being a stickler for punctuation these days. One almost dare not get up in the mornings. True, one occasionally hears a marvellous punctuation-fan joke about a panda who 'eats, shoots and leaves', but in general the stickler's exquisite sensibilities are assaulted from all sides, causing feelings of panic and isolation. A sign at a health club will announce, 'I'ts party time, on Saturday 24th May we are have a disco/party night for free, it will be a ticket only evening.' Advertisements offer decorative services to 'wall's – ceiling's – door's ect'. Meanwhile a newspaper placard announces 'FAN'S FURY AT STADIUM INQUIRY', which sounds quite interesting until you look inside the paper and discover that the story concerns a quite large mob of fans, actually – not just the lone hopping-mad fan so promisingly indicated by the punctuation.

Everywhere one looks, there are signs of ignorance and indifference. What about that film *Two Weeks Notice?* Guaranteed to give sticklers a very nasty turn, that was – its posters slung along the sides of buses in letters four feet tall, with no apostrophe in sight. I remember, at the start of the *Two Weeks Notice* publicity campaign in the spring of 2003, emerging cheerfully from Victoria Station (was I whistling?) and stopping dead in my tracks with my fingers in my mouth. Where was the apostrophe? Surely there should be an apostrophe on that bus? If it were 'one month's notice' there would be an apostrophe (I reasoned); yes, and if it were 'one week's notice' there would be an apostrophe. Therefore 'two weeks' notice' requires an apostrophe! Buses that I should have caught (the 73; two 38s) sailed off up Buckingham Palace Road while I communed thus at length with my inner stickler, unable to move or, indeed, regain any sense of perspective.

Part of one's despair, of course, is that the world cares nothing for the little shocks endured by the sensitive stickler. While we look in horror at a badly punctuated sign, the world carries on around us, blind to our plight. We are like the little boy in *The Sixth Sense* who can see dead people, except that we can see dead punctuation. Whisper it in petrified little-boy tones: dead punctuation is invisible to everyone else – yet we see it *all the time*.

- From *Eats, Shoots & Leaves* (adapted)

Opposing Views

(2) Punctuation: The Case Against Rules
by AA Gill

AA Gill is a celebrated social commentator and TV and restaurant critic for *The Sunday Times*. He is also dyslexic. Gill writes, 'I am a dyslexic. A dyslexic who writes a lot – 1,500 words, give or take, a day … The spellchecker would say 1,000 are spelt wrongly. I am a grammar cripple, a functioning illiterate. Literally.' Gill's dyslexia is so challenging that he has to dictate his articles to his secretary.

The following extract is taken from AA Gill's article 'A Pioneering New Way to Face up to Dyslexia'. In this piece Gill describes visiting a school for dyslexic children.

I stood in front of this sea of blameless little faces, knowing that behind each of them there was already a room full of low esteem, full of catalogues of failure, a great weight of parental concern, and I wondered again at the horrible obstacle course we make of other people's childhoods.

And I caught sight of one student, and I felt the anger, the hot fury for the wasted, tearful, silently worried, failed years of school, and I had a Spartacus moment. I started talking, rather too loudly. I told them this was their language, this English, this most marvellous and expressive cloak of meaning and imagination. This great, exclamatory, illuminating song, it belonged to anyone who found it in their mouths. There was no wrong way to say it, or write it, the language couldn't be compelled or herded, it couldn't be tonsured or pruned, pollarded or plaited, it was as hard as oaths and as subtle as rhyme. It couldn't be forced or bullied or policed by academics; it wasn't owned by those with flat accents; nobody had the right to tell them how to use it or what to say. There are no rules and nobody speaks incorrectly, because there is no correctly: no high court of syntax. And while everyone can speak with the language, nobody speaks for the language. Not grammars, not dictionaries. They just run along behind, picking up discarded usages. This English doesn't belong to examiners or teachers. All of you already own the greatest gift, the highest degree this country can bestow. It's on the tip of your tongue.

And then I caught sight of myself, standing like a declamatory ticktack man, bellowing like a costermonger, and I stopped and stared at the faces staring at me with expressions of utter incomprehension. From the back of the room, a teacher coughed.

- From *The Sunday Times*, 2010 (adapted)

Questions

Exploring *The Punctuation Vigilante*

1. Lynne Truss describes herself as a 'stickler'. What do you think she means by this?
2. Explain the joke about the panda who 'eats, shoots and leaves'.
3. **(a)** What is Lynne Truss's general argument in this extract?
   (b) Do you agree with her?
4. **(a)** Lynne Truss is often considered a humorous writer. Find two phrases from this extract that readers may find humorous.
   (b) Do you personally find these examples amusing? Why/Why not?
5. Truss makes a strong case for punctuation. Write a paragraph calling for improved punctuation in text messages.
   Or
   Write a paragraph arguing that punctuation rules should be abandoned while texting.

Exploring *Punctuation: The Case Against Rules*

6. What evidence is there in the article to suggest AA Gill did not enjoy school?
7. Describe the tone used by the author in this piece.
8. Do you agree with AA Gill's view, that, for language, there is 'no wrong way to say it, or write it'?
9. Comment on the last sentence of the extract. Does this undermine Gill's general point?
10. Gill's writing style here is flamboyant and revels in the use of interesting words. Using a dictionary, find the meanings of the following words: exclamatory, tonsure, pollard, syntax, bestow, declamatory, costermonger.

Comparison

11. Which article did you find the most persuasive? Explain your answer.

Writers' Workshop

1. Poor punctuation is obviously a source of great annoyance for Lynne Truss. Write an essay about something that greatly annoys you.
2. Write a letter to AA Gill responding to the views expressed in his article.

Language Lesson: References

References to popular culture provide the reader with something to relate to and help illustrate the writer's point. They may encourage a reader to relate to a writer. Writers need to be aware who they are writing for. For example, particular 'pop culture references' such as teen films, modern celebrities and new music stars may have more relevance to a younger readership.

In the extract from *Eats, Shoots & Leaves*, Lynne Truss makes reference to popular films: 'We are like the little boy in *The Sixth Sense* who can see dead people, except that we can see dead punctuation'. This well known film allows Truss to explain her point of view as well as amuse the reader.

Paddy's Day by Peter Cunningham

This article from the *Irish Daily Mail* tackles the issue of alcohol in Irish society. The writer, Peter Cunningham, strongly condemns how Ireland deals with this serious problem.

It was the expression 'drunken mob' used in media reports earlier this week to describe what occurred in Finglas that was surprisingly shocking. Last Monday, St Patrick's Day, the Garda riot squad moved into an area of south Finglas that had been taken over by young thugs running amok. Cars were hijacked and torched, their occupants beaten up. Children as young as 10 years old were reported to have been intoxicated.

Loutish behaviour on St Patrick's Day, particularly in Dublin, has become pretty much standard in recent years and therefore to hear about it again shouldn't come as much of a surprise. Yet, nowadays in the wider world you don't hear much about 'drunken mobs'. Riots and political demonstrations that get out of control, yes. Crowds of rampaging dissenters where the abuse of power has provoked despair and violence, certainly. But drunken mobs? Crowds whose behaviour is fuelled by drinking so much alcohol that the riot police have to be called in? It's a modern rarity – except in Ireland.

When it comes to doing drunk, we still do it better and more consistently than anyone. Alcohol abuse is an Irish epidemic. We binge drink on an epic scale and we pay the consequences: at least half of all fatal and serious road accidents are linked to drink-driving. Drunken brawls are commonplace. Recently, two Polish men were murdered when they refused to buy drinks for local youths. Drunkenness in Ireland is not new, but the link between drink and violence is a worrying modern phenomenon.

It wasn't always like this. Drink has truly become the demon in our midst. Alcohol abuse has devastating consequences: depression, anxiety, suicide, marriage breakdown, criminal behaviour, unemployment and poverty all come after the hangover. The community too pays a high price. Alcohol misuse is estimated to cost the economy more than €2.7 billion a year in health costs and lost productivity. Irish men cannot moralise about excess drinking and I am no exception. We have all grown up in what is known as the drink culture, in reality a dingy subculture where alcohol is the major form of recreation; where the system of measuring alcohol in units is seen as a scorecard rather than a medical imperative.

Alcohol is Ireland's biggest public conspiracy. We are all in it and we all sustain it. We laugh knowingly at the booze-soaked fossil that is Father Jack, but the truth is, we all know a Father Jack. Drink is everywhere in Ireland and in the battle to try and weave a path through it and not be swallowed up, we have eulogised and celebrated 'the jar' for generations. We have presented ourselves to the world as the only people who truly know how to have fun and are mystified when we encounter cultures who seem to have fun without getting legless. We feel sorry for such people. They haven't discovered the magic potion, as we have.

Yet, the fact that a drunken mob can take over a residential area of Dublin in the 21st Century should ring alarm bells in the heads of anybody who cares about Irish society. This image, like a throwback to that of a medieval mob, should at the very least cause us to have a long hard look at ourselves. Isn't it high time that we admitted that our freewheeling alcohol consumption is both personally ruinous and a devastating example to the younger generations? We are the inheritors of centuries of alcohol abuse, but we are not alone. In Georgian London it was estimated that a quarter of all households were used for the production or sale of gin. 'Drunk for a penny, dead drunk for twopence' was the catchy advertising slogan of the day.

By 1838, the caricature of the drunken Irishman was well established when Father Theobald Mathew went on a nationwide crusade to exhort people to take a pledge not to drink. At its height, just before the Famine, Father Mathew's temperance drive had enrolled nearly three million people. The abuse of alcohol was so widespread and destructive in the United States in the early twentieth century that a national prohibition on the manufacture and sale of alcohol was imposed from 1920 to 1933.

Today the sale of alcohol is still outlawed in many towns and communities across the United States. In Norway, Sweden, Finland and Iceland, the sale of liquor to consumers takes place only through government monopolies. Many countries of the Middle East, North Africa and Central Asia, either partially or totally, ban the sale and consumption of alcohol. Similar restrictions exist in South Asia and South-East Asia. And even parts of Australia have a tradition of alcohol prohibition. What all this is saying is that alcohol is a dangerous drug that most societies feel it necessary to legislate for. Not here. In Ireland today, where taking the pledge and Father Mathew sound like embarrassing sound bites from an era of ignorance and poverty best forgotten, alcohol roars in the ears of the nation. We all enjoy it, we are all complicit. If a home teams wins a coveted trophy, or a horse trained in the home village wins a big race, the media interview with the locals usually ends with the line: 'And I've no doubt that there'll be plenty of sore heads here tomorrow!' We take it for granted that celebration and drunkenness are natural companions. The craic, that term that seems to encompass all any of us could ever wish for, means only one thing.

The myth of drink is rooted in us as fiery, goblet-swilling Celts. Drink was long celebrated too as being synonymous with genius: Brendan Behan and Flann O'Brien, both of whom I remember as sad and paralytic, were writers whose genius was overtaken by their tragic alcohol-led destiny. This Irish-drink myth gets carried forward by the likes of Shane McGowan, whose self-destruction from alcohol is worn as a badge of distinction. But when I hear about drunken mobs on the rampage, attacking innocent bystanders and 10-year-old kids throwing up because they're drunk, I have to wonder where we all went wrong.

It's as if Ireland is still in the era of Gin Lane or Oliver Twist. There's no point in complaining that we're victims of our genes or of our tragic past. There's little pride in blaming the Irish weather, or the lack of alternative activities to being in a pub in Ireland, or the wisdom found at the end of a row of pints. We need to try and think our way soberly out of this mess, which is no longer just a drunken mess but has become a murderous one as well.

'People are no closer to the acceptance of alcoholism as a disease than they were when this centre opened in 1978,' says John Donohoe, senior counsellor at the Hanly Centre. 'The focus now is all on drugs. It goes without saying that drink is the biggest drug of all but, of course, the government gets a lot of money from alcohol sales.' More than €2 billion every year, to be exact. What the government should do, but won't, is ban all advertising and sports sponsorship of alcohol. What else can kids think of but a future on the booze when whatever sport they have chosen to play or watch is intrinsically interwoven with intoxicating liquor? It comes at them from every quarter.

We have made things this bad. I wish we hadn't. But there comes a time when we should stand up as a nation and assert ourselves as more than just part of a drunken mob.

- From the *Irish Daily Mail*, 2008 (adapted)

Glossary

eulogised: praised highly

Brendan Behan and **Flann O'Brien:** famous Irish writers

Shane McGowan: former lead-singer of The Pogues

Gin Lane: an 18th-century print by Hogarth depicting the damage caused by drinking gin

Oliver Twist: a 19th-century novel by Charles Dickens in which alcohol is portrayed as a destructive influence on some of the characters

Hanly Centre: an organisation that deals with alcohol-related harm

Questions

Exploring *Paddy's Day*

1. What reportedly happened on St Patrick's Day in south Finglas?
2. According to the writer, how does the Irish drinking culture impact on the community?
3. **(a)** What image of Irish society is presented in this article?
   (b) Do you believe this is a fair representation of Ireland? Explain your viewpoint.
4. Why, according to John Donohoe of the Hanly Centre, does the Irish government do little to address the problem of alcohol in Ireland?
5. **(a)** What solution to excessive drinking amongst young people does the writer offer at the end of the article?
   (b) Do you believe that this solution would help deal with the problems outlined in this article? Give a reason for your answer.
6. **(a)** Find three emotive phrases in this article.
   (b) Why do you think Peter Cunningham uses emotive language?
7. **(a)** Find an example of a rhetorical question in this piece.
   (b) Why do you think the writer chooses to use rhetorical questions in this article?
8. **(a)** Which Irish writers and singers does the article refer to?
   (b) What point does Peter Cunningham make in relation to these artists?
9. Are you persuaded by this article? Refer to the text in your answer.

Writers' Workshop

Write an article that deals with a social issue that you feel is important.

Language Lesson: Argument and Persuasion

In an opinion piece, a writer will try to convince the reader of their point of view by arguing in a logical, factual manner or they will attempt to persuade the reader using suggestion and emotive language. It is not uncommon to see both strategies present in a single piece of writing. In *Paddy's Day*, Peter Cunningham uses both.

Argument

The language of argument uses logic and factual information to convince the reader. Examples of this type of writing can be found in newspaper articles, legal writing, debating, philosophy, scientific journals etc. The following are common features of the language of argument:

* **Facts:** Peter Cunningham uses hard facts to support his ideas. For example, he notes that 'Alcohol misuse is estimated to cost the economy more than €2.7 billion a year.'
* **Logic:** In this article, the writer offers a number of logical arguments. He states that young people are exposed to advertising for alcohol which affects the choices they make in life. Therefore, Cunningham argues, the government should 'ban all advertising and sports sponsorship of alcohol.'
* **Anticipatory arguments:** The writer anticipates some objections people may raise to his ideas. He then tries to dismiss them: 'There's no point in complaining that we're victims of our genes or of our tragic past. There's little pride in blaming the Irish weather, or the lack of alternative activities to being in a pub in Ireland'.
* **Reliable authorities:** Cunningham appeals to reliable experts to add weight to his argument. For example, he quotes a counsellor from the Hanly Centre who illustrates how serious the problem of alcohol is in Ireland.

Persuasion

Persuasive language works by appealing to a reader's emotions, suggesting ideas and using language such as rhetorical questions. This type of language is found in newspaper articles, speeches, debating, advertising, sermons, propaganda etc.

* **Emotive language:** Peter Cunningham regularly uses emotive language in *Paddy's Day*. This helps to arouse the reader's emotions and encourages moral outrage. For example: 'Alcohol abuse is an Irish epidemic'. The writer also includes imagery that is bound to provoke an emotional response such as the images of drunken children, car accidents and violent riots.
* **Suggestion:** 'Loutish behaviour on St Patrick's Day, particularly in Dublin, has become pretty much standard in recent years'. This line suggests that Dublin is beset by violent behaviour every March 17th. This is not necessarily true but the suggestion helps the writer to add drama and emotion to the article.
* **Comparisons:** Cunningham unfavourably compares Ireland to Georgian London, and the drunk individuals on St Patrick's Day to a 'medieval mob'. Such dramatic comparisons are used to persuade the reader of the writer's point of view.
* **Repetition:** Although not used to great effect here, repeating a phrase or word can be an effective way to emphasise an idea.
* **Rhetorical questions:** A question where the answer is implied is known as a 'rhetorical question'. For example, Cunningham writes: 'Isn't it high time that we admitted that our free-wheeling alcohol consumption is both personally ruinous and a devastating example to the younger generations?' Here the reader knows that the implied answer is an emphatic 'Yes!'

Seaside Society by Conor Goodman

Conor Goodman is the editor of the *Irish Times*' supplement *The Ticket*. In this article he reflects on the experience of swimming in Dublin Bay.

My wife bought Jimmy for me. He's a portly, unsmiling man. On a sunless day he stands by the sea with his ample torso exposed, drying the back of his head with a towel. He may not be a real person; I know Jimmy only as a figure on a canvas that hangs on my wall. It's one of a series of paintings of Dublin Bay swimmers, and I like it because I'm a swimmer too.

Some day I want to be Jimmy, but I've a long way to go. When people like him started swimming, the bay was far less hospitable – for humans anyway – than it is today. As Brendan Behan said: 'People don't actually swim in Dublin Bay. They are merely going through the motions.' Today the veterans of dirty old Dublin Bay sit at the Forty Foot in all weathers, passing the time of day and taking the odd dip in water now only slightly less pure than Ballygowan.

These are men with barnacles on their bottoms, whose hides can withstand jellyfish stings and seal bites, who could eat bowls of E.coli for breakfast and utter satisfied burps, who, like some freaks from Darwin's diary, have developed layers of Dublin Bay-repellent blubber that inures them to changes in temperature. They could wade through lava pools with only Speedos for protection, or camp out on glaciers wearing nothing at all, and declare either experience 'only gorgeous'. They are Dublin's Crocodile Dundees.

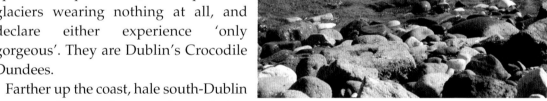

Farther up the coast, hale south-Dublin women who are wise enough to take it a little easier, breaststroking serenely through the shallower waters of Seapoint. This is one of the few places in the capital that has been left unmolested by commercial Ireland; it is completely free of shops, cafes or pubs. And maybe it's the atmosphere, or maybe the bracing water affects the voice box somehow, but even the 'Dart accent' seems to have passed it by. I hear only courtly tones and faded country accents. It's no Copacabana – one-piece swimsuits and sensible swimming caps seem to rule the waves here – but it has its own genteel glamour.

Into this venerable atmosphere come people like me, the new generation of swimmers, interlopers in Aussie board shorts and wetsuits. Playacting, lepping off rocks and making pathetic attempts at the butterfly stroke. We reward ourselves with full Irish breakfasts or elaborate brunches after morning swims, and a slew of pints after evening ones.

In summer and autumn we little dippers flock to the sea. We'll drop everything to take a quick dip, even scheduling our meals around the changing tides. But from November to April, when the Jimmies of this world are still enjoying daily dunkings, some crucial task always seems to prevent us joining them. Only on Christmas Day, emboldened by festive hot whiskeys, might we brave the wintry waters. But most of us have yet to develop the seal-pelt skin or yogic mind-control required to become year-round swimmers.

Sometimes the generations connect in conversation. 'Any jelliers today?' 'I've a good mind to ring the coastguard about those jet-skiers.' 'A friend got a nip from a seal last week.' 'I'm sure I saw dolphins out there the other day.' And, of course, people on their way into the water ask those on the way out how they found it. The water's always either 'lovely' (survivable) or 'lovely when you get in' (polar).

Overt suggestions that it may be cold are strictly taboo, as are allusions to the Mediterranean, Indian Ocean or other warm waters in which you may have swum; references to naked swimming, either in the past or now (a number of men at the Forty Foot still swim au naturel, out of public view); and speculation about that brown stuff floating in the water.

But, mostly, you don't have to say anything. There's a silent bond between all who take to the sea. We are united in sympathy for the Muggles, those people who pass by, shake their heads and ask: 'Are you mad?' We share a secret nobody else knows about. We know the shock of cold water on our bodies, but we also know it feels warm by the time you get out. We know the freedom of floating in the sunshine and looking back at the shore, with its passing traffic. We know what it is to be part of a classless society, where, for the half-hour you spend at the seaside, your house, car, job and education count for nothing. And we know the warm afterglow when you put your clothes back on and head for home.

It's a sneak preview of heaven. One day I'll enjoy it all day – and all year – long. I just can't wait to grow old.
                                                                                    - From the *Irish Times*, 2005

Questions

Exploring *Seaside Society*

1. Conor Goodman begins the article by referring to Jimmy. Who is Jimmy?
2. Where are the two bathing spots mentioned in the article?
3. **(a)** Which famous Irish writer is quoted in the article?
    (b) What do you think this quotation means?
4. In what way are the author's fellow swimmers depicted?
5. The author writes that swimming in the sea is 'a sneak preview of heaven.' In particular, what does he enjoy about the experience of swimming in the sea?
6. This article makes use of humorous language. Find three examples of humour in the article and comment on their effectiveness.
7. Describe the tone of *Seaside Society*.
8. Using a dictionary, find the meaning of the following words from the article: ample, genteel, venerable, interlopers, taboo.

Writers' Workshop

Using *Seaside Society* as a model, write a personal essay about a pastime that you have.

Language Lesson: Register

The register of a piece of writing refers to the style, tone and language used by the writer. Different writing tasks require different registers. Writers need to make sure that they are using the most appropriate register for the task. Broadly speaking, register can be thought of as formal (legal documents, academic writing, letters of complaint, wedding invitations etc.) or informal (text messages, personal writing, tweets, advertising etc.). The following obituary shows how it is important to adopt the appropriate register in writing.

Formal Register	Informal Register
Joe Blogs passed away in the loving care of his wife Jane late yesterday evening. He will be sadly missed…	Joe kicked the bucket last night. Poor old Jane, what'll she do with herself now? Sure we'll miss him altogether; he was a great lad…

In *Seaside Society*, Conor Goodman adopts an informal register: 'Some day I want to be Jimmy, but I've a long way to go', 'One day I'll enjoy it all day – and all year – long. I just can't wait to grow old.' The comic tone adds to this informality: 'These are men with barnacles on their bottoms, whose hides can withstand jellyfish stings and seal bites, who could eat bowls of E.coli for breakfast and utter satisfied burps, who, like some freaks from Darwin's diary, have developed layers of Dublin Bay-repellent blubber'.

In your own writing you should think about (a) the purpose of the piece and (b) who the intended audience is. This will help you to find the correct register for the task.

The Boy Soprano by Bernard Farrell

Bernard Farrell is an Irish playwright. He is most celebrated for his play *I Do Not Like Thee, Doctor Fell*. In this personal piece he fondly recalls an episode from his youth.

When I was growing up, the back garden of our house backed onto the bigger houses and bigger back gardens of Spencer Villas. In these houses lived richer people, more aloof people, people we seldom saw and, when we did, we silently and respectfully passed them by. The house at the end of our garden was owned by Mrs Brennan who, despite her Irish name, was a most aristocratic lady – 'Like the Queen of England,' my father would whisper whenever we saw her, as she promenaded down Adelaide Road with an air of majesty and entitlement. She spoke to no one, ever – but all that changed the year that my sister began to take singing lessons, the year when I turned twelve.

In our family, my sister Margaret had an exceptionally beautiful singing voice and, in her early teens, she was already taking lessons in operatic interpretation, vocal training and choral work. And every afternoon, in that last summer of my pre-teen years, she would be out in our back garden, practising her scales, rehearsing her exam pieces and occasionally, with so little effort, soaring into something by Puccini or Offenbach.

And this was the time that Mrs Brennan and I first met and spoke.

I remember I was walking up Adelaide Road when suddenly she was standing in front of me, saying loudly and firmly: 'Good morning, Bernard.' I stopped in wordless amazement but now, more like Lady Bracknell than the Queen, she was continuing, 'I was in my back garden yesterday and I heard you singing and I must say that you have the most beautiful boy-soprano voice I have ever heard.'

I looked at her, knowing that I should immediately explain that she was listening to my sister, not to me, but, at that time of my life, I was so starved of compliments that I suddenly heard myself humbly saying, 'Thank you very much, Mrs Brennan.'

And so began our relationship as, in the weeks that followed, whenever she appeared, she consistently praised me, encouraged me and assured me of how gifted I was. As I accepted these compliments, my youthful confidence continued to grow and grow, as weeks turned into months and the seasons changed, and winter drove us indoors, and spring reunited us, and then we were into a new summer. And it was at this time, with my confidence at its zenith that my voice broke.

Suddenly, I was speaking hoarser and harsher and in a tone lower than I thought possible. But as I self-consciously monitored these adolescent changes, I never once questioned the effect they would have on my relationship with Mrs Brennan – until, quite suddenly, I met her again.

She greeted me with her usual enthusiasm and it was only when I replied, 'Good Morning, Mrs Brennan,' that she stopped and asked what had happened to my voice. I politely told her that, over the past few weeks, my voice had begun to break and this was now how it would be for the rest of my life. She looked puzzled.

'But,' she said, 'I heard you singing yesterday, in your back garden.' I was trapped. I had to think quickly – and I did.

I said, 'Ah yes, Mrs Brennan – what has happened is that I have had to stop singing – but my sister, Margaret, has now started and it was probably her you heard.'

She looked at me for a moment and then said, 'Well, she does sing quite well – but she will never be as good as you.'

In the years that followed, I saw less and less of Mrs Brennan – she no longer promenaded along

Adelaide Road and then I heard of her illness and, soon after, that she had passed away. By then, my sister's singing career had begun to blossom and, for many years, she revelled in the appreciation and the applause, until she relinquished it all for love, parenthood and family. And some months ago, at too young an age, she too died. At her funeral, as I remembered her, I also remembered Mrs Brennan and I wondered if they were now together, speaking to each other at long last. And I smiled at the thought of Margaret telling her who was really singing in our back garden all those years ago – and Mrs Brennan now knowing that the boy soprano never really existed, that he was just a young, insecure impostor who had once tried to live in the shadow of his much more gifted sister.

- From RTÉ's *Sunday Miscellany* (adapted)

Questions

Exploring *The Boy Soprano*

1. According to the writer, what were the people who lived in Spencer Villas like?
2. How is Mrs Brennan presented in the first paragraph of the passage?
3. Based on your reading of the whole passage, how would you describe Mrs Brennan?
4. According to Bernard Farrell, why did he allow Mrs Brennan to think that he was singing?
5. After his voice broke, how did the writer explain the singing Mrs Brennan heard from her back garden?
6. At the end of the passage, the writer reveals how he felt about his sister. Describe these feelings.

Writers' Workshop

Bernard Farrell fondly remembers an episode from his childhood. Write a personal essay about a memory that you warmly cherish.

Language Lesson: Features of Personal Writing

Through personal writing, authors reflect on aspects of their lives. A piece of personal writing will usually have all of the following features:

- **Autobiographical:** What defines *The Boy Soprano* most clearly as **personal writing** is its autobiographical nature. Bernard Farrell recalls a moment from his childhood that is amusing but also allows him to reflect personally on the recent death of his sister.
- **Personal tone:** Farrell adopts a personal tone by writing in the first person. This means the story is told directly from his point of view using 'I': 'I remember I was walking up Adelaide Road', 'I also remembered Mrs Brennan and I wondered if they were now together'.
- **Expresses personal emotions and thoughts:** The personal quality is also achieved through the writer's expression of personal emotions or thoughts. Farrell tells us regularly how he was feeling: 'at that time of my life, I was so starved of compliments that I suddenly heard myself humbly saying, "Thank you very much, Mrs Brennan."'
- **Reflective quality:** Finally, personal writing often has a reflective quality. This means that the writer thinks about the significance of an event in their lives. In the last paragraph of *The Boy Soprano*, Bernard Farrell considers the life of Mrs Brennan and also reflects on what a wonderful woman his sister was.

The Enamel Jug by Peter Jankowsky

Peter Jankowsky is a German-born writer living in Ireland. He has translated numerous poems for Irish and German publications as well as publishing a memoir, *Myself Passing By*. In this piece he recalls an incident from his childhood in post-war Berlin.

In winter, the playground of the kindergarten was reduced to a few grassy square metres rising, just about, over low-lying ground which, from autumn onwards, turned into a morass, the remnant of a number of allotments, now devastated by war action. All around the mud loomed the typical four-storey houses of Berlin, many of them now in ruins. A group of children were playing on the little patch of green, five-, six-year olds, a single boy and half a dozen girls. It wasn't peaceful play: it consisted of chases and scuffles, the girls nagging the boy, he making them scream by pulling their sleeves and their hair – all bitterly enjoyable in the dim November light of the first winter after the end of the war.

   Unnoticed by the playing children, another boy had appeared on the scene; like an emanation of their grim surroundings, a tall, scraggy lad of maybe fourteen years, poorly dressed in something uniform-like that hung down from his shoulders, as did his long arms. His right hand clutched the handle of an enamel jug, the kind you would take to a field kitchen for a ladle-full of soup. He stood there motionless, watching, a pale face without expression.

   The little boy had just burst into a wild dervish dance, making the girls scatter and scream, when the din was cut as if by a knife, by the tall boy's voice.

   'Look away!' he ordered the girls calmly. The children all froze and looked at him. The small boy stood in front of the tall one, looking up at him. He saw him raise his right arm slowly, the handle of the chipped enamel jug clenched in his fist, he saw him swing his arm back as far as he could. And then the stranger, with all his might, brought the pot down on the little boy's head, hitting it just above his right eyebrow and cutting down to the bone.

   They all could hear the short, hard knock, as if on wood; the little boy heard it from within. Blood spurted out promptly, then after a moment of silent shock came a howl, more of horror than of pain. Fingers covering the violated face were flooded with blood and tears and saliva. He stumbled forward, calling for the kindergarten nurse, the girls fluttering all around him, now screaming with genuine terror. They completely forgot about the tall boy who had vanished, unseen, back from where he had first appeared, the ruined city. The bleeding boy was brought to a first-aid station in the neighbourhood. The wound needed a few stitches and with a big bandage, like a turban, he was delivered home into the arms of mother and grandmother.

   And that's where that day ended for me – in a nest of warmth and nourishment and care. Where did the tall boy go? Where had he come from? For half a century now, his darkly looming figure, his right arm swung back, has been a regular visitor to my sleepless hours. Why had he wanted to erase me from his world? For that had been his intention, no doubt about that; had he had an axe instead of that enamel jug, he would have used it, such was his ferocity. Over the years I have brooded over every one of the few details I can remember. Those uniform bits, for instance. Had he perhaps been one of the unfortunate teenage boys the Nazis had drafted in at the very end of the war, had taught to kill, to be heroes, to defend their mothers and sisters? Had he, in his confused mind, wanted to rescue those little girls from their tormentor? Even then I had felt that jealousy had been a motif, not so much of me being with girls, but of me not being alone.

And that pitiful enamel jug – had he no one to feed him? Were his parents dead, maybe still buried under the rubble? Was he just roaming around, homeless, gone feral, after all he had seen, all he had lost? Was he, when we met, as impregnated with death and killing as I was as yet untouched by it? I will never get the answers to these questions, but over a lifetime they have brought him ever closer to me, my would-be executioner.

- From RTÉ's *Sunday Miscellany*

Glossary

morass: marshy ground

Questions

Exploring *The Enamel Jug*

1. Briefly summarise what happened to the writer in the story.
2. What possible motivations does the writer offer to explain his attacker's behaviour?
3. What are the writer's feelings towards the boy? Refer to the article in your answer.
4. **(a)** The narration of the story changes from the third person ('he'/'the boy') to the first person ('I'). Identify where this happens.
   (b) Why do you think the writer chose to begin the story in the third person and then change to the first person?
5. Would you agree that this episode from his life had a profound or serious effect on the writer? Explain your viewpoint.

Writers' Workshop

Imagine you are the older boy in *The Enamel Jug*. Write a diary entry for the day described in the story. Try and explore the boy's motivation for attacking the younger child.

Descriptive Language

When writers want to bring a scene to life or portray an image vividly, they make use of a number of descriptive writing techniques.

Adjectives – Adjectives are describing words that qualify a noun, giving more information about an object. For example, the sentence, **The door swung open suddenly to reveal a hallway,** can be made much more descriptive by introducing adjectives: **The** ancient **door swung open to reveal a** damp, gloomy **hallway.**

Adverbs – Adverbs are usually used to tell the reader more about a verb. They show how something is done. For example, the sentence, **The fox walked across the field,** can be made more descriptive by introducing adverbs such as quickly, warily, recklessly to show how the fox walked: **The fox walked** cautiously **across the field.**

Similes – A simile is a comparison that uses the words **like** or **as.** An effective simile can help the reader to imagine what is being described. In the following example a volcano is compared to a sleeping giant using the word **like: The volcano loomed above them** like **a sleeping giant.**

Metaphor – Like similes, metaphors are also a type of comparison. The difference is that the words like or as are not used. In the following example a bedroom is compared to a bombsite: **My bedroom was a real mess; it was a bombsite.**

Personification – This is a particular type of metaphor, where a non-human thing is given human qualities. For example, a writer may describe how the sun shined by giving the sun human qualities: **The sun smiled down on the children.** The sun can't literally smile, but the use of personification is a more interesting way of explaining that the sun was shining.

Extended metaphor – This is when a writer continues a metaphor over a number of sentences. Read 'Fire on the Mountain' by William Golding on page 35 for an excellent example of this.

Appeals to the senses – Writers often describe an item by referring to the senses other than vision. For example, a reader may learn how something tastes, sounds, smells or feels.

Attention to detail – By providing lots of detail, a writer can build an image in a reader's mind. However, too much detail can become dull after a while, so a writer needs to be careful how they use this device by choosing to focus on significant details.

Word choices – Writers can agonise over their work, looking for just the right verb or noun to express their ideas. The words **walked, strolled, ambled, sauntered, wandered, rambled, promenaded** all mean roughly the same thing, but each one has its own resonance. Writers are careful to choose the best word to help them describe a scene or an event.

The following three extracts show how these writing devices can be put to use.

Descriptive Language

(1) from *Lord of the Flies*
by William Golding

Smoke was rising here and there among the creepers that festooned the dead or dying trees. As they watched, a flash of fire appeared at the root of one wisp, and then the smoke thickened. Small flames stirred at the bole of a tree and crawled away through leaves and brushwood, dividing and increasing. One patch touched a tree trunk and scrambled up like a bright squirrel. The smoke increased, sifted, rolled outwards. The squirrel leapt on the wings of the wind and clung to another standing tree, eating downwards. Beneath the dark canopy of leaves and smoke the fire laid hold on the forest and began to gnaw. Acres of black and yellow smoke rolled steadily towards the sea. At the sight of the flames and the irresistible course of the fire, the boys broke into shrill, excited cheering. The flames as though they were a kind of wild life, crept as a jaguar creeps on its belly towards a line of birch-like saplings that fledged an outcrop of the pink rock. They flapped at the first of the trees, and the branches grew a brief foliage of fire. The heart of flame leapt nimbly across the gap between the trees and then went swinging and flaring along the whole row of them. Beneath the capering boys a quarter of a mile square of forest was savage with smoke and flame. The separate noises of the fire merged into a drum-roll that seemed to shake the mountain.

(2) from *Hard Times* by Charles Dickens

It was a town of red brick, or of brick that would have been red if the smoke and ashes had allowed it; but, as matters stood it was a town of unnatural red and black like the painted face of a savage. It was a town of machinery and tall chimneys, out of which interminable serpents of smoke trailed themselves for ever and ever, and never got uncoiled. It had a black canal in it, and a river that ran purple with ill-smelling dye, and vast piles of building full of windows where there was a rattling and a trembling all day long, and where the piston of the steam-engine worked monotonously up and down, like the head of an elephant in a state of melancholy madness. It contained several large streets all very like one another, and many small streets still more like one another, inhabited by people equally like one another, who all went in and out at the same hours, with the same sound upon the same pavements, to do the same work, and to whom every day was the same as yesterday and tomorrow, and every year the counterpart of the last and the next.

(3) from *The Wave* by Liam O'Flaherty

The wave advanced, slowly at first, with a rumbling sound. That awful mass of water advanced simultaneously from end to end of its length without breaking a ripple on its ice-smooth breast. But from its summit a shower of driven foam arose, from east to west, and fell backwards on to the shoulders of the sea that came behind the wave in mountains pushing it to the cliff. The giant cliff looked small in front of that moving wall of blue and green and white water.

Then there was a roar. The wave sprang upwards to its full height. Its crest broke and points of water stuck out, curving downwards like fangs. It seemed to bend its head as it hurtled forward to ram the cliff. In a moment the wave and the cliff had disappeared in a tumbling mass of white water that yawned and hissed and roared. The whole semi-circle of the cliff vanished in the white water and the foam mist that rose above it blotting out the sky. Just for one moment it was thus. In another moment the broken wave had fallen, flying to the sea in a thousand rushing fragments. The cliff appeared again.

But a great black mouth had opened in its face, at the centre, above the cavern. The cliff's face stood ajar, as if it yawned, tired of battle. The mouth was vertical in the cliff, like a ten-foot wedge stuck upwards from the edge of the cavern. Then the cliff tried to close the mouth. It pressed in on it from either side. But it did not close. The sides fell inwards and the mouth grew wider. The whole centre of the cliff broke loose at the top and swayed forward like a tree being felled. There was a noise like rising thunder. Black dust rose from the tottering cliff through the falling foam of the wave. Then with a soft splash the whole centre of the cliff collapsed into the cavern. The sides caved in with another splash. A wall of grey dust arose shutting out everything. The rumbling of moving rocks came through the cloud of dust. Then the cloud rose and went inland.

The cliff had disappeared. The land sloped down to the edge of the cove. Huge rocks stood awkwardly on the very brink of the flat rock, with the rim of the sea playing between them. Smoke was rising from the fallen cliff. And the wave had disappeared. Already another one was gathering in the cove.

Questions

Exploring the extract from *Lord of the Flies*

1. Write down two similes from this extract.
2. Find three adverbs in this extract.
3. Explain how William Golding makes use of extended metaphor in this text.
4. Do you think Golding's choice of verbs is interesting? Give examples from the text in your answer.

Exploring the extract from *Hard Times*

5. Find two examples in this extract where Charles Dickens appeals to the senses.
6. The writer uses a number of adjectives in this extract. Write down five.
7. What is life like for the people of the town described in this text?

Exploring the extract from *The Wave*

8. Where does Liam O'Flaherty use personification in this extract?
9. Write down two similes from the extract.
10. Find two phrases in the text where the writer appeals to the senses.

Writers' Workshop

1. Modelling your answer on Extract 1 from *Lord of the Flies,* write your own descriptive paragraph using an extended metaphor. Choose one of the following as the title: A Savage Storm, Lightning Bolt, The Lake, Dog Fight, A Roaring Crowd.
2. Write a descriptive composition inspired by one of the pictures A, B or C below. Make use of the descriptive techniques outlined on page 34.

Descriptive Language: Advertorial

Fjord Focus by Warren Baillie

Trailfinders' Warren Baille uncovers a slice of paradise in Alaska's Kenai Fjords National Park.

Every once in a while you come across a very special place; a truly unique and magical place. Somewhere so beautiful, so incredible, that you feel you just have to tell everybody about it (but would secretly love to tell nobody about it). Alaska, and more specifically in this instance, the Kenai Fjords is just such a place.

Alaska is an infinitely beautiful state of epic proportions. It's a land where nature dominates, offering you the chance to reconnect with the natural world and a reminder that life does not have to be bound by office walls and ring-roads. Here the sound of tapping keyboards is replaced by the high-pitched cry of bald eagles, the delicate smells of spruce trees take the place of exhaust fumes and the shadows are cast by towering mountains rather than tower blocks.

Alaska remains gratifyingly wild and remote, indeed Juneau is the only state capital in the world not accessible by road. In large parts of the state, people are as likely to commute to work by float-plane as they are by bus or train. So it's perhaps no surprise to find the pristine wilderness of The Kenai Fjords National Park with its magnificent glaciers, mirror-like waters and imposing mountains is just four hours south of Anchorage, the largest city in the state.

Accessible only by boat, the adventure starts long before you arrive at the beautifully crafted Kenai Fjords Lodge in the heart of the park. The 'transfer' is a marine wildlife and glacier cruise along the rugged coastline that beggars belief. The blow of humpbacks breaks the still air, the towering fins of orcas slice through the calm waters and puffins, cute sea otters, and Steller sea lions hop amongst the rocks of the shoreline. As we cruised along, the wake of our boat provided a perfect natural stage for a pod of Dall's porpoises to demonstrate their natural exuberance and athleticism.

The backdrop of the lodge is equally awe-inspiring right on the lake's edge. Gazing out over soaring, snow-capped mountains, rising majestically from the ice-berg strewn waters below, the thunderous roar of calving glaciers is one of the few sounds interrupting the silence in this pristine location. Just 16 log cabins are sensitively placed to remain hidden amongst the forest yet still enjoy the sensational views and inside all is cosy and comfortable.

A range of included activities helps you to make the most of this unique environment. Guided walks along pristine beaches in search of fresh bear paw prints in the sand, or lagoon explorations by voyager canoe allow you to get close to nature. However, I soon discovered that the kayak is the perfect way to explore this magical place and one that allows you to glide almost unnoticed by the local wildlife in the gentle waters around the lodge. Kayaking allows near silent movement that allowed us to hear the crackle of bergy-bits as we paddled ever closer to the icy-blue face of massive glaciers, passing by sea otters floating on their backs, harbour seals popping up from time to time behind our boats to see what the fuss was about.

The beauty of the landscape was complemented by the encyclopaedic knowledge of the lodge's guides who ensured that each day was an education as well as an experience, and the communal style fine dining at the lodge provided the perfect opportunity to swap stories of the day's adventures over a dish of grilled salmon and a chilled glass of wine.

I had only got to see a fraction of what this immense state had to offer. However, such was the impression that Alaska had made on me, that I felt that my internal compass would certainly lead me back north, and I vowed to return one day to this land of the midnight sun the next time city life got too dark to bear.

Flights: to Anchorage cost from **€979pp** with Trailfinders. A 3 day/2 night package at the stunning Kenai Fjords Glacier Lodge costs from **€899pp** including the cruise from Seward, full board and guided activities. Your Trailfinders consultant can advise you on transfers from Anchorage. A 5 day private self guided tour, 'The Denali Highlights', including Anchorage, Denali National Park and a ride aboard the famous Alaska Railroad costs from **€769pp.**

Cruise: With more coastline than the rest of the 49 states put together, a cruise is the natual way to explore Alaska. We have a wide choice of cruise lines, ships and itineraries to choose from. Ask your consultant for details.

Questions

Exploring *Fjord Focus*

1. What is the purpose of this article?
2. According to the article, what does Alaska have to offer tourists?
3. Explain the pun used in this article's title. (A **pun** is a play on words).
4. **(a)** The article contains many positive words and pleasing expressions. Find three examples of this type of language.
   (b) Why does the writer use this type of language?
5. **(a)** How does the writer compare Alaska to life at home?
   (b) Why does he make this comparison?
6. Find two examples of descriptive language in the article and explain which descriptive devices the writer uses. Refer back to the guide to descriptive language on page 34.
7. Comment on the three photographs above that accompany the article.
8. Who do you think is the target audience for this travel brochure article? Why do you think so?

Writers' Workshop

Modelling the article on page 38, write a travel brochure article for a sun holiday. You may wish to use the internet or magazines to find images for your article.

Advertising

Bulging handbags. Mobile phones. Emotional **baggage.**

That's quite enough to schlep around, without a heavy conditioner adding the **extra burden** of follicle flatness.

But hark! Who's this tripping lightly into view? Enter **Aussie 3 Minute Miracle** deep conditioners.

Rich, bouncy, post-shampoo pick-me-ups that leave you buzzing with what we call **Luscious Light**-ness.

Not just a look, it's a whole way of life. With just one not-unpleasant side-effect: **light-headedness.**

"There's more to life than hair but it's a good place to start."

Questions

Exploring the Aussie Hair advertisement

1. What product is being advertised here?
2. Looking at the advertisement's visual impact, comment on:
   (a) the colour scheme
   (b) the background images
3. **(a)** Find two examples of alliteration[1] in this advertisement.
   (b) Why do you think the advertisers chose to use alliteration?
4. What tone is used in this advertisement? Refer to the text in your response.
5. **(a)** The advertisement contains many pleasing words and phrases. Write down three.
   (b) In the case of each, explain what the word or phrase suggests about the product.
6. Who do you think this advertisement is aimed at? Explain your answer by referring to the text.
7. Explain the advertisement's final line, 'With just one not-unpleasant side-effect: light-headedness'.
8. Do you think this advertisement uses the language of argument or persuasion? (See page 26) Refer to the advertisement in your response.

   [1] Alliteration is the repetition of consonant sounds in neighbouring words.
   For example, **Don't dream it, Drive it**. Here, the repeated **d** sound has a pleasing sound and grabs the attention of the reader.

Writers' Workshop

Despite the importance of the visual elements, this advertisement relies heavily on the words (or **copy**) to convey its message. Use a similar strategy to create an advertisement for a product of your choice.

Looking Towards the Leaving Cert:
The Five Language Styles

It is not easy to categorise a piece of writing as styles and formats sometimes overlap. However, in the Leaving Certificate course you will be asked to consider language in terms of five separate categories. This is a helpful way of focusing on how you write.

The five categories are:
(1) the Language of Information
(2) the Language of Persuasion
(3) the Language of Argument
(4) the Language of Narrative
(5) the Aesthetic Use of Language

→ The language of **information** aims to provide factual ideas. It is vital that this type of writing is clear and concise. The language of information is used in report writing, scientific writing, business memos, policy documents, instruction manuals and unbiased accounts.

→ The language of **persuasion** aims to convince the reader by using non-rational ideas like suggestion, emotive language and other manipulative writing devices. You find persuasive language in newspaper articles, advertising, speech making, politics and debating. Chapters 1 and 2 of this book contain many examples of this type of language.

→ Like persuasive language, the language of **argument** aims to convince the reader that a particular claim is true. However, the language of argument makes a case using logic and factual information. This language style is used in the world of politics, science, media, law and debating. Chapter 1 contains examples of this type of language.

→ The language of **narrative** is about telling stories. This type of writing makes use of descriptive language, dialogue and characterisation; it pays close attention to structure. The short stories in Chapter 4 of this book are good examples of this language style as is some of the personal writing in Chapter 1.

→ The **aesthetic** use of language appeals to the imagination by using descriptive devices and imagery. The poems in Chapter 3 display this type of language as does the section on descriptive language in Chapter 1. You will also see this use of language in fiction such as the short stories in Chapter 4.

It would be incorrect to say that each style is wholly separate: a speaker in a debate is likely to use the language of argument as well as persuasive language; short stories may make use of both narrative and aesthetic language. However, it is helpful to see language in terms of different styles in order to make you conscious of a writer's style and intention.

The following examples each discuss an oak tree. You will see how the language style used can radically change the way each topic is dealt with.

The Language of **Information:** There are over 600 varieties of oak. The fruit of an oak is called an acorn. Its flowers are known as catkins. Oak is often used in furniture and floor manufacturing.

The Language of **Persuasion:** Is oak the most beautiful of all the trees? I certainly think so. There is nothing more magnificent than seeing the grandeur of a mature, sturdy oak. It brings a sense of calm to any streetscape. In its more natural setting, there is truly something magical about a forest of oak trees; the way the light filters through the leaves is both captivating and enchanting.

The Language of **Argument:** Oak trees and other native tree species are becoming increasingly scarce as valuable forest land is used by developers. According to the World Resources Institute, 15 million hectares of forest are destroyed annually around the world. It is therefore vital that Ireland acts to conserve its native species and resists this trend of deforestation.

The Language of **Narrative:** In the beginning there was an acorn. It fell from the branches of its parent tree and against the odds landed somewhere fertile, moist and protected. As the months went by the acorn germinated, slowly at first, testing the soil and then confidently laid down roots. After a couple of years it grew to be a sapling, bending and flexing with the push and pull of the wind. Many decades later, towering over the landscape it produced a tiny acorn. The acorn fell from its branches and landed somewhere fertile, moist and protected.

The **Aesthetic** Use of Language: On windy nights, I hear the rustle of its branches scratch and tap against my window. And then, when the weather settles, it seems to whisper outside. I watch the occasional play of its leafy fingers in the streetlight throw shadows on my bedroom wall. The tree is always there, always just outside. I take comfort from its presence: the stout trunk, the deep roots, the way it shields my house from view. I live peacefully in its shadow.

Mechanics
Capital Letters, Full Stops and Commas

Capital Letters

Capital letters should be used:

1. **To begin a sentence**
   When the concert ended the crowd roared in approval.

2. **For proper nouns**
   Proper nouns refer to a specific person, place or thing: **E**mma, **C**ork, **S**ony. All proper nouns are given a capital letter. Proper nouns include:

   > **People's names:** *Aidan, Nina, Doctor Murphy*
   > **Days of the week:** *Monday, Wednesday, Saturday*
   > **Months and holidays:** *June, October, Christmas, Easter* (Seasons are not given capital letters:
   > *spring, summer, autumn, winter*)
   > **Place names:** *Galway, Australia, New York, Moneygall*
   > **Brands:** *Nokia, Apple, Pepsi, Nike*
   > Adjectives formed from proper nouns are also capitalised: *Irish, American, Spanish*

3. **For initials**
   *For many years **A.J.** O'Neill had worked in counter-intelligence for the **C.I.A.***

4. **For all the main words of titles of books, films, songs etc.**
   'The Old Man and the Sea,' 'Harry Potter and the Deathly Hallows'

5. **For the first word of direct speech**
   The farmer roared, 'Get off my property!'

6. **For 'I' as the first person singular**
   *That was the first time since the storm that **I** had seen the ruined house.*

Practising Capital Letters

Rewrite the following passage, inserting capital letters in the correct place. There are 39 missing capitals in total.

   i remember that christmas like it was yesterday, particularly the cold weather: the way my breath seemed to freeze instantly in the air. the biting wind seemed as if it could cut through my eleven year old bones and my mother insisted on wrapping me in layers of clothing before i could even consider leaving the house. that was also the winter when i learnt the true meaning of fear, the winter when i first met master khan.

   master khan was an illusionist. i was never sure where he was from. i suspected china but if somebody had told me korea, america or alaska, i wouldn't have been the least bit surprised. he seemed to exude a kind of worldliness, the sense that he was from another place or another time.

   the first time i saw him, master khan's eyes seemed to bore into my soul, like he was looking at me, through me and inside me, all at the same time. i'd bumped into him on main street, quite by accident, just outside the local burger king. having just read dickens' oliver twist, i was reminded of the character of fagin.

'come here boy,' he said as one of his long, bony fingers beckoned me to approach. he grinned at me like some kind of devil. his voice made me feel like an iceberg had eclipsed the sun, blocking out the meagre winter light. as he did his best impression of a smile, his lips seemed to peel back from his mouth revealing a frightening set of pointed yellow teeth. he spoke in a low, threatening voice, 'do you want me to ask you again boy?'

Full stops
A full stop is placed at the end of a sentence.

Commas
Commas are used:
- ❖ to separate items in a list
  He bought flour, eggs, milk, butter and a lemon.
- ❖ to divide up sentences, making them easier to understand
  The stuntman, despite the fact he was injured, still decided to jump from the burning building.

Practising Capital Letters, Commas and Full Stops

Rewrite the following passage, inserting capital letters, commas and full stops in the correct places.
the kitchen was squalid dark and hidden from the view of the street by thick black curtains tony stared around him and felt the cold creep into his bones the only source of light or heat was a sputtering candle that appeared dangerously close to being blown out by a cold draft panic rose up in his throat as he realised he was locked in

feeling tired and hungry tony resigned himself to sitting on the stone tiles as he was thirsty he fished out the half empty bottle of pepsi from his bag the sugar seemed to sharpen his senses and gave him the energy to search the room for something to help him escape after rifling through the grimy drawers and cabinets he placed his acquisitions on the table: a bread knife a can opener the flex from a kettle and a box of matches it didn't seem promising

above him he could hear the floorboards creak as his captors paced around upstairs 'how long will they keep me here?' he whispered aloud suddenly as if in response a key turned sharply in the lock behind him

2 Speaking Out:
Speeches & Debating

'There are always three speeches,
for every one you actually gave.
The one you practiced, the one
you gave, and the one you
wish you gave.'

Dale Carnegie, American writer

www.CartoonStock.com

Gerald sensed that more than just his reputation
was riding on the success of the presentation.

Making a Speech

Successful speeches are crafted carefully to win over the audience. Speech-writers use language that strengthens their argument, persuades or entertains. The following language devices are commonly found in speeches:

∗ **Rhetorical questions:** These are questions in which the answer is already implied. They are used to make a statement. For example, instead of the statement, 'I don't believe that', a rhetorical question can be used, 'Do you expect me to believe that?' Asking questions of an audience is an effective and persuasive tool in making speeches and debating.

∗ **Repetition:** This can help to emphasise a point.

∗ **Hyberbole (exaggeration):** Hyperbole is the use of exaggeration to create strong feelings or to make an impression. It is not meant to be taken literally: 'I've told you a million times'; 'I'm so hungry I could eat a horse'; 'I've a ton of homework to do'.

∗ **Humour:** When it is suitable, a joke can help to entertain and win over a crowd.

∗ **Identification with the audience:** Sometimes speakers may want to identify themselves with the crowd. Speakers, therefore, often say 'we' to include the audience in the speech. The speaker may also use references or place names known to the audience.

∗ **Metaphor:** Metaphorical language can add colour to a speech. Look at Martin Luther King's *I Have a Dream* speech on page 56 for an excellent example of this.

∗ **Anecdote/Illustration:** Sometimes an idea may need an example to bring it to life or make a point more relevant. Speech-writers often use an anecdote to illustrate a point.

∗ **Facts:** It is difficult to argue with hard facts; they help to strengthen a point but become less effective if overused.

∗ **Emotive language:** Language that stirs the emotions may help to rouse an audience. For example, a speech about animal rights may use emotive language to evoke sympathy in the audience: 'These helpless animals are subjected to torture on a daily basis.'

∗ **Anticipatory statements:** By predicting the counter-argument and dismissing it, a speaker can deal with any potential opposition to their ideas.

The delivery of a speech is also vital. Appearing confident and at ease can help to reassure the audience. Similarly, there are times when the speaker must appear passionate. Speech makers therefore need to think about:

∗ The rise and fall of their voice (cadence)
∗ Body language
∗ Pausing
∗ The speed at which they speak
∗ How they move

'Teach Every Child About Food'
by Jamie Oliver

The TED (Technology, Entertainment and Design) Prize is awarded annually to help spread 'wishes big enough to change the world'. It presents the winner with a prize of $100,000 [€74,000] and, more importantly, a platform from which to spread his/her ideas. The recipient of the TED prize is given 18 minutes to address an audience of leading figures in America. The prize is awarded by a non-profit organisation: the Sapling Foundation. In 2010, Jamie Oliver was awarded the TED prize to spread his message about addressing childhood obesity.

Sadly, in the next 18 minutes, four Americans that are alive will be dead from the food that they eat.

My name's Jamie Oliver. I'm 34 years old. I'm from Essex in England and for the last 7 years I've worked fairly tirelessly to save lives in my own way. I'm not a doctor. I'm a chef. I don't have expensive equipment or medicine; I use information, education.

I profoundly believe that the power of food has a primal place in our homes that binds us to the best bits of life. We have an awful, awful reality right now. America, you're at the top: this is one of the most unhealthy countries in the world.

Can I please just see a raise of hands for how many of you have children in this room today? Please put your hands up. Aunties, uncles, put your hands up as well. Most of you. OK. We, the adults of the last four generations, have blessed our children with the destiny of a shorter lifespan than their own parents. Your child will live a life 10 years younger than you because of the landscape of food that we've built around them. Two thirds of this room, today, in America, are statistically overweight or obese.

The statistics of bad health are clear, very clear. We spend our lives being paranoid about death, murder, homicide, you name it. It's on the front page of every paper. But diet-related disease is the biggest killer in the United States, right now. This is a global problem. It's a catastrophe. It's sweeping the world. England is right behind you, as usual.

We need a revolution. Mexico, Australia, Germany, India, China, all have massive problems of obesity and bad health. Think about smoking. It costs less than obesity now. Obesity costs you Americans 10% of your healthcare bills. 150 billion dollars a year. In 10 years, it's set to double. 300 billion dollars a year. And let's be honest, guys, you ain't got that cash.

I came here to start a food revolution that I so profoundly believe in. We need it. The time is now. We're at a tipping-point. I've been trying in America for 7 years. Now is the time when it's ripe – ripe for the picking.

I want to introduce you to some of the people that I care about. Your public. Your children. I want to show a picture of my friend Brittany. She's 16 years old. She's got 6 years to live because of the food that she's eaten. She's the third generation of Americans that hasn't grown up within a food environment where they've been taught to cook at home or in school. Neither was her mum, neither was her mum's mum. She has 6 years to live. She's eating her liver to death.

Stacy, the Edwards family. This is a normal family, guys. Stacy does her best, but she's third-generation as well: she was never taught to cook at home or in school. The family's obese. Justin, here, 12 years old. He's 350 pounds. He gets bullied, for God's sake. The daughter there, Katie, she's 4 years old. She's obese before she even gets to primary school. Marissa. She's all right. But you know what?

Her father, who was obese, died in her arms. And then the second-most-important man in her life, her uncle, died of obesity. And now her step-dad is obese. You see, the thing is obesity and diet-related disease doesn't just hurt the people that have it: it's all of their friends, families, brothers, sisters.

This is our landscape of food. I need you to understand it. You've probably heard all this before, but let's just go back over it. Over the last 30 years, what's happened that's ripped the heart out of this country? Let's be frank and honest: modern-day life.

Let's start with the Main Street. Fast food has taken over the whole country. We know that. The big brands are some of the most important powers in this country. Supermarkets as well. Big companies. 30 years ago, most of the food was largely local and largely fresh. Now it's largely processed and full of all sorts of additives and extra ingredients. Portion size is obviously a massive, massive problem. Labelling is an enormous problem. The labelling in this country is a disgrace. The industry wants to self-police themselves. What, in this kind of climate? They don't deserve it. How can you say something is low-fat when it's full of so much sugar?

Home. The biggest problem with the home is that it used to be the heart of passing on food culture, what made our society. That isn't happening anymore. Hasn't happened for 30 years. And you know, life changes, life always evolves, but we have to step back for a moment, and readdress the balance.

Now, the reality is, the food that your kids get every day is fast food, it's highly processed, there's not enough fresh food in there at all. You know, the amount of additives, E-numbers, ingredients you wouldn't believe. There's not enough veggies at all. French fries are considered a vegetable. Pizza for breakfast. They don't even get given crockery. Knives and forks? No, they're too dangerous. They have scissors in the classroom but knives and forks, no! And the way I look at it is, if you don't have knives and forks in your school, you're purely endorsing, from a state level, fast food because it's handheld.

I want to tell you about something that epitomises the trouble that we're in, guys. I want to talk about something so basic: milk. Every kid has the right to milk at school. Your kids should be having milk at school, breakfast and lunch. Right? They should be having two bottles. Ok? And most kids do. But milk isn't good enough anymore. Because someone at the milk board probably paid a lot of money for some geezer to work out that if you put loads of flavourings and colourings and sugar in milk, more kids will drink it.

And obviously now that's going to catch on. The apple board is going to work out that if they make toffee apples they'll eat more apples as well. Do you know what I mean? For me, there's no need to flavour the milk. There is sugar in everything. It's in everything. Even the milk hasn't escaped the kind of modern day problems. In one carton of flavoured milk there is nearly as much sugar as one of your favourite cans of fizzy pop. And they are having two a day! Now, any judge in the whole world would look at the statistics and the evidence, and they would find any government that allows this guilty of child abuse. That's my belief.

Now, if I came up here with a cure for AIDS or cancer, you'd be fighting and scrambling to get to me. This, all this bad news, is preventable. That's the good news. It's very preventable.

Under the circumstances, it's profoundly important that every single American child leaves school knowing how to cook 10 recipes that will save their life. Life skills.

That means students, young parents, should be taught the basics of cooking, no matter what recession hits them next time. If you can cook, recession money doesn't matter. If you can cook, time doesn't matter. Now, look, if we do all this stuff, and we can, it's so achievable. Absolutely. But the home needs to start passing on cooking again, for sure. For sure, pass it on as a philosophy.

If one person teaches three people how to cook something, and they teach three of their mates, that only has to repeat itself 25 times, and that's the whole population of America. Romantic, yes, but, most importantly, it's about trying to get people to realise that every one of your individual efforts makes a difference. We've got to put back what's been lost.

It's about free cooking lessons guys, free cooking lessons in the Main Street. This is real, tangible change. Around America there are plenty of wonderful things going on. There are angels around America doing great things in schools, farm to school set-ups, garden set-ups, education. There are amazing people doing this already. The problem is they all want to roll out what they're doing to the next school, and the next. But there is no cash. We need to recognise the experts and the angels quickly, identify them, and allow them to easily find the resources to keep rolling out what they're already doing, and doing well.

And look, I know it's weird having an English person standing here before you talking about all this. All I can say is I care. I'm a father. And I love this country. And I believe truly that if change can be made in this country, beautiful things will happen around the world. If America does it, other people will follow. It's incredibly important.

I thought if I had a magic wand what would I do? And I thought, you know what? I'd just love to be put in front of some of the most amazing movers and shakers in America. And a month later TED phoned me up and gave me this award. I'm here. So, my wish is for you to help a strong sustainable movement to educate every child about food, to inspire families to cook again, and to empower people everywhere to fight obesity.

Thank you.

- California, 10 February 2010 (adapted)

Questions

Exploring 'Teach Every Child About Food'

1. **(a)** What is Jamie Oliver's opening statement in this speech?
   (b) What effect do you think this statement has on the audience?
2. What is Jamie Oliver's view of fast food?
3. According to Oliver, how is modern-day home-life different to home-life thirty years ago?
4. In Oliver's opinion, how can the problem of obesity be addressed by society?
5. **(a)** Write down three facts Jamie Oliver includes in this speech.
   (b) Do you feel that his use of facts strengthens his argument? Explain your view.
6. Apart from the use of facts, how else does Jamie Oliver try to persuade the audience?
7. Describe the tone of this speech. Choose examples from the text to support your opinion.
8. Some commentators on this issue believe a 'junk food' tax should be introduced. Do you agree? Explain why/why not.

Writers' Workshop

Choose another problem facing society today. Write a speech outlining the problem and offering solutions to address it.

Go Find Out

Learn more about the TED Prize and hear the winners' speeches at www.tedprize.org.

'How Great I Am' by Muhammad Ali

Muhammad Ali (formerly Cassius Clay) unashamedly dubbed himself 'the greatest' boxer of all time. In 1974, at the age of thirty-two, Ali regained the title of Heavyweight Champion of the World in a fight against George Foreman. The match took place in Zaire in Africa and was famously referred to as 'The Rumble in the Jungle'. The address below is taken from a press conference in the pre-match build-up.

It is befitting that I leave the game just like I came in, beating a big bad monster who knocks out everybody and no one can whup him. So when little Cassius Clay from Louisville, Kentucky, came up to stop Sonny Liston (the man who annihilated Floyd Patterson twice) he was gonna kill me! But he hit harder than George. His reach is longer than George's. He's a better boxer than George. And I'm better now than I was when you saw that twenty-two year old undeveloped kid running from Sonny Liston. I'm experienced now, professional. Jaw's been broke, been knocked down a couple of times, I'm bad!

Been chopping trees. I done something new for this fight. I done wrestled with an alligator. That's right. I have wrestled with an alligator. I done tussled with a whale. I done handcuffed lightning, thrown thunder in jail. That's bad! Only last week I murdered a rock, injured a stone, hospitalised a brick! I'm so mean I make medicine sick!

Bad. Fast. Fast! Fast! Last night I cut the light off in my bedroom, hit the switch and was in the bed before the room was dark. Fast. And you George Foreman, all of you chumps are gonna bow when I whup him. All of ya! I know you got him. I know you got him picked but the man's in trouble. I'm gonna show you how great I am!

- New York, September 1974

Exploring 'How Great I Am'

1. Which of his skills and qualities does Muhammad Ali draw attention to in his press address?
2. **(a)** Muhammad Ali uses much hyperbole (exaggeration) in this press statement. Find three examples of this.
   (b) Do you feel this type of language is effective here? Why/why not?
3. Describe the tone used by Muhammad Ali in this piece.
4. What is your impression of Muhammad Ali from his press address above?
5. Imagine you are a journalist at the press conference. Write down three questions you would ask Ali and the answers you think he would give.

Writers' Workshop
Imagine you are a boxer preparing to fight Muhammad Ali. Write the short talk you would deliver to the media to intimidate your opponent.

Activity
Watch This Speaker
Go to Youtube to watch the video of this press conference with Muhammad Ali.

'Eve-Of-Battle Speech' by Tim Collins

Colonel Tim Collins is the former Commanding Officer of the Royal Irish Regiment of the British Army. This famous speech was delivered to his men on the eve of going to battle against Suddam Hussein's Iraqi forces in 2003. The speech was not recorded but survives because a single journalist transcribed it in shorthand as Collins spoke to his men.

We go to liberate, not to conquer. We will not fly our flags in their country. We are entering Iraq to free a people and the only flag which will be flown in that ancient land is their own. Show respect for them.

There are some who are alive at this moment who will not be alive shortly. Those who do not wish to go on that journey, we will not send. As for the others, I expect you to rock their world. Wipe them out if that is what they choose. But if you are ferocious in battle remember to be magnanimous in victory.

Iraq is steeped in history. It is the site of the Garden of Eden, of the Great Flood and the birthplace of Abraham. Tread lightly there.

You will see things that no man could pay to see and you will have to go a long way to find a more decent, generous and upright people than the Iraqis. You will be embarrassed by their hospitality even though they have nothing. Don't treat them as refugees for they are in their own country. Their children will be poor, in years to come they will know that the light of liberation in their lives was brought by you.

If there are casualties of war then remember that when they woke up and got dressed in the morning they did not plan to die this day. Allow them dignity in death. Bury them properly and mark their graves.

It is my foremost intention to bring every single one of you out alive. But there may be people among us who will not see the end of this campaign. We will put them in their sleeping bags and send them back. There will be no time for sorrow.

The enemy should be in no doubt that we are his nemesis and that we are bringing about his rightful destruction. There are many regional commanders who have stains on their souls and they are stoking the fires of hell for Saddam. He and his forces will be destroyed by this coalition for what they have done. As they die they will know their deeds have brought them to this place. Show them no pity.

It is a big step to take another human life. It is not to be done lightly. I know of men who have taken life needlessly in other conflicts. I can assure you they live with the mark of Cain upon them. If someone surrenders to you then remember they have that right in international law and ensure that one day they go home to their family. The ones who wish to fight, well, we aim to please. If you harm the regiment or its history by over-enthusiasm in killing or in cowardice, know it is your family who will suffer. You will be shunned unless your conduct is of the highest – for your deeds will follow you down through history. We will bring shame on neither our uniform or our nation.

As for ourselves, let's bring everyone home and leave Iraq a better place for us having been there. Our business now is north.
- Kuwait, 19 March 2003 (adapted)

Questions
Exploring Collins's 'Eve-Of-Battle Speech'

1. What is the purpose of this speech?
2. How are the Iraqi people portrayed by Colonel Collins?
3. According to Tim Collins, how should the men behave in Iraq?
4. Describe the tone of this speech.
5. **(a)** This speech makes a number of biblical references. Identify two such references.
   (b) Why do you think the speaker makes these references?
6. Why do you think Collins refers to the men's families?
7. How does Collins justify the armed action against Iraqi forces?
8. Do you find this speech to be persuasive? Why/why not?
9. Prince Charles described this speech as 'extraordinarily stirring, civilised and humane.' Do you agree with this statement? Explain your viewpoint.

Writers' Workshop

Imagine you are the journalist who transcribed this speech. Write an article for your newspaper reporting on the experience of hearing this speech.

'The Ireland That We Dreamed Of'
by Éamon de Valera

Éamon de Valera was both a former President and Taoiseach of Ireland. 'The Ireland That We Dreamed Of' was his St Patrick's Day address given on RTÉ radio to mark the 50th anniversary of the Gaelic League, a group who promoted Irish culture and its language. This speech is often incorrectly quoted as containing the phrase 'comely maidens dancing at the crossroads'. De Valera does mention 'happy maidens', but there is no mention of crossroads.

The ideal Ireland that we would have, the Ireland that we dreamed of, would be the home of a people who valued material wealth only as a basis for right living, of a people who, satisfied with frugal comfort, devoted their leisure to the things of the spirit – a land whose countryside would be bright with cosy homesteads, whose fields and villages would be joyous with the sounds of industry, with the romping of sturdy children, the contest of athletic youths and the laughter of happy maidens, whose firesides would be forums for the wisdom of serene old age. The home, in short, of a people living the life that God desires that men should live.

With the tidings that make such an Ireland possible, St. Patrick came to our ancestors fifteen hundred years ago, promising happiness here no less than happiness hereafter. It was the pursuit of such an Ireland that later made our country worthy to be called the island of saints and scholars. It was the idea of such an Ireland – happy, vigorous, spiritual – that fired the imagination of our poets; that made successive generations of patriotic men give their lives to win religious and political liberty; and that will urge men in our own and future generations to die, if need be, so that these liberties may be preserved.

We of this time, if we have the will and active enthusiasm, have the opportunity to inspire and move our generation in like manner. We can do so by keeping this thought of a noble future for our country constantly before our eyes, ever seeking in action to bring that future into being, and ever remembering that it is for our nation as a whole that future must be sought.

- RTÉ Radio, 17 March 1943 (adapted)

Questions

Exploring 'The Ireland That We Dreamed Of'

1. Describe Éamon de Valera's vision of an ideal Ireland.
2. **(a)** This speech contains many positive and pleasing phrases. Identify three such phrases.
   (b) Why do you think de Valera includes such phrases?
3. Why do you think de Valera refers to St Patrick?
4. Other than the reference to St Patrick, would you agree that this speech has a religious tone? Explain your viewpoint.
5. Would you like to live in the kind of Ireland that Éamon de Valera imagines? Explain your view with reference to the speech.
6. Do you think modern Ireland has become the Ireland that Éamon de Valera dreamed of? Why/why not?

Writers' Workshop

Write a speech entitled 'The Ireland of Tomorrow'. In your speech, give your vision of what Ireland could be like in the future.

Activity

Listen to de Valera's 1943 Speech Online

This speech is available via RTÉ's archive link. Go to http://www.rte.ie/laweb/ll/ll_t09b.html and scroll down to the play button for his 1943 speech.

I Have a Dream' by Martin Luther King, Jr.

Dr Martin Luther King made this impassioned speech at an American civil rights rally in Washington in 1963. Five years later he was assassinated. Martin Luther King was a Baptist preacher who called for a peaceful, equal and respectful coexistence between all races. He won the Nobel Peace Prize the year after he made this speech. Today he stands as a symbol for civil rights and Americans celebrate his contribution to society on Martin Luther King Day which falls on the third Monday of each January.

Five score years ago, a great American, in whose symbolic shadow we stand today signed the Emancipation Proclamation. This momentous decree came as a great beacon light of hope to millions of Negro slaves, who had been seared in the flames of withering injustice. It came as a joyous daybreak to end the long night of their captivity.

But one hundred years later, the Negro still is not free. One hundred years later, the life of the Negro is still sadly crippled by the manacles of segregation and the chains of discrimination. One hundred years later, the Negro lives on a lonely island of poverty in the midst of a vast ocean of material prosperity. One hundred years later, the Negro is still languishing in the corners of American society and finds himself an exile in his own land. And so we've come here today to dramatise a shameful condition. One hundred years later, the Negro still is not free. In a sense we have come to our nation's capital to cash a cheque. When the architects of our republic wrote the magnificent words of the Constitution and the Declaration of Independence, they were signing a promissory note to which every American was to fall heir. This note was a promise that all men, yes, black men as well as white men, would be guaranteed the unalienable rights of life, liberty, and the pursuit of happiness. It is obvious today that America has defaulted on this promissory note, insofar as her citizens of colour are concerned. Instead of honouring this sacred obligation, America has given the Negro people a bad cheque, a cheque which has come back marked 'insufficient funds'.

But we refuse to believe that the bank of justice is bankrupt. We refuse to believe that there are insufficient funds in the great vaults of opportunity of this nation. And so we have come to cash this cheque, a cheque that will give us upon demand the riches of freedom and the security of justice.

We have also come to this hallowed spot to remind America of the fierce urgency of Now. This is no time to engage in the luxury of cooling off or to take the tranquillising drug of gradualism. Now is the time to make real the promises of democracy. Now is the time to rise from the dark and desolate valley of segregation to the sunlit path of racial justice. Now is the time to lift our nation from the quicksands of racial injustice to the solid rock of brotherhood. Now is the time to make justice a reality for all of God's children.

It would be fatal for the nation to overlook the urgency of the moment. This sweltering summer of the Negro's legitimate discontent will not pass until there is an invigorating autumn of freedom and equality. 1963 is not an end but a beginning. Those who hope that the Negro needed to blow off steam and will now be content will have a rude awakening if the nation returns to business as usual. There will be neither rest nor tranquillity in America until the Negro is granted his citizenship rights. The whirlwinds of revolt will continue to shake the foundations of our nation until the bright day of justice emerges.

But there is something that I must say to my people who stand on the warm threshold which leads into the palace of justice. In the process of gaining our rightful place we must not be guilty of wrongful deeds. Let us not seek to satisfy our thirst for freedom by drinking from the cup of bitterness and hatred. We must ever conduct our struggle on the high plane of dignity and discipline. We must not allow our creative protest to degenerate into physical violence. Again and again we must rise to the majestic heights of meeting physical force with soul force.

The marvellous new militancy which has engulfed the Negro community must not lead us to a distrust of all white people, for many of our white brothers, as evidenced by their presence here today, have come to realize that their destiny is tied up with our destiny. And they have come to realize that their freedom is inextricably bound to our freedom. We cannot walk alone.

And as we walk, we must make the pledge that we shall always march ahead. We cannot turn back. There are those who are asking the devotees of civil rights, 'When will you be satisfied?' We can never be satisfied as long as the Negro is the victim of the unspeakable horrors of police brutality. We can never be satisfied as long as our bodies, heavy with the fatigue of travel, cannot gain lodging in the motels of the highways and the hotels of the cities. We cannot be satisfied as long as a Negro in Mississippi cannot vote and a Negro in New York believes he has nothing for which to vote. No, no, we are not satisfied and we will not be satisfied until justice rolls down like waters and righteousness like a mighty stream.

I am not unmindful that some of you have come here out of great trials and tribulations. Some of you have come fresh from narrow jail cells. Some of you have come from areas where your quest for freedom left you battered by the storms of persecutions and staggered by the winds of police brutality. You have been the veterans of creative suffering. Continue to work with the faith that unearned suffering is redemptive. Go back to Mississippi, go back to Alabama, go back to South Carolina, go back to Georgia, go back to Louisiana, go back to the slums and ghettos of our northern cities, knowing that somehow this situation can and will be changed. Let us not wallow in the valley of despair. I say to you today, my friends, so even though we face the difficulties of today and tomorrow, I still have a dream. It is a dream deeply rooted in the American dream.

I have a dream today. I have a dream that one day this nation will rise up and live out the true meaning of its creed: We hold these truths to be self-evident that all men are created equal.

I have a dream that one day on the red hills of Georgia the sons of former slaves and the sons of former slave owners will be able to sit down together at the table of brotherhood. I have a dream that one day even the state of Mississippi, a state sweltering with the heat of injustice, sweltering with the heat of oppression, will be transformed into an oasis of freedom and justice.

I have a dream that my four little children will one day live in a nation where they will not be judged by the colour of their skin but by the content of their character. I have a dream today!

I have a dream that one day, down in Alabama, with its vicious racists, with its governor having his lips dripping with the words of interposition and nullification; one day right down in Alabama little black boys and black girls will be able to join hands with little white boys and white girls as sisters and brothers. I have a dream today!

I have a dream that one day every valley shall be exalted, and every hill and mountain shall be made low, the rough

places will be made plain, and the crooked places will be made straight, and the glory of the Lord shall be revealed and all flesh shall see it together.

This is our hope. This is the faith that I will go back to the South with. With this faith we will be able to hew out of the mountain of despair a stone of hope. With this faith we will be able to transform the jangling discords of our nation into a beautiful symphony of brotherhood. With this faith we will be able to work together, to pray together, to struggle together, to go to jail together, to stand up for freedom together, knowing that we will be free one day. And this will be the day, this will be the day when all of God's children will be able to sing with new meaning, 'My country 'tis of thee, sweet land of liberty, of thee I sing. Land where my fathers died, land of the Pilgrim's pride, from every mountainside, let freedom ring!' And if America is to be a great nation, this must become true.

'From every mountainside, let freedom ring!'
And so let freedom ring from the prodigious hilltops of New Hampshire.
Let freedom ring from the mighty mountains of New York.
Let freedom ring from the heightening Alleghenies of Pennsylvania.
Let freedom ring from the snow-capped Rockies of Colorado.
Let freedom ring from the curvaceous slopes of California.
But not only that. Let freedom ring from Stone Mountain of Georgia.
Let freedom ring from Lookout Mountain of Tennessee.
Let freedom ring from every hill and molehill of Mississippi, from every mountainside, let freedom ring!

And when this happens, when we allow freedom to ring, when we let it ring from every village and every hamlet, from every state and every city, we will be able to speed up that day when all of God's children, black men and white men, Jews and Gentiles, Protestants and Catholics, will be able to join hands and sing in the words of the old Negro spiritual, 'Free at last, free at last. Thank God Almighty, we are free at last.'

- Washington, 28 August 1963

Questions
Exploring 'I Have a Dream'

1. What is Martin Luther King's message in this speech?
2. What kind of relationship does King want to see between black and white people?
3. How does Martin Luther King identify with the audience?
4. **(a)** Repetition is used to great effect in this speech. Identify two examples of this.
   (b) What effect does King's use of repetition have on the listener?
5. What effect do you think Martin Luther King's references to songs have on the audience?
6. **(a)** This speech employs a number of striking metaphors. Identify two examples of metaphorical language in this speech.
   (b) Do you feel that these metaphors are effective?
7. Choose a phrase that you felt was particularly stirring or striking from this speech. Explain why you found this phrase interesting.

Writers' Workshop

Imagine you were present in Washington for this famous speech. Write a diary entry describing the experience and the effect the speech had on you.

Activity

Watch This Speech Online

Go to Youtube and watch the video of Martin Luther King delivering this historic speech.

Activity

Learn About the Speaker

Read Martin Luther King's acceptance speech for the Nobel Peace Prize at www.nobelprize.org

Debating

Although it can be nerve-wracking at times to stand up in front of an audience, debating can be a fun way of speaking in public and using persuasive language. There are many ways to hold a debate as rules can differ between competitions. The basic rules laid out in this book are used by many organisations in Ireland, including Concern who run a national competition for schools.

The Rules

Two teams of four debate a **motion** that has been given to them in advance. The motion is the issue that will be debated, e.g. school uniforms should be banned. One team known as the **proposition** supports the motion. The other team, the **opposition**, argues against the motion.

The teams are judged by three **adjudicators**. Each speaker is given 4 ½ minutes to talk. Speeches less than 4 minutes or greater than 4 ½ minutes incur a penalty.

Each team has a captain who introduces the team's argument and sums up at the end of the debate.

A **chairperson** is in charge of running the debate. The **timekeeper** ensures that the speakers are aware of the time by giving the speaker a warning at 4 minutes and again at 4½ minutes. The timekeeper also makes a note if any speaker goes over time.

Procedure

- ☐ Chairperson welcomes the audience, teams and adjudicators, and introduces the motion.
- ☐ Captain of the Proposition (speaker 1) opens by giving an overview of his/her team's argument.
- ☐ Captain of the Opposition (speaker 1) opens by giving an overview of his/her team's argument.
- ☐ Speaker 2 from the Proposition speaks.
- ☐ Speaker 2 from the Opposition speaks.
- ☐ Speaker 3 from the Proposition speaks.
- ☐ Speaker 3 from the Opposition speaks.
- ☐ Speaker 4 from the Proposition speaks.
- ☐ Speaker 4 from the Opposition speaks.
- ☐ Captain of the Opposition closes by summing up the team's argument and makes some final points.
- ☐ Captain of the Proposition closes by summing up the team's argument and makes some final points.
- ☐ Adjudicators add up scores and decide upon a winner.
- ☐ The Chairperson opens out the discussion to the audience.
- ☐ The Chief Adjudicator announces the winning team.

> I won't lie, the first time I stood up to talk I was petrified. My hands shook and my throat was dry. But after a few times, my confidence kicked in. Now I get a real buzz from getting up and arguing. - James, 4th Year debater

Rebuttal

The difference between a speech and debating is that a counter-argument is offered during a debate. Rebuttal is when a speaker takes on a point of the other team and discredits it. Good rebuttal will be convincing and undermine the ideas of the other team. As team captains speak twice, they only rebut in their final address.

Room Layout

The room should be laid out as indicated in the diagram below.

Adjudicator's Score Sheet

Score sheets can be downloaded from www.mentorbooks.ie/Teachers' Resources

Motion:

_____

Proposition team's names	Captain	Speaker 2	Speaker 3	Speaker 4
Opposition team's names	Captain	Speaker 2	Speaker 3	Speaker 4

Proposition Team

	Content Marks out of 10	Delivery Marks out of 10	Rebuttal Marks out of 5	Penalties Deduct 5 marks for being under 4 mins or over 4 ½ mins	Total Scores
Captain Opening					
Speaker 2					
Speaker 3					
Speaker 4					
Captain Closing					
Total Team Score (max120)					

Tips

◎ **Be prepared.** Write your main points on cue cards. Practise your speech in the mirror. Try and anticipate the opposing team's arguments; this will aid your rebuttal. Research the topic well.

◎ **Speak clearly.**

◎ **Use your body.** Communication is more than just the words used. Try and use hand gestures, facial expressions and body language to help communicate your ideas and show your confidence. Think about how you stand and move.

◎ **Use humour.** Humour, where appropriate, can help to win the audience over. It provides entertainment and keeps the listeners engaged.

◎ **Take notes.** As the opposing speakers are talking, jot down ideas for rebuttal. Notes can be passed between team members.

Opposition Team

	Content Marks out of 10	Delivery Marks out of 10	Rebuttal Marks out of 5	Penalties Deduct 5 marks for being under 4 mins or over 4 ½ mins	Total Scores
Captain Opening					
Speaker 2					
Speaker 3					
Speaker 4					
Captain Closing					
Total Team Score (max120)					

Debating Motions

Debating topics can vary considerably; some are serious, others less so. A good topic will provoke vigorous debate and invite a number of different viewpoints. Often motions begin with a reference to 'This house'. This is a convention in debating that refers to the people in the room (i.e. the house) where the debate is taking place.

The ten suggested motions below can be used in your own debates or can serve as models to write your own motions.

1. *That this house believes all music should be free to download.*
2. *That this house would make Irish an optional Leaving Certificate subject.*
3. *That this house would ban vivisection.*
4. *That this house believes social networking sites are damaging to society.*
5. *That this house would charge students to attend university.*
6. *That this house would introduce legislation guaranteeing that 50% of TDs are women.*
7. *That this house believes in extending the voting age to 16.*
8. *That this house would ban all alcohol advertising.*
9. *That this house would reintroduce the death penalty.*
10. *That this house would change the national anthem.*

Activity

Get Involved in Debating

There are many debating competitions for schools. Two popular competitions for Transition Year students are the Concern Debates (www.concern.net/debates) and the Denny All Ireland Schools' Debating Competition (www.irishschoolsdebating.com).

Mechanics:
Exclamation Marks and Question Marks

Exclamation Marks

The exclamation mark is used to show strong emotions such as surprise, anger or excitement. It also indicates loudness. For example:

I can't believe it!	Surprise
Bang! The gun exploded in the alleyway.	Loudness
'Help! Somebody help me!' shouted the frantic child.	Urgency
That's it! I can't take this anymore!	Anger

Overuse of the exclamation mark takes away its power and meaning, therefore it should be used sparingly. As the writer F. Scott Fitzgerald commented, 'Cut out all those exclamation points. An exclamation point is like laughing at your own jokes.'

One exclamation mark is enough. Avoid doing the following:
The boy shouted, 'Wow!!! What an incredible car!!! I have to get one!!!!!!'

Question Marks

A question mark is placed at the end of a question.

Both exclamation marks and question marks are placed inside the inverted commas in direct speech:
'Stop!' shouted the man.
'How much does it cost?' asked the woman.

Exclamation marks and question marks are used in place of commas and full stops:
'Help,' cried a voice from inside the well. (A comma is used.)
'Help!' cried a voice from inside the well. (The comma is replaced by an exclamation mark.)

Practising Exclamation Marks and Question Marks

Rewrite the sentences below using exclamation marks and question marks. For some examples, either punctuation mark will fit. Remove commas and full stops where necessary.

1. 'Would you like a cup of tea,' the woman gently enquired.
2. 'The lotto. I just won 5 million euro in the lotto,' shrieked the man.
3. If I ever see your face around here again, you're dead. Do you hear me. Dead.
4. 'Where have you been,' the irritated boss snapped.
5. How many soldiers have the enemy sent.
6. Now. Push the eject button now. This plane is going down.
7. That's incredible.
8. 'Is everyone alright down there,' the rescue worker shouted.
9. Crash. The entire building collapsed in a cloud of dust.
10. I can't believe it. You won. That's fantastic.

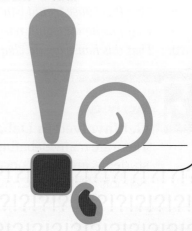

Mechanics:
Homophones

Homophones are words that sound similar but have very different meanings. The following ten homophones commonly cause confusion.

We're / Were
> *We're* = we are.
> *Were* is the past tense of *are*.

Ensure / Insure
> *Ensure* means *to make sure*.
> *Insure* is what an insurance company does.

Who's / Whose
> *Who's* = who is.
> *Whose* is concerned with ownership: *Whose football is this?*

Threw / Through
> *Threw* is the past tense of *throw*. It is a verb.
> *Through* is used in every other case.

Weather / Whether
> *Weather* refers to the climate: raining, windy, humid etc.
> *Whether* means *if*: *Do you know whether or not he is coming?*

Past / Passed
> *Passed* is the past tense of *pass*.
> *Past* refers to a period of time that has already happened.

Principal / Principle
> *Principal* is an adjective meaning the most important or main person, as in a school principal.
> *Principle* is a noun meaning law, rule or standard: *He was an idealistic person with unshakable principles.*

Their / They're / There
> *Their* is used to indicate possession, *their house*.
> *They're* = they are.
> *There* is used to indicate a place or is used with the verb to be: *The house is over there. There are too many people in this car.*

Too / To
> *Too* means *also* or *excessively*: *Can I come too? The cake was far too sweet.*
> *To* is used in all other cases.

Advice / Advise
> *Advice* is a noun: *The man gave great advice.*
> *Advise* is a verb: *I advise you to leave that job.*

Practising Homophones

Rewrite the following sentences using the correct homophones.

1. '_____ lost,' complained the irritable husband. (We're/Were)
2. 'Please _____ you keep your heads inside the windows,' ordered the bus driver. (Ensure/Insure)
3. He was the kind of man _____ eyes were bigger than his stomach. (Who's/Whose)
4. The child _____ the rock with incredible force _____ the double glazed window. (Threw/Through)
5. The _____ forecast was unclear. The fishermen were uncertain _____ to go out to sea or not. (Weather/Whether)
6. The mother hoped that her son had _____ his exams. He hadn't been hugely successful in the _____. (Past/Passed)
7. The _____ supervised the students' physics class as their teacher was absent. He tried in vain to explain Einstein's _____ of relativity. (Principal/Principle)
8. _____ car broke down just over _____. I think _____ going to walk. (Their/They're/There)
9. I'm driving _____ Galway today; you can come _____ if you like. (To/Too)
10. I'd _____ you to listen to your doctor. He gives great _____. (Advice/Advise)

3 Poetry:
The Packsack of Invisible Keepsakes

> 'Poetry is a packsack of invisible keepsakes.'
>
> Carl Sandburg, American poet

" I hope you'll dump me . . I want to start writing poetry. "

A Violent World

Stealing by Carol Ann Duffy

The most unusual thing I ever stole? A snowman.
Midnight. He looked magnificent; a tall, white mute
beneath the winter moon. I wanted him, a mate
with a mind as cold as the slice of ice
within my own brain. I started with the head.

Better off dead than giving in, not taking
what you want. He weighed a ton; his torso,
frozen stiff, hugged to my chest, a fierce chill
piercing my gut. Part of the thrill was knowing
that children would cry in the morning. Life's tough.

Sometimes I steal things I don't need. I joy-ride cars
to nowhere, break into houses just to have a look.
I'm a mucky ghost, leave a mess, maybe pinch a camera.
I watch my gloved hand twisting the doorknob.
A stranger's bedroom. Mirrors. I sigh like this – Aah.

It took some time. Reassembled in the yard,
he didn't look the same. I took a run
and booted him. Again. Again. My breath ripped out
in rags. It seems daft now. Then I was standing
alone among lumps of snow, sick of the world.

Boredom. Mostly I'm so bored I could eat myself.
One time, I stole a guitar and thought I might
learn to play. I nicked a bust of Shakespeare once,
flogged it, but the snowman was the strangest.
You don't understand a word I'm saying, do you?

Questions

Exploring *Stealing*

1. According to the speaker, what is the most unusual thing he/she ever stole?
2. Name three other things the speaker has stolen in the past.
3. What do you think the thief means when he/she says, 'a mate/with a mind as cold as the slice of ice/within my own brain'? Explain your answer.
4. Looking at the second stanza, what evidence can you find that shows the speaker is a cruel individual?
5. What do you think the speaker means when he/she says, 'I'm a mucky ghost'?
6. **(a)** The poem contains one violent incident. Describe this incident in your own words.
   (b) What does this incident reveal about the speaker?
7. Describe the attitude of the speaker. In your answer, consider the speaker's tone and his/her ideas about the world.
8. Do you feel any sympathy for the speaker? Why/why not?

Writers' Workshop

Imagine you are the snowman's owner who has just discovered your snowman has been stolen. Write an account of the theft from your perspective.

Things To Think About: Persona

Sometimes a poet may adopt a character's voice to speak in a poem. This other voice is called a persona. In *Stealing*, the persona of the thief allows Carol Ann Duffy to look at the world from another person's perspective and gives the reader an insight into a particular type of individual.

Things To Think About: Run-On Line (enjambment)

A **run-on** line (also called **enjambment**) is when the end of one line flows onto the next line without a punctuation mark. Sometimes poets do this to create a sense of rhythm or for rhyme. In *Stealing*, the run-on line has a very particular effect. At times it adds to or qualifies an idea, for example: 'I joy-ride cars/to nowhere'. Here the break between 'cars' and 'to nowhere' emphasises the pointlessness of the speaker's behaviour.

Go Find Out

This poem explores the issue of crime in society. Find an article from a newspaper that deals with this issue. Summarise the article and write your thoughts on how society can deal with the problem of crime.

The One Twenty Pub by Wisława Szymborska (translated by Dennis O'Driscoll)

The bomb is primed to go off at one twenty.
A time-check: one sixteen.
There's still a chance for some to join
the pub's ranks, for others to drop out.

The terrorist watches from across the street.
Distance will shield him
from the impact of what he sees:

A woman, turquoise jacket on her shoulder,
enters; a man with sunglasses departs.
Youths in tee-shirts loiter without intent.

One seventeen and four seconds.
The scrawny motorcyclist, revving up
to leave, won't believe his luck;
but the tall man steps straight in.

One seventeen and forty seconds.
That girl, over there with the walkman
– now the bus has cut her off.
One eighteen exactly.
Was she stupid enough to head inside?
Or wasn't she? We'll know before long,
when the dead are carried out.

It's one nineteen.
Nothing much to report
until a muddled barfly hesitates,
fumbles with his pockets, and, like
a blasted fool, stumbles back
at one nineteen and fifty seconds
to retrieve his goddamn cap.

One twenty
How time drags when…
Any moment now.
Not yet.
Yes.
    Yes,
        there
           it
             goes.

Glossary
barfly: a drunk; a person who frequents
bars regularly

Questions

Exploring *The One Twenty Pub*

1. **(a)** There are two voices speaking in this poem: the terrorist's and the poet's. Find a line that shows the terrorist's view of the situation.
    (b) Find an example of the poet's voice in the poem.
2. **(a)** Describe the patrons who enter and exit the pub.
    (b) How does Wisława Szymborska show that these are very ordinary people?
    (c) Why do you think she chooses to emphasise their ordinariness?
3. The terrorist describes the motorcyclist as 'scrawny', a girl as 'stupid' and a man as a 'muddled barfly'. Why do you think the terrorist uses such negative words to describe the people?
4. In your own words, describe the event depicted in this poem.
5. Describe the attitude of the terrorist. Quote from the poem in your answer.
6. How does the poet build the tension in the poem?
7. This could be any pub, anywhere, at any time. Why do you think the poet chooses not to identify a particular place, group of people or terrorist organisation?
8. The final four lines of the poem are placed in a slanting pattern on the page. What effect does this create?

Writers' Workshop

Write a speech condemning the use of terrorism.

Find Out About the Poet

Wisława Szymborska won the Nobel Prize for Literature in 1996. Go to www.nobelprize.org and discover some of her other poems.

The Highwayman by Alfred Noyes

PART ONE

I

The wind was a torrent of darkness among the gusty trees,
The moon was a ghostly galleon tossed upon cloudy seas,
The road was a ribbon of moonlight over the purple moor,
And the highwayman came riding—
      Riding—riding—
The highwayman came riding, up to the old inn-door.

II

He'd a French cocked-hat on his forehead, a bunch of lace at his chin,
A coat of the claret velvet, and breeches of brown doe-skin;
They fitted with never a wrinkle: his boots were up to the thigh!
And he rode with a jewelled twinkle,
      His pistol butts a-twinkle,
His rapier hilt a-twinkle, under the jewelled sky.

III

Over the cobbles he clattered and clashed in the dark inn-yard,
And he tapped with his whip on the shutters, but all was locked and barred;
He whistled a tune to the window, and who should be waiting there
But the landlord's black-eyed daughter,
      Bess, the landlord's daughter,
Plaiting a dark red love-knot into her long black hair.

IV

And dark in the dark old inn-yard a stable-wicket creaked
Where Tim the ostler listened; his face was white and peaked;
His eyes were hollows of madness, his hair like mouldy hay,
But he loved the landlord's daughter,
      The landlord's red-lipped daughter,
Dumb as a dog he listened, and he heard the robber say—

V

'One kiss, my bonny sweetheart, I'm after a prize to-night,
But I shall be back with the yellow gold before the morning light;
Yet, if they press me sharply, and harry me through the day,
Then look for me by moonlight,
      Watch for me by moonlight,
I'll come to thee by moonlight, though hell should bar the way.'

VI

He rose upright in the stirrups; he scarce could reach her hand
But she loosened her hair i' the casement! His face burnt like a brand
As the black cascade of perfume came tumbling over his breast
And he kissed its waves in the moonlight,
 (Oh, sweet, black waves in the moonlight!)
Then he tugged at his rein in the moonlight, and galloped away to the West.

PART TWO

I

He did not come in the dawning; he did not come at noon;
And out o' the tawny sunset, before the rise o' the moon,
When the road was a gypsy's ribbon, looping the purple moor,
A red-coat troop came marching—
 Marching—marching—
King George's men came marching, up to the old inn-door.

II

They said no word to the landlord, they drank his ale instead,
But they gagged his daughter and bound her to the foot of her narrow bed;
Two of them knelt at her casement, with muskets at their side!
There was death at every window;
 And hell at one dark window;
For Bess could see, through her casement, the road that he would ride.

III

They had tied her up to attention, with many a sniggering jest;
They had bound a musket beside her, with the barrel beneath her breast!
"Now, keep good watch!" and they kissed her.
She heard the dead man say—
Look for me by moonlight;
 Watch for me by moonlight;
I'll come to thee by moonlight, though hell should bar the way!

IV

She twisted her hands behind her; but all the knots held good!
She writhed her hands till her fingers were wet with sweat or blood!
They stretched and strained in the darkness, and the hours crawled by like years,
Till, now, on the stroke of midnight,
 Cold, on the stroke of midnight,
The tip of one finger touched it! The trigger at least was hers!

V

The tip of one finger touched it; she strove no more for the rest!
Up, she stood up to attention, with the barrel beneath her breast,
She would not risk their hearing; she would not strive again;
For the road lay bare in the moonlight;
 Blank and bare in the moonlight;
And the blood of her veins in the moonlight throbbed to her love's refrain.

VI

Tlot-tlot; tlot-tlot! Had they heard it? The horse-hoofs ringing clear;
Tlot-tlot, tlot-tlot in the distance? Were they deaf that they did not hear?
Down the ribbon of moonlight, over the brow of the hill,
The highwayman came riding,
      Riding, riding!
The red-coats looked to their priming! She stood up, straight and still!

VII

Tlot-tlot, in the frosty silence! *Tlot-tlot*, in the echoing night!
Nearer he came and nearer! Her face was like a light!
Her eyes grew wide for a moment; she drew one last deep breath,
Then her finger moved in the moonlight,
      Her musket shattered the moonlight,
Shattered her breast in the moonlight and warned him—with her death.

VIII

He turned; he spurred to the West; he did not know who stood
Bowed, with her head o'er the musket, drenched with her own red blood!
Not till the dawn he heard it, his face grew grey to hear
How Bess, the landlord's daughter,
      The landlord's black-eyed daughter,
Had watched for her love in the moonlight, and died in the darkness there.

IX

Back, he spurred like a madman, shrieking a curse to the sky,
With the white road smoking behind him and his rapier brandished high!
Blood-red were his spurs i' the golden noon; wine-red was his velvet coat,
When they shot him down on the highway,
      Down like a dog on the highway,
And he lay in his blood on the highway, with the bunch of lace at his throat.

X

And still of a winter's night, they say, when the wind is in the trees,
When the moon is a ghostly galleon tossed upon cloudy seas,
When the road is a ribbon of moonlight over the purple moor,
A highwayman comes riding—
      Riding—riding—
A highwayman comes riding, up to the old inn-door.

XI

Over the cobbles he clatters and clangs in the dark inn-yard;
He taps with his whip on the shutters, but all is locked and barred;
He whistles a tune to the window, and who should be waiting there
But the landlord's black-eyed daughter,
      Bess, the landlord's daughter,
Plaiting a dark red love-knot into her long black hair.

Glossary

galleon: a type of sailing ship
ostler: a stableman
harry: to trouble; to harass
tawny: yellow-brown colour
red-coat: British soldier
casement: a type of window
refrain: a reoccurring phrase. In this case: the Highwayman's promise to Bess.
priming: gunpowder
musket: a gun
rapier: a type of sword

Questions
Exploring *The Highwayman*

1. What promise did the highwayman make to Bess?
2. How do you think the soldiers learned that the highwayman would be at the inn at midnight?
3. How did Bess warn the highwayman of the soldiers' presence?
4. In *The Highwayman*, Alfred Noyes frequently appeals to the senses. Find three examples of this in the poem.
5. **(a)** This poem contains a number of striking images or pictures. For this reason it can be described as highly cinematic. Describe two images from the poem that you found memorable.
    (b) Why were these images particularly striking to you?
6. A metaphor is a comparison that does not use like or as. Alfred Noyes includes metaphors throughout this poem.
    (a) Write down three metaphors from Part One that you found effective. Explain why you found one of these particularly effective.
    (b) Write down three metaphors from Part Two of the poem. Comment on the effectiveness of one of these metaphors.
7. **(a)** In your opinion, is the highwayman portrayed in a positive or negative light? Explain your viewpoint.
    (b) How are the red-coat soldiers portrayed?
8. Describe the rhythm and rhyming scheme of this poem.
9. Explain what occurs in stanza XI of Part Two.

Writers' Workshop
Imagine you are a newspaper reporter sent to investigate the event described in the poem. Write the article you would submit to the newspaper.

Things To Think About: Ballad
The Highwayman is a type of poem known as a ballad. Ballads were originally set to music (the word 'ballad' has its roots in the French word 'ballares', which means 'dance-song'). For this reason, ballads are very rhythmic with regular rhyme patterns. Ballads are also narrative poems; this means that they tell a story. Often they recount tales of adventure, romance, comedy or an historical event.

Find Out About the Poet
Alfred Noyes is best remembered for *The Highwayman*. Go to www.poetryfoundation.org to learn about his life and read some of his other poems.

Lipstick by Rosita Boland

Home from work one evening, the summer
Before I went to Iran,
I switched the radio on as usual,
Chose a knife and started to slice
Red peppers, spring onions, wild mushrooms.

It was a while before I started listening.
Propped up against a tin of Lapsang tea,
The radio on the far shelf
Was narrating a documentary about Iran.

After the Shah fled, Revolutionary Guards
Patrolled the streets of Teheran.
They were looking for stray hairs, exposed ankles
And other signs of female disrespect.
When they discovered women wearing lipstick
They razor-bladed it off,
Replacing one red gash with another.

The programme ended.
I was left standing there in my kitchen
With the vegetables half-chopped on the table:
The scarlet circles of the peppers
Delicate mouths, scattered at random.

Glossary
Lapsang tea: a type of Chinese tea with a smoky flavour.
Shah: the King of Iran. The last Shah was overthrown by an Islamic revolution in 1979.
The Revolutionary Guards: Members of a military group that enforces Sharia Law in Iran.
Teheran: the capital of Iran. Sometimes spelt 'Tehran'.

Questions

Exploring *Lipstick*

1. In the first stanza, the poet describes a very ordinary evening. How does she communicate the ordinariness of the scene?
2. **(a)** What types of behaviour did the Revolutionary Guards see as examples of 'female disrespect'?
   (b) How did the Revolutionary Guards punish this behaviour?
3. **(a)** Describe the attitude of the poet before she started to listen to the radio documentary.
   (b) How does her attitude change?
4. In *Lipstick*, the red peppers take on new meaning towards the end of the poem. Explain the significance of the red peppers and how their meaning changes.
5. What is your personal response to this poem?
6. Write about a radio or television programme that made you feel sympathy for people you don't know. Describe the programme and what it made you think about.

Discussion Topics

Do men and women have equal status in Irish society?

OR

Discuss the mistreatment of women in some societies abroad.

A Violent World

Hotel Room, 12th Floor by Norman MacCaig

This morning I watched from here
a helicopter skirting like a damaged insect
the Empire State building, that
jumbo size dentist's drill, and landing
on the roof of the PanAm skyscraper.
But now Midnight has come in
from foreign places. Its uncivilised darkness
is shot at by a million lit windows, all
ups and acrosses.

But midnight is not
so easily defeated. I lie in bed, between
a radio and a television set, and hear
the wildest of warwhoops continually
ululating through
the glittering canyons and gulches –
police cars and ambulances racing
to broken bones, the harsh screaming
from coldwater flats, the blood
glazed on the sidewalks.

The frontier is never
somewhere else. And no stockades
can keep the midnight out.

Glossary
Empire State building: famous
building in New York City
PanAm: an American airline
ululating: howling or wailing
canyon: deep valley
gulches: ravines; steep valleys
stockades: wooden fortresses

Questions

Exploring *Hotel Room, 12th Floor*

1. **(a)** Where is the speaker in this poem?
   (b) How do you know?
2. Norman MacCaig uses similes and metaphors to great effect in this poem. Write down one simile and one metaphor from the first stanza and comment on their effectiveness.
3. **(a)** The poet brings the city to life by appealing to the senses. Find three examples of this in the poem.
   (b) Do you think the sounds the speaker hears are real or are they his imagined fears? Explain your viewpoint.
4. **(a)** *Hotel Room, 12th Floor* contains a number of violent images and references to the wild west. Identify three examples of this.
   (b) How do these references affect MacCaig's portrayal of the city?
5. Midnight is referred to in all three stanzas. What do you think midnight represents in the poem?
6. The words no and never in the final stanza indicate that a strong conclusion has been reached. What conclusion do you think the speaker comes to in this poem?

Writers' Workshop

Write about an experience where you felt unsettled or unsure of your surroundings. This may be an experience you had abroad or at home.

Activity

Visual Response

Create a poster to represent this poem. Use cut-outs from magazines, photographs or your own artistic skills to illustrate the ideas in the poem. Include the words of the poem in your poster to accompany your images. You don't need to stick literally to the poem: try to capture the spirit and mood of the poet's words and ideas.

Those Winter Sundays by Robert Hayden

Sundays too my father got up early
and put his clothes on in the blueblack cold,
then with cracked hands that ached
from labor in the weekday weather made
banked fires blaze. No one ever thanked him.

I'd wake and hear the cold splintering, breaking.
When the rooms were warm, he'd call,
and slowly I would rise and dress,
fearing the chronic angers of that house,

Speaking indifferently to him,
who had driven out the cold
and polished my good shoes as well.
What did I know, what did I know
of love's austere and lonely offices?

Glossary
austere: stern and forbidding; self-denying
offices: duty or task; a service carried out for another;
a position of responsibility

The Song of the Old Mother
by William Butler Yeats

I rise in the dawn, and I kneel and blow
Till the seed of the fire flicker and glow;
And then I must scrub and bake and sweep
Till stars are beginning to blink and peep;
And the young lie long and dream in their bed
Of the matching of ribbons for bosom and head,
And their day goes over in idleness,
And they sigh if the wind but lift a tress:
While I must work because I am old,
And the seed of the fire gets feeble and cold.

Glossary
tress: a lock of hair; a plait

Questions
Exploring *Those Winter Sundays* and *The Song of the Old Mother*

Those Winter Sundays
1. The poem begins with the words, 'Sundays too my father got up early'. What does the word 'too' suggest?
2. **(a)** What chores did the father perform for his son?
   (b) How does Robert Hayden show that these chores were unpleasant?
3. What kind of relationship do you think the father and son had?
4. **(a)** Describe the tone of the poem's final two lines.
   (b) What does this suggest about the feelings of the speaker in the poem?

The Song of the Old Mother
5. What chores does the old mother perform?
6. What is the old mother's view of young people?
7. In the poem's final line, the old mother describes how 'the seed of the fire gets feeble and cold'. Seed is an unusual word to use to describe a fire's embers. Considering the poem as a whole, why do you think Yeats chose this word?

Comparison
8. '*Those Winter Sundays* and *The Song of the Old Mother* offer us different perspectives on the same theme.' Discuss this statement with reference to both poems.
9. Which poem do you prefer? Explain your answer.

Writers' Workshop
Thinking about both poems, write your own poem entitled *Song of the Old Father*.

Activity
1. **Recite a Poem:** Learn one of these poems off by heart and recite it in your next English class.
2. **Listen to the Poet:** Listen to W.B. Yeats read *The Song of the Old Mother* at www.poetryarchive.org

About The Poet: W.B. Yeats' Life
W.B. Yeats was born in Dublin but spent much of his childhood in London and Sligo.

He fell in love with the Irish nationalist Maud Gonne while in his early twenties. He proposed to her five times but was always rejected. His infatuation with her provided inspiration for much of his poetry.

After meeting influential figures such as Lady Gregory, Yeats became increasingly supportive of Irish nationalism. This, coupled with his interest in Irish folklore and mythology, shaped much of his poetry. He was part of a group of writers who spearheaded the Irish Literary Revival and he was a cofounder of the Abbey Theatre.

Yeats held an interest in mysticism and the occult. He was a member of the paranormal research organisation called **The Ghost Club.** This aspect of his life also influenced his poetry.

At the age of 51, he married Georgie Hydes-Lee whom he met through occult circles. They had two children together.

Yeats was elected to the Seanad in 1922, eventually serving for two terms. A year later he was awarded the Nobel Prize for Literature. The Nobel Committee commented that his poetry 'gives expression to the spirit of a whole nation.'

He died in France in 1939 but his body was returned to Ireland and is buried in Sligo. The epitaph on his tombstone is from his poem *Under Ben Bulben*: 'Cast a cold Eye/On Life, on Death./Horseman, pass by.'

The Back Seat of My Mother's Car
by Julia Copus

We left before I had time
to comfort you, to tell you that we nearly touched
hands in that vacuous half-dark. I wanted
to stem the burning waters running over me like tiny
rivers down my face and legs, but at the same time I was reaching out
for the slit in the window where the sky streamed in,
cold as ether, and I could see your fat mole-fingers grasping
the dusty August air. I pressed my face to the glass;
I was calling to you – *Daddy*! – as we screeched away into
the distance, my own hand tingling like an amputation.
You were mouthing something I still remember, the noiseless words
piercing me like that catgut shriek that flew up, furious as a sunset
pouring itself out against the sky. The ensuing silence
was the one clear thing I could decipher –
the roar of the engine drowning your voice,
with the cool slick glass between us.

With the cool slick glass between us,
the roar of the engine drowning, your voice
was the one clear thing I could decipher –
pouring itself out against the sky, the ensuing silence
piercing me like that catgut shriek that flew up, furious as a sunset.
You were mouthing something: I still remember the noiseless words,
the distance, my own hand tingling like an amputation.
I was calling to you, Daddy, as we screeched away into
the dusty August air. I pressed my face to the glass,
cold as ether, and I could see your fat mole-fingers grasping
for the slit in the window where the sky streamed in
rivers down my face and legs, but at the same time I was reaching out
to stem the burning waters running over me like tiny
hands in that vacuous half-dark. I wanted
to comfort you, to tell you that we nearly touched.
We left before I had time.

Questions

Exploring *The Back Seat of My Mother's Car*

1. (a) Who is speaking in the first stanza?
    (b) Who is speaking in the second stanza?
2. What do you think is happening in the lives of these characters? Refer to the poem in your answer.
3. Describe the feelings of either of the speakers in the poem.
4. Explain what you understand by each of the following phrases from the poem:
    (a) 'my own hand tingling like an amputation' (Stanzas 1 and 2)
    (b) 'I wanted/to stem the burning waters running over me like tiny/rivers down my face and legs' (Stanza 1)
    (c) 'the ensuing silence/piercing me like that catgut shriek that flew up, furious as a sunset' (Stanza 2)
5. Aside from the examples in Question 4, choose two phrases from the poem that you feel are striking. Write down these phrases and explain why you find them striking.
6. (a) Describe the structure of *The Backseat of My Mother's Car*.
    (b) Do you feel this is an effective way to structure the poem. Why/why not?
7. Julia Copus includes a number of interesting words in this poem. Using a dictionary find the meaning of each of the following: vacuous, ether, ensuing, decipher.

Writers' Workshop

Write a stanza of poetry or a prose paragraph from the point of view of the mother in the poem.

Listen To The Poet

Go to www.poetryarchive.org and listen to Julia Copus read this poem.

Parents and Children

Mother of the Groom by Seamus Heaney

What she remembers
Is his glistening back
In the bath, his small boots
In the ring of boots at her feet.

Hands in her voided lap,
She hears a daughter welcomed.
It's as if he kicked when lifted
And slipped her soapy hold.

Once soap would ease off
The wedding ring
That's bedded forever now
In her clapping hand.

Questions

Exploring Mother of the Groom

1. What are the mother's earliest memories of her son?
2. What do you understand by the line, 'It's as if he kicked when lifted/And slipped her soapy hold'?
3. How do you think the mother feels about her son's marriage? Refer to the poem in your answer.
4. (a) In your own words describe the imagery of the final stanza.
    (b) What is being suggested about the mother's life through this image?
5. How important is the title of the poem? Explain your answer.

Writers' Workshop

Imagine you are the mother of the groom from this poem. Write a diary entry for the night before your son's wedding.

Learn About The Poet

Seamus Heaney won the Nobel Prize for Literature in 1995. Go to www.nobelprize.org to learn more about Heaney and to hear his acceptance speech for the award.

Parents and Children

Weakness by Alden Nowlan

Old mare whose eyes
are like cracked marbles,
drools blood in her mash,
shivers in her jute blanket.

My father hates weakness worse than hail;
in the morning
    without haste
he will shoot her in the ear, once,
shovel her under in the north pasture.

Tonight
    leaving the stables
he stands his lantern on an overturned water pail,
turns,
    cursing her for a bad bargain,
and spreads his coat
carefully over her sick shoulders.

Glossary
jute: a coarse material often used for making sacks

Questions

Exploring *Weakness*

1. In your own words, describe the horse from this poem.
2. Why is the father planning to shoot the horse?
3. What is your impression of the father in this poem? Refer to the poem in your response.
4. Choose a phrase from the poem that you feel is striking. Explain why you find this phrase striking.
5. Why do you think Alden Nowlan chose to entitle this poem '*Weakness*'?
6. Write a paragraph beginning with the following statement: This poem shows that kindness can be found in the most surprising of places.

Writers' Workshop

Imagine you are the father. Write a diary entry recording your thoughts on the night this poem is set.

Things To Think About: Biography

Poets' lives and experiences help to shape the content and emotions of their poems. In *Weakness*, Alden Nowlan draws on memories of his father for inspiration.

Alden Nowlan was born into extreme poverty in Canada. His mother left the family home when he was very young and Nowlan was raised by his father and grandmother. Nowlan's family were tough individuals who saw no value in education, let alone poetry. He completed only four years of school.

As a teenager, Nowlan discovered the library located eighteen miles from his home. He hitchhiked there every weekend and read in secret, hiding the fact from his father. As the poet remembers, 'My father would as soon have seen me wear lipstick.'

Parents and Children

Do Not Go Gentle into That Good Night
by Dylan Thomas

Do not go gentle into that good night,
Old age should burn and rave at close of day;
Rage, rage against the dying of the light.

Though wise men at their end know dark is right,
Because their words had forked no lightning they
Do not go gentle into that good night.

Good men, the last wave by, crying how bright
Their frail deeds might have danced in a green bay,
Rage, rage against the dying of the light.

Wild men who caught and sang the sun in flight,
And learn, too late, they grieved it on its way,
Do not go gentle into that good night.

Grave men, near death, who see with blinding sight
Blind eyes could blaze like meteors and be gay,
Rage, rage against the dying of the light.

And you, my father, there on the sad height,
Curse, bless, me now with your fierce tears, I pray.
Do not go gentle into that good night.
Rage, rage against the dying of the light.

Questions
Exploring *Do Not Go Gentle into That Good Night*

1. **(a)** Who do you think Dylan Thomas is addressing when he says, 'Do not go gentle into that good night'?
   (b) What does he mean by this phrase?
2. The poet mentions many other men who 'rage against the dying of the light'. List three.
3. The second stanza states that 'Though wise men at their end know dark is right…they/ Do not go gentle into that good night'. What do you understand by these lines?
4. Choose two images from the poem that you find memorable or striking. Explain why these images stood out for you.
5. Describe the poet's tone in *Do Not Go Gentle into That Good Night.* Support your answer with examples from the poem.

Writers' Workshop
Imagine you are a radio broadcaster presenting a show called *Great Poets of the 20th Century.* Write an introduction to this poem. Alternatively you could record your introduction and play it to the class.

Things To Think About: Refrain
A refrain is a line or phrase that reoccurs throughout a poem. The refrain often comes at the end of a stanza. In the poem above, the refrain, 'Rage, rage against the dying of the light' emphasises the poem's central idea.

Listen to the Poet
Go to www.poets.org and listen to Dylan Thomas read this poem.

Find Out About the Poet
Dylan Thomas died at the early age of 39. Go online and research the poet's troubled life. You may wish to consult www.dylanthomas.com, www.poetryarchive.org or www.poetryfoundation.org.

Activity
Recite a Poem
Learn this poem off by heart and recite it in your next English class.

Parents and Children

Prayer Before Birth by Louis MacNeice

I am not yet born; O hear me.
Let not the bloodsucking bat or the rat or the stoat or the
   club-footed ghoul come near me.

I am not yet born, console me.
I fear that the human race may with tall walls wall me,
   with strong drugs dope me, with wise lies lure me,
      on black racks rack me, in blood-baths roll me.

I am not yet born; provide me
With water to dandle me, grass to grow for me, trees to talk
   to me, sky to sing to me, birds and a white light
      in the back of my mind to guide me.

I am not yet born; forgive me
For the sins that in me the world shall commit, my words
   when they speak me, my thoughts when they think me,
      my treason engendered by traitors beyond me,
         my life when they murder by means of my
            hands, my death when they live me.

I am not yet born; rehearse me
In the parts I must play and the cues I must take when
   old men lecture me, bureaucrats hector me, mountains
      frown at me, lovers laugh at me, the white
         waves call me to folly and the desert calls
            me to doom and the beggar refuses
               my gift and my children curse me.

I am not yet born; O hear me,
Let not the man who is beast or who thinks he is God
   come near me.

I am not yet born; O fill me
With strength against those who would freeze my
   humanity, would dragoon me into a lethal automaton,
      would make me a cog in a machine, a thing with
         one face, a thing, and against all those
            who would dissipate my entirety, would
               blow me like thistledown hither and
                  thither or hither and thither
                     like water held in the
                        hands would spill me.

Glossary
dandle: pet
automaton: robot; a non-thinking person
dissipate: to disperse; to scatter; to break up;
to use wastefully

Let them not make me a stone and let them not spill me.
   Otherwise kill me.

Questions

Exploring *Prayer Before Birth*

1. Who is speaking in this poem?
2. Rewrite each of the following phrases in your own words:
    (a) 'provide me/With water to dandle me, grass to grow for me, trees to talk/to me, sky to sing to me, birds and a white light/in the back of my mind to guide me'
    (b) 'O fill me/With strength against those who would freeze my/humanity, would dragoon me into a lethal automaton,/would make me a cog in a machine, a thing with/one face'
3. In the fourth stanza, Louis MacNeice writes, 'forgive me/For the sins that in me the world shall commit.' What do you think he means by this line?
4. Explain how the speaker's attitude towards the world is largely negative.
5. Does the poem highlight any positive aspects of the world? Explain your viewpoint.
6. Choose a phrase that you find striking or memorable (other than the ones in Q2 and Q3). Explain why you find this phrase striking.
7. Louis MacNeice uses many interesting words in this poem. Using a dictionary, find the meanings of the following words: console, engender, bureaucrats, hector, dragoon.

Writers' Workshop

Write a letter to the poet, Louis MacNeice, which includes one of the following sentences:
- I enjoyed your poem *Prayer Before Birth*.
- I found your poem *Prayer Before Birth* thoroughly depressing.

Listen to the Poet

Go to www.poetryarchive.org and listen to Louis MacNeice read this poem.

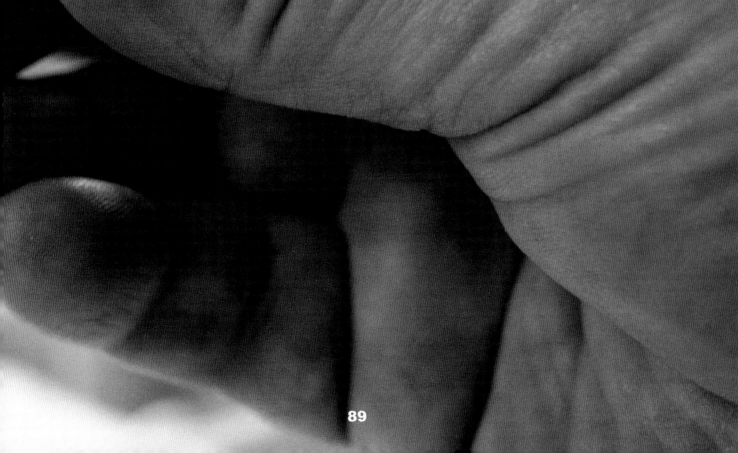

Love

I Am Very Bothered by Simon Armitage

I am very bothered when I think

of the bad things I have done in my life.

Not least that time in the chemistry lab

when I held a pair of scissors by the blades

and played the handles

in the naked lilac flame of the Bunsen burner;

then called your name, and handed them over.

O the unrivalled stench of branded skin

as you slipped your thumb and middle finger in,

then couldn't shake off the two burning rings. Marked,

the doctor said, for eternity.

Don't believe me, please, if I say

that was just my butterfingered way, at thirteen,

of asking you if you would marry me.

Questions
Exploring *I Am Very Bothered*

1. Why is the poet 'very bothered'?
2. Explain what the poet did with the scissors in chemistry class.
3. What does the poet mean when he says, 'that was just my butterfingered way, at thirteen,/of asking you if you would marry me'?
4. Considering what the poet says in the final stanza, what is the significance of the phrases 'finger' and 'burning rings' in the second stanza?
5. Do you feel the poem realistically describes the way boys try to attract the attention of girls? Explain your viewpoint.
6. Simon Armitage chose the title *I Am Very Bothered* for this poem. Suggest an alternative title. Explain your choice with reference to the poem.

Writers' Workshop

1. Write a short composition about a school experience that you remember well.
2. Write a poem from the perspective of the girl in *I Am Very Bothered*, beginning with the phrase, 'I too am very bothered …'

Find Out About the Poet
Learn about Simon Armitage and read more of his work at www.poetryarchive.org, www.poetryfoundation.org and www.simonarmitage.com.

Lovebirds by Jo Shapcott

So she moved into the hospital the last nine days
to tend him with little strokes and murmurs
as he sank into the sheets. Nurse
set out a low bed for her, night-times, next to his.
He nuzzled up to her as she brushed
away the multiplying cells with a sigh,
was glad as she ignored the many
effluents and the tang of death. The second
last morning of his life he opened
his eyes, saying, 'I can't wake up'
but wouldn't close them for his nap
until he was sure she was there.
Later he moved quietly to deeper sleep,
as Doctor said he would, still listening
to her twittering on and on until the last.

The Vacuum by Howard Nemerov

The house is so quiet now
The vacuum cleaner sulks in the corner closet,
Its bag limp as a stopped lung, its mouth
Grinning into the floor, maybe at my
Slovenly life, my dog-dead youth.

I've lived this way long enough,
But when my old woman died her soul
Went into that vacuum cleaner, and I can't bear
To see the bag swell like a belly, eating the dust
And the woollen mice, and begin to howl

Because there is old filth everywhere
She used to crawl, in the corner and under the stair.
I know now how life is cheap as dirt,
And still the hungry, angry heart
Hangs on and howls, biting at air.

Exploring *Lovebirds* **and** *The Vacuum*

Lovebirds

1. Explain in your own words what happens in the poem *Lovebirds*.
2. How would you describe the relationship between the couple in the poem. Refer to the poem in your answer.
3. Why wouldn't the man close his eyes 'until he was sure she was there'?
4. **(a)** Describe the final image of the poem.
    (b) What emotions does this image stir in you as a reader?

The Vacuum

5. Why is the house 'so quiet now'?
6. **(a)** Personification is a type of metaphor when a non-human thing is given human qualities. Find an example of personification in this poem.
    (b) Why do you think the poet chose to use personification?
7. **(a)** A simile is a comparison that uses the words like or as. Write down two similes from this poem.
    (b) Do you feel that these are effective comparisons? Explain your answer.
8. What do you think the poet means in the last two lines of this poem?

Comparison

9. Which poem do you prefer? Explain your answer.
10. '*Lovebirds* and *The Vacuum* both explore the pain of losing a loved one.' Discuss this statement with reference to both poems.

Write a short story inspired by one of these poems.

Love

My Mistress' Eyes are Nothing Like the Sun
by William Shakespeare

My mistress' eyes are nothing like the sun;
Coral is far more red than her lips' red;
If snow be white, why then her breasts are dun;
If hairs be wires, black wires grow on her head.
I have seen roses damasked, red and white,
But no such roses see I in her cheeks;
And in some perfumes is there more delight
Than in the breath that from my mistress reeks.
I love to hear her speak, yet well I know
That music hath a far more pleasing sound;
I grant I never saw a goddess go;
My mistress, when she walks, treads on the ground.
    And yet, by heaven, I think my love as rare
    As any she belied with false compare.

Glossary
dun: dull grayish brown
damasked: containing layers of colour
belie: to show to be false, to contradict

My Funny Valentine
lyrics by Lorenz Hart

My funny valentine
Sweet comic valentine
You make me smile with my heart

Your looks are laughable, unphotographable
Yet you're my favorite work of art

Is your figure less than Greek
Is your mouth a little bit weak
When you open it to speak, are you smart?

Don't change a hair for me
Not if you care for me
Stay little valentine stay

Each day is Valentine's Day

Glossary
Greek: in this case meaning classically perfect

Questions
Exploring *My Mistress' Eyes are Nothing Like the Sun* and *My Funny Valentine*

My Mistress' Eyes are Nothing Like the Sun
1. In your own words, describe the woman depicted in *My Mistress' Eyes are Nothing Like the Sun*.
2. In this poem, Shakespeare gives an image of his mistress through a series of contrasts. Find three examples of such contrasts.
3. Write out the rhyming scheme of this poem.
4. The poem ends with a rhyming couplet: 'And yet, by heaven, I think my love as rare/As any she belied with false compare'. What do you think Shakespeare means by these lines?
5. Do you feel the woman in the poem would be complimented or insulted by this sonnet? Explain with reference to the poem.

My Funny Valentine

6. Write a response to this song beginning with one of the following lines:
   - *My Funny Valentine* is a song that could cause great offence…
   - *My Funny Valentine* is a beautiful love song…
7. Write out the lyrics of a song that appeals to you. Write a personal response to this song. You may wish to consider the song's theme, imagery, subject matter, language, rhythm, melody etc.

Comparison

8. These texts both have similar ideas about love and beauty. Explain how the song and the poem are alike, quoting from both texts.
9. Which do you feel is more effective, the song or the poem? Justify your choice.

Writers' Workshop

Write a letter from the perspective of either of the women in the two poems. The letter should be addressed to the relevant poet/lyricist and provide a reaction to the song/poem.

Things To Think About: Sonnet

A sonnet is a 14-line-poem written using iambic pentameter (see below). Sonnets date back to the thirteenth century and often deal with the theme of love. The sonnet form requires poets to write with great skill and control. There are two main types of sonnet: Petrarchan and Shakespearean.

Petrarchan sonnets are named after the Italian poet Petrarch. They are dived into an eight-line section called an octet, followed by a six-line stanza called a sestet.

A Shakespearean sonnet, like the one above, has three four-line sections called quatrains, followed by a rhyming couplet. The rhyming scheme for a Shakespearean sonnet is *ababcdcdefefgg*.

Things To Think About: Iambic Pentameter

Iambic pentameter is a type of rhythm often found in Shakespeare's works. A line of iambic pentameter contains ten syllables, five of which are stressed. If you read the line below and clap your hands to every **DUM**, you will hear where the stresses lie.

da	DUM	da	DUM	da	DUM	da	DUM	da	DUM

When this is applied to a line from the poem it sounds like this:

da	DUM	da	DUM	da	DUM	da	DUM	da	DUM
My	mis-	tress'	eyes	are	noth-	ing	like	the	sun

Traditionally, iambic pentameter has been a very popular rhythm in poetry because it reflects the rhythms of human speech while retaining the musicality of poetry.

Listen to the Song

My Funny Valentine had been recorded by many celebrated singers including Chet Baker, Frank Sinatra, Ella Fitzgerald and Elvis Costello. See if a member of your class has a version at home or listen to it on the internet.

Love

Leaning into the Afternoons
by Pablo Neruda (translated by W.S. Merwin)

Leaning into the afternoons I cast my sad nets
towards your oceanic eyes.

There in the highest blaze my solitude lengthens and flames,
its arms turning like a drowning man's.

I send out red signals across your absent eyes
that move like the sea near a lighthouse.

You keep only darkness, my distant female,
from your regard sometimes the coast of dread emerges.

Leaning into the afternoons I fling my sad nets
to that sea that beats on your marine eyes.

The birds of night peck at the first stars
that flash like my soul when I love you.

The night gallops on its shadowy mare
shedding blue tassels over the land.

Questions
Exploring *Leaning into the Afternoons*

1. Who do you think is speaking in this poem?
2. **(a)** Personification is when a non-human thing is given a human quality. Find two examples of personification in the poem.
    (b) What does Neruda's use of personification tell you about the feelings of the speaker in the poem?
3. **(a)** Choose a phrase or image from the poem that expresses the speaker's loneliness or sense of longing.
    (b) Do you feel that these lines effectively communicate his loneliness? Why/why not?
4. How do you think the speaker feels about the woman he is describing? Explain why you think so.
5. **(a)** This poem contains some images that are energetic, and at times even violent. Identify two such images.
    (b) Why do you think Neruda includes these kinds of ideas in his poem?
6. '*Leaning into the Afternoons* contrasts darkness with brilliant colour and light.' Do you agree with this statement? Refer to the poem in your answer.
7. Suggest a different title for this poem. Explain why you suggested this title.

Writers' Workshop
Imagine you have been asked to make a video version of this poem. Describe what your finished video would be like. You may wish to comment on the types of visuals you would use, the music and the possibility of a voiceover. Refer to the poem in your response.

Things To Think About: Imagery
Leaning into the Afternoons has a strong painterly quality. This means that Neruda uses vivid imagery to convey the ideas in his poem and to provide the reader with a detailed mental picture. The poem captures the transition from afternoon to evening to night in its beautiful descriptions of light and colour: 'in the highest blaze my solitude lengthens and flames,/its arms turning like a drowning man's'. At the centre of this image is the lone figure of the fisherman casting his nets into the sea with resignation and longing.

Activity
Visual Response
Choose one stanza from the poem. Draw a picture or make a collage inspired by your chosen lines. Include the words of the stanza as part of your picture.

Find Out About the Poet
Pablo Neruda won the Nobel Prize for Literature in 1971. Go to www.nobelprize.org and discover some of his other poems.

A Barred Owl by Richard Wilbur

The warping night-air having brought the boom

Of an owl's voice into her darkened room,

We tell the wakened child that all she heard

Was an odd question from a forest bird,

Asking of us, if rightly listened to,

"Who cooks for you?" and then "Who cooks for you?"

Words, which can make our terrors bravely clear,

Can also thus domesticate a fear,

And send a small child back to sleep at night

Not listening for the sound of stealthy flight

Or dreaming of some small thing in a claw

Borne up to some dark branch and eaten raw.

Glossary
Barred: a type of owl; or a verb
meaning excluded; or perhaps a
pun on 'bard'

Questions
Exploring *A Barred Owl*

1. Why did the child awaken?
2. Explain the relevance of the phrase, 'Who cooks for you?'
3. What does the poet mean when he writes, 'Words … Can also domesticate a fear'?
4. Do the parents succeed in getting the child back to sleep? Explain with reference to the poem.
5. What is the poem's rhyming scheme?
6. The poem's title is a pun: the Barred Owl is a species of owl found all over America, but the word 'bar' also means to prevent or exclude. Explain how this second meaning of the word is relevant to the poem.
7. **(a)** Describe the image of the owl as it is presented in the poem's final three lines.
   (b) Explain how this image is at odds with what the parents have told their child.
   (c) What point do you feel the poet is making about parents and children in these final lines?

Writers' Workshop

1. Write a dialogue recreating the conversation between the parents and the child of this poem.
2. An anthology (collection) of nature poetry called *The Big Wild World* is being published. You have been invited to nominate a poem for the selection. Write a letter to the publishers explaining why you would or would not choose *A Barred Owl* for inclusion.

Things To Think About: Iambic Pentameter
This poem is written in iambic pentameter. Look back at page 95 to read about iambic pentameter.

Find Out About the Poet
You can learn more about Richard Wilbur and read his poetry at www.poetryfoundation.org.

Nature

Mushrooms by Sylvia Plath

Overnight, very
Whitely, discreetly,
Very quietly

Our toes, our noses
Take hold on the loam,
Acquire the air.

Nobody sees us,
Stops us, betrays us;
The small grains make room.

Soft fists insist on
Heaving the needles,
The leafy bedding,

Even the paving.
Our hammers, our rams,
Earless and eyeless,

Perfectly voiceless,
Widen the crannies,
Shoulder through holes. We

Diet on water,
On crumbs of shadow,
Bland-mannered, asking

Little or nothing.
So many of us!
So many of us!

We are shelves, we are
Tables, we are meek,
We are edible,

Nudgers and shovers
In spite of ourselves.
Our kind multiplies:

We shall by morning
Inherit the earth.
Our foot's in the door.

Glossary
loam: soil
meek: submissive; weak and
compliant

Questions

Exploring *Mushrooms*

1. Who is speaking in this poem? Explain your answer.
2. **(a)** List two phrases from the poem that you feel accurately capture the idea of mushrooms.
   (b) Explain why you chose these phrases.
3. Sylvia Plath makes much use of assonance (repeated vowel sounds in neighbouring words) in *Mushrooms*. Find two more examples of this in the poem.
4. The poet uses personification to give the mushrooms human qualities. Find three examples of this in the poem.
5. **(a)** How are the mushrooms portrayed as powerful in this poem?
   (b) How are the mushrooms depicted as vulnerable?
   (c) Which of the mushrooms' qualities do you feel is stressed more, their power or their vulnerability? Explain why you think so.
6. In *Mushrooms*, we can hear an echo of Psalm 37 from the Bible which says 'the meek shall inherit the earth'. Where is this idea present in the poem?
7. 'The mushrooms in this poem are portrayed as persistent and vaguely menacing.' Do you agree with this statement? Give reasons for your answer.
8. Can this poem by read as a comment on humanity? Explain your viewpoint.

Writers' Workshop

Make use of personification to write your own poem from the perspective of an object or something from nature. You may use *Mushrooms* as a model to help you.

Learn More About the Poet

Read Plath's poetry and find out more about her life at www.poets.org.

Nature

Bags of Meat by Thomas Hardy

'Here's a fine bag of meat,'
Says the master-auctioneer,
As the timid, quivering steer,
Starting a couple of feet
At the prod of a drover's stick,
And trotting lightly and quick,
A ticket stuck on his rump,
Enters with a bewildered jump.

'Where he's lived lately, friends,
I'd live till lifetime ends:
They've a whole life everyday
Down there in the Vale, have they!
He'd be worth the money to kill
And give away Christmas for goodwill.'

'Now here's a heifer – worth more
Than bid, were she bone-poor;
Yet she's round as a barrel of beer';
'She's a plum,' said the second auctioneer.

'Now this young bull – for thirty pound?
Worth that to manure your ground!'
'Or to stand,' chimed the second one,
'And have his picter done!'

The beast was rapped on the horns and snout
To make him turn about.
'Well,' cried a buyer, 'another crown –
Since I've dragged here from Taunton Town!'

'That calf, she sucked three cows,
Which is not matched for bouse
In the nurseries of high life
By the first-born of a nobleman's wife!'
The stick falls, meaning, 'A true tale's told,'
On the buttock of the creature sold,
And the buyer leans over and snips
His mark on one of the animal's hips.

Each beast, when driven in,
Looks round at the ring of bidders there
With a much-amazed reproachful stare,
As at unnatural kin,
For bringing him to a sinister scene
So strange, unhomelike, hungry, mean;
His fate the while suspended between
A butcher, to kill out of hand,
And a farmer, to keep on the land;
One can fancy a tear runs down his face
When the butcher wins, and he's driven from the place.

Glossary
steer: a castrated bull
bouse: alcoholic drink ('booze')

102

Nature

At the Bomb Testing Site by William Stafford

At noon in the desert a panting lizard
waited for history, its elbows tense,
watching the curve of a particular road
as if something might happen.

It was looking at something farther off
than people could see, an important scene
acted in stone for little selves
at the flute end of consequences.

There was just a continent without much on it
under a sky that never cared less.
Ready for a change, the elbows waited.
The hands gripped hard on the desert.

Questions

Exploring *Bags of Meat* and *At the Bomb Testing Site*

Bags of Meat

1. In your own words, describe the event depicted in *Bags of Meat*.
2. How is the steer (bull) portrayed in the first stanza?
3. Give two reasons why the cattle are good value, according to the auctioneers.
4. **(a)** Describe the tone of the auctioneers. Give examples from the poem.
   (b) Is their tone at odds with the experience of the cattle? Give reasons for your answer.
5. Do you feel sorry for the animals? Why/why not?

At the Bomb Testing Site

6. What is the lizard waiting for in this poem?
7. **(a)** Stafford gives the lizard some human qualities. Find an example of this.
   (b) What effect does this have on the reader?
8. How important is the title of this poem? Give reasons for your answer.
9. What do you think the poet means when he says, 'little selves/at the flute end of consequences'? Give reasons for your answer.
10. How does the poet create an air of tension and expectancy in the poem?
11. Write a fourth stanza for this poem, describing what happened next.

Comparison

12. 'Thomas Hardy's *Bags of Meat* and William Stafford's *At the Bomb Testing Site* explore humanity's relationship with animals and nature.' Discuss this statement, supporting your view with reference to the poem.

Debate
Research the issue of animal rights and debate the following motion: *That this house believes humanity has little respect for the environment and the creatures that live in it.*

The Past

Death of an Irishwoman by Michael Hartnett

Ignorant, in the sense
she ate monotonous food
and thought the world was flat,
and pagan, in the sense
she knew the things that moved
at night were neither dogs nor cats
but *pucas* and darkfaced men,
she nevertheless had fierce pride.
But sentenced in the end
to eat thin diminishing porridge
in a stone-cold kitchen
she clenched her brittle hands
around a world
she could not understand.
I loved her from the day she died.
She was a summer dance at the crossroads.
She was a card game where a nose was broken.
She was a song that nobody sings.
She was a house ransacked by soldiers.
She was a language seldom spoken.
She was child's purse, full of useless things.

Glossary
monotonous: boring; tedious; lacking in variety
pagan: here it refers to pre-Christian beliefs and traditions
pucas: mischievous spirits from Irish folklore
diminishing: decreasing; becoming weaker or smaller
ransacked: plundered; a house thoroughly searched, often damaged in the process

Questions

Exploring *Death of an Irishwoman*

1. In the poet's eyes, why is the woman 'ignorant'?
2. For what reason does the poet see the woman as 'pagan'?
3. What do you think the poet means when he writes, 'she clenched her brittle hands/around a world/she could not understand'? Give reasons for your answer.
4. What evidence is there that the poet was very fond of the old woman?
5. Describe the tone of the last six lines.
6. What do you think the poet means by each of the following metaphors?
   (a) 'She was a summer dance at the crossroads.'
   (b) 'She was a card game where a nose was broken.'
   (c) 'She was a language seldom spoken.'
   (d) 'She was child's purse, full of useless things.'
7. The old woman in this poem has been described as 'representing an Ireland of a previous age.' Write a response agreeing or disagreeing with this statement.

Writers' Workshop

Write a composition entitled 'Looking Back on the Past'.

The Past

Ozymandias by Percy Bysshe Shelley

I met a traveller from an antique land
Who said: Two vast and trunkless legs of stone
Stand in the desert… Near them, on the sand,
Half sunk, a shattered visage lies, whose frown,
And wrinkled lip, and sneer of cold command,
Tell that its sculptor well those passions read
Which yet survive, stamped on these lifeless things,
The hand that mocked them, and the heart that fed:
And on the pedestal these words appear:
'My name is Ozymandias, king of kings:
Look on my works, ye Mighty, and despair!'
Nothing beside remains. Round the decay
Of that colossal wreck, boundless and bare
The lone and level sands stretch far away.

Glossary
antique: ancient
visage: face; appearance

Questions

Exploring *Ozymandias*

1. How do we know that the original monument was large?
2. What evidence is there that the sculptor was a skilled craftsman?
3. Explain how this poem is a sonnet. Look back to page 95 for the definition of a sonnet.
4. Shelley makes much use of alliteration in this poem. Find three examples of this.
5. (a) Describe the carved face of Ozymandias as it is portrayed in the poem.
   (b) What does this suggest about Ozymandias?
6. What does the inscription on the pedestal suggest about the personality of Ozymandias?
7. The inscription on the pedestal seems to be at odds with the surrounding landscape. Explain how this is so.
8. What do you think is the theme of this poem?

Writers' Workshop

Ozymandias is another name for the Egyptian pharaoh, Ramses II. Imagine Ozymandias/Ramses II kept a diary. Write an entry for his diary the day the carving of his monument was completed.

The History of the Poem

Percy Bysshe Shelley wrote this sonnet in a competition with his friend, the poet Horace Smith, in 1818. Both poems deal with the same subject matter and make the same moral point but Smith's version lacks the brilliance of Shelley's.

The Past

Blankets by Ruth Fainlight

The stuffy ground-floor bedroom
at the back of our flat. The bed,
covered with blue Witney blankets
bound with paler blue velvet.

Measles, scarlet fever,
influenza, whooping cough.
The night I tripped over the oilstove
Mother lit to warm the bathroom.

From hip to heel, burning
paraffin splashed. Weeks in bed
under a sort of cradle made
to hold the weight of the blankets off.

Bunches of flowers, orange and red,
climbed the faded papered walls
up to the ceiling. My eyes rolled back
in their sockets, counting the nosegays.

Nightmares under the blankets.
Like sodden tufts of moss
bulging virulently green,
mounting the window ledge

and oozing through the open gap,
sooty spores clogging my
nostrils and mouth, the touch
of velvet would make me scream.

I still sleep under those blankets
(their velvet binding rubbed bare)
the self-same ones I pulled around
my shoulders and hid beneath:

now potent and dangerous
as plague-infected blankets thrown
over the walls of a city besieged,
or exchanged for the sacred land

of people with no more immunity
to the pathogens they carried, than I
to the fevers of memory in the folds
and the weave of these old blue blankets.

Glossary
Witney blankets: a type of blanket made from wool and nylon
paraffin: a type of fuel that can burn the skin
nosegays: small bunches of flowers
virulently: poisonously; spitefully hostile; maliciously
potent: powerful
pathogen: something that causes a disease such as a virus or bacterium

Questions

Exploring *Blankets*

1. How are the blankets described in the first stanza of the poem?
2. What illnesses does the poet associate with the blankets?
3. (a) Why was the poet confined to bed for a number of weeks in her childhood?
   (b) How is this experience portrayed by the poet?
4. (a) How do you think the poet feels about the old blankets? Quote from the poem to support your answer.
   (b) The blankets in this poem are a metaphor. Explain this metaphor.
5. The poet mentions people with no immunity to 'pathogens' exchanging their sacred land for blankets. To whom do you think she is referring?
6. What do you think is the message of this poem?

Writers' Workshop

Write about an object that brings back memories of the past for you.

Listen to the Poet

Go to **www.poetryarchive.org** and listen to Ruth Fainlight read her poem.

The Past

Death of a Naturalist by Seamus Heaney

All year the flax-dam festered in the heart
Of the townland; green and heavy-headed
Flax had rotted there, weighted down by huge sods.
Daily it sweltered in the punishing sun.
Bubbles gargled delicately, bluebottles
Wove a strong gauze of sound around the smell.
There were dragonflies, spotted butterflies,
But best of all was the warm thick slobber
Of frogspawn that grew like clotted water
In the shade of the banks. Here, every spring
I would fill jampotfuls of the jellied
Specks to range on window-sills at home,
On shelves at school, and wait and watch until
The fattening dots burst into nimble-
Swimming tadpoles. Miss Walls would tell us how
The daddy frog was called a bullfrog
And how he croaked and how the mammy frog
Laid hundreds of little eggs and this was
Frogspawn. You could tell the weather by frogs too
For they were yellow in the sun and brown
In rain.

Then one hot day when fields were rank
With cowdung in the grass the angry frogs
Invaded the flax-dam; I ducked through hedges
To a coarse croaking that I had not heard
Before. The air was thick with a bass chorus.
Right down the dam gross-bellied frogs were cocked
On sods; their loose necks pulsed like sails. Some hopped:
The slap and plop were obscene threats. Some sat
Poised like mud grenades, their blunt heads farting.
I sickened, turned, and ran. The great slime kings
Were gathered there for vengeance and I knew
That if I dipped my hand the spawn would clutch it.

Glossary
flax: a type of plant fibre that is spun into linen
flax-dam: a pool where flax is held down by sods and softened before it's processed. The smell is strong and unpleasant.
festered: rotted
gauze: a thin haze; netted material often used to dress wounds
nimble: quick and agile
rank: having a strong smell

Questions

Exploring *Death of a Naturalist*

1. **(a)** In your own words, describe the flax-dam as it is depicted in the first stanza.
    (b) What did Miss Walls teach her pupils about frogspawn?
    (c) Explain how the young Heaney was able to judge the weather by looking at the frogs.
2. Identify four verbs from the first stanza that you feel help bring the scene to life. In the case of each, explain why you think these verbs are well chosen.
3. Describe the scene that is presented in the second stanza.
4. Heaney remembers how his attitude towards frogs changed. Describe this change and why it occurred.
5. Why do you think the poem is called *Death of a Naturalist*?
6. **(a)** Find two phrases in this poem where the poet appeals to the senses.
    (b) What effect does this kind of language have on the reader?
7. 'Seamus Heaney has impressive powers of observation and a sharp eye for detail.' Discuss this statement using evidence from the poem.

Writers' Workshop

1. In *Death of a Naturalist*, Seamus Heaney reflects on a moment from his childhood, when his view of the world changed. Write about a moment from your childhood that was significant to you.
2. Your class has decided to make a video to accompany the text of this poem. Describe what this video would look like. You may wish to refer to the images, music, colour, voiceover or any other feature of video. Refer to the poem throughout your answer.

Poetry Projects

Project 1: An Anthology of the Class's Work

Task

- **As a class,** your task is to create an anthology of the class's poems.
- **Each student** in the group must compose a poem to be included in the anthology.
- **Each student** must write a short introduction to another person's poem.

Guidelines

- The website www.poetryireland.ie may offer some help.
- Set a clear date for submission of poems.
- Consider having a theme for your anthology (maybe: transition, identity, the future, teenage kicks etc.)
- Decide who should write the introductions for which poems.
- Make decisions democratically on which poems to include by voting.
- You may want to appoint an editor, design team, production team, chairperson (for meetings), secretary (for meetings).

Project 2: Study of a Poet

This project allows you to independently explore a poet's work. The poems you include in your project will say something about you. To complete this project, you will need regular access to the internet.

Task

- Choose a poet (from this book or another book) that you find interesting and write a report on that poet.

Project Guidelines

Your study should contain all of the following:

- A **short biography** of the poet. Where is the poet from? Has his/her life been interesting, unusual or controversial? Has the poet won any major awards?
- An **anthology of six poems** by the poet that you found interesting. This will be printed from the internet, photocopied from books or copied from sources.
- An **overview of the poet's work.** Look at the themes the poet explores, interesting stylistic features and the poems' subject-matter.
- A **personal response** to one poem. Write an in-depth response to one poem. You may wish to discuss the poem's theme, subject-matter, imagery, language, emotions, mood, tone or any other features you find interesting.
- A **bibliography.** This is a list of all the books and websites that you used while writing this project.

Research Guidelines

- To get you started, some website addresses have been suggested below. These contain helpful information about many poets and samples of their work.
- Do not rely solely on the websites listed here. You will need to visit other websites, use the library or find books at home to complete your study.
- Keep a list of every website you visit for your bibliography (see above).
- Plagiarism: This is when you claim somebody else's work is your own. It is important that you do not plagiarise. Use the internet to find information and ideas, but these must be expressed in your own words.

Helpful Websites

The following websites contain useful information and anthologise thousands of poems.

- www.poetryarchive.org
- www.poets.org
- www.poetryfoundation.org
- www.poetsgraves.co.uk

Mechanics:
Inverted Commas

Inverted commas are also called quotation marks. **They are used:**
- in direct speech
- for quotations
- for titles of poems, articles etc.
- to emphasise a word

Inverted commas may be single: 'Good morning' or double: "Good morning". Both styles are acceptable but you must remain consistent.

Direct Speech

When a character speaks out loud, inverted commas are placed around the words spoken. This separates the character's words from the narrator's. For example: 'You better give me that back,' he threatened, 'I won't tell you again.'

Punctuation such as question marks, exclamation marks, commas and full stops are placed inside the inverted commas.
'Is anybody there?' asked the terrified man.

If more than one person is speaking, a new line is started for each speaker.
'Did you do your homework?' asked Rachael.
'Of course I did,' replied Sarah, 'Didn't you?'

Quotations

When quoting somebody, you should use inverted commas to indicate that the words are not your own. For example:
   Homer Simpson reminds the audience of his stupidity when he tells Lisa, 'Vampires are make-believe, like elves, gremlins and Eskimos.'

Single inverted commas have been used in the example above. For a quote within a quote, double inverted commas should be used:
   'Dad said, "Vampires are make-believe,"' recalled Lisa.

Titles

To avoid confusion, you should place titles inside inverted commas. The following examples show how inverted commas can change the meaning of a sentence. The first example is about the play 'Hamlet', the second is about the character of Hamlet.

'Hamlet' radically changed my outlook on life.
Hamlet radically changed my outlook on life.
   When typing, titles of books and films can be italicised or underlined instead of using inverted commas: *Hamlet*, *The Great Gatsby*, *The Dark Knight*.

Emphasis

Look at how inverted commas change the meaning of the following sentence:

She served me her food with a grin.

She served me her 'food' with a grin.

Most people would rather eat the food in the first example. The inverted commas radically change the meaning of the sentence.

Look at the following sentence:

The teacher shared his wisdom about life with the class.

The teacher shared his 'wisdom' about life with the class.

Most people would rather not listen to the teacher in the second example.

Practising Inverted Commas

Rewrite these sentences using inverted commas.

1. Where do the inverted commas go? asked the student.
2. We're over here! shouted the stranded climbers.
3. My favourite book of all time has to be Oliver Twist.
4. Stop that man, the hysterical woman shrieked, he's stolen my purse!
5. Albert Einstein celebrated innovative thinkers when he said, Anyone who has never made a mistake has never tried anything new.
6. Children really brighten a home, stated the father, They never turn the lights off.
7. It was Pádraig Pearse who proclaimed, Ireland unfree shall never be at peace.
8. Although released a few years ago, The Dark Knight has remained thrilling to watch.
9. As Marie Antoinette was led to the guillotine, her last words were: Pardon me, sir. I did not do it on purpose. She had accidently stepped on the executioner's foot.
10. I went to a bookstore and asked the saleswoman, Where's the self help section? She replied, If I tell you, that would defeat the purpose. (George Carlin)

Short Fiction:

4 The Truth that Didn't Happen

> *But it's the truth even if it didn't happen.*
>
> – The Chief, from Ken Kesey's
> One Flew Over the Cuckoo's Nest

The Trout by Seán Ó Faoláin

One of the first places Julia always ran to when they arrived in G— was The Dark Walk. It is a laurel walk, very old; almost gone wild; a lofty midnight tunnel of smooth, sinewy branches. Underfoot the tough brown leaves are never dry enough to crackle: there is always a suggestion of damp and cool trickle.

She raced right into it. For the first few yards she always had the memory of the sun behind her, then she felt the dusk closing swiftly down on her so that she screamed with pleasure and raced on to reach the light at the far end; and it was always just a little too long in coming so that she emerged gasping, clasping her hands, laughing, drinking in the sun. When she was filled with the heat and glare she would turn and consider the ordeal again.

This year she had the extra joy of showing it to her small brother, and of terrifying him as well as herself. And for him the fear lasted longer because his legs were so short and she had gone out at the far end while he was still screaming and racing.

When they had done this many times they came back to the house to tell everybody that they had done it. He boasted. She mocked. They squabbled.

'Cry babby !'

'You were afraid yourself, so there!'

'I won't take you any more.'

'You're a big pig.'

'I hate you.'

Tears were threatening, so somebody said, 'Did you see the well?' She opened her eyes at that and held up her long lovely neck suspiciously and decided to be incredulous. She was twelve and at that age little girls are beginning to suspect most stories: they have already found out too many, from Santa Claus to the stork. How could there be a well! In The Dark Walk? That she had visited year after year? Haughtily she said, 'Nonsense.'

But she went back, pretending to be going somewhere else, and she found a hole scooped in the rock at the side of the walk, choked with damp leaves, so shrouded by ferns that she uncovered it only after much searching. At the back of this little cavern there was about a quart of water. In the water she suddenly perceived a panting trout. She rushed for Stephen and dragged him to see, and they were both so excited that they were no longer afraid of the darkness as they hunched down and peered in at the fish panting in his tiny prison, his silver stomach going up and down like an engine.

Nobody knew how the trout got there. Even old Martin in the kitchen garden laughed and refused to believe that it was there, or pretended not to believe, until she forced him to come down and see. Kneeling and pushing back his tattered old cap he peered in.

'Be cripes, you're right. How the divil in hell did that fella get there?'

She stared at him suspiciously.

'You knew?' she accused; but he said, 'The divil a' know,' and reached down to lift it out. Convinced, she hauled him back. If she had found it, then it was her trout.

Her mother suggested that a bird had carried the spawn. Her father thought that in the winter a small streamlet might have carried it down there as a baby, and it had been safe until the summer came and the water began to dry up. She said, 'I see,' and went back to look again and consider the matter in private. Her brother remained behind, wanting to hear the whole story of the trout, not really interested in the actual trout but much interested in the story which his mummy began to make up for him on the lines of, 'So one day Daddy Trout and Mammy Trout...' When he retailed it to her she said, 'Pooh.'

It troubled her that the trout was always in the same position; he had no room to turn; all the time the silver belly went up and down; otherwise he was motionless. She wondered what he ate, and in between visits to Joey Pony and the boat, and a bathe to get cool, she thought of his hunger. She brought him down bits of dough; once she brought him a worm. He ignored the food. He just went on panting. Hunched over him she thought how all the winter, while she was at school, he had been in there. All the winter, in The Dark Walk, all day, all night, floating around alone. She drew the leaf of her hat down around her ears and chin and stared. She was still thinking of it as she lay in bed.

It was late June, the longest days of the year. The sun had sat still for a week, burning up the world. Although it was after ten o'clock it was still bright and still hot. She lay on her back under a single sheet, with her long legs spread, trying to keep cool. She could see the D of the moon through the fir tree – they slept on the ground floor. Before they went to bed her mummy had told Stephen the story of the trout again, and she, in her bed, had resolutely presented her back to them and read her book. But she had kept one ear cocked.

'And so, in the end, this naughty fish who would not stay at home got bigger and bigger and bigger, and the water got smaller and smaller…'

Passionately she had whirled and cried, 'Mummy, don't make it a horrible old moral story!' Her mummy had brought in a fairy godmother then, who sent lots of rain, and filled the well, and a stream poured out and the trout floated away down to the river below. Staring at the moon she knew that there are no such things as fairy godmothers and that the trout, down in The Dark Walk, was panting like an engine. She heard somebody unwind a fishing reel. Would the *beasts* fish him out !

She sat up. Stephen was a hot lump of sleep, lazy thing. The Dark Walk would be full of little scraps of moon. She leaped up and looked out the window, and somehow it was not so lightsome now that she saw the dim mountains far away and the black firs against the breathing land and heard a dog say *bark-bark*. Quietly she lifted the ewer of water and climbed out the window and scuttled along the cool but cruel gravel down to the maw of the tunnel. Her pyjamas were very short so that when she splashed water it wet her ankles. She peered into the tunnel. Something alive rustled inside there. She raced in, and up and down she raced, and flurried, and cried aloud, 'Oh, gosh, I can't find it,' and then at last she did. Kneeling down in the damp she put her hand into the slimy hole. When the body lashed they were both mad with fright. But she gripped him and shoved him into the ewer and raced, with her teeth ground, out to the other end of the tunnel and down the steep paths to the river's edge.

All the time she could feel him lashing his tail against the side of the ewer. She was afraid he would jump right out. The gravel cut into her soles until she came to the cool ooze of the river's bank where the moon mice on the water crept into her feet. She poured out, watching until he plopped. For a second he was visible in the water. She hoped he was not dizzy. Then all she saw was the glimmer of the moon in the silent-flowing river, the dark firs, the dim mountains, and the radiant pointed face laughing down at her out of the empty sky.

She scuttled up the hill, in the window, plonked down the ewer, and flew through the air like a bird into bed. The dog said *bark-bark*. She heard the fishing reel whirring. She hugged herself and giggled. Like a river of joy her holiday spread before her.

In the morning Stephen rushed to her, shouting that 'he' was gone, and asking 'where' and 'how'. Lifting her nose in the air she said superciliously, 'Fairy godmother, I suppose?' and strolled away patting the palms of her hands.

Glossary
Ewer: a large jug

Questions
Exploring *The Trout*

1. **(a)** In your own words, describe 'The Dark Walk'.
   (b) Why do you think Julia is drawn to this place?
2. **(a)** What is her mother's explanation as to how the trout got into the little cavern?
   (b) What is her father's explanation?
3. How do you know that Julia is concerned for the trout?
4. What evidence can you find that shows Julia is growing up?
5. Why do you think Julia sneaks out at night to rescue the trout?
6. What kind of person do you think Julia is?
7. What point do you think is being made in the story's final paragraph?
8. **(a)** Seán Ó Faoláin's writing is often highly descriptive. Give three examples of descriptive writing in this short story that you find to be vivid or striking.
   (b) Explain why these sentences stand out for you.
9. Using a dictionary, match the following words from the story with their definitions.

1.	Lofty	a.	Partial darkness; shade; gloom
2.	Sinewy	b.	Doubtful; not willing to believe; sceptical
3.	Dusk		
4.	Incredulous	c.	Ran hurriedly; scampered
5.	Shrouded	d.	To do something with determination
6.	Streamlet	e.	Tough; interwoven
7.	Resolutely	f.	Elevated
8.	Scuttled	g.	Emitting light
9.	Radiant	h.	A small river
10.	Superciliously	i.	Haughtily; to act with superiority
		j.	Covered over; hidden from view

Writers' Workshop

The Trout captures a moment in which the story's character takes an important step towards adulthood. Write about a time in your life when you felt you matured as an individual or started to leave your childhood behind.

Language Lesson: Feature of Fiction – Omniscient Narrator

It is important to distinguish between the author of a story and the narrator. The author is the person who wrote the story; the narrator is the voice telling the story. The narrator's point of view may be different to the author's. For example, a story could be narrated by an angry male car thief but the author could be a happy woman who has never committed a crime in her life.

There are two types of narrator commonly used in fiction:
⇨ **First person** narrator: I said, I thought, I see.
⇨ **Third person** or omniscient narrator: She said, he thought, Julia sees.
   Note: The **second person** (you said, you thought, you see) is only occasionally used.

An omniscient narrator is one who tells a story but does not get involved in the action. An omniscient narrator reports the thoughts and feelings of the characters.

Omniscient means all knowing. An omniscient narrator, therefore, knows everything that occurs in a story. He can see all that happens and can relay a character's most private thoughts and feelings.

Although *The Trout* focuses on the experiences of one character (Julia), the story is not told directly from her point of view. Instead, the writer has used an omniscient narrator: One of the first places <u>Julia</u> always ran to when they arrived in G— was The Dark Walk; <u>She</u> wondered what he ate; <u>She</u> scuttled up the hill.

The omniscient narrator is not necessarily a neutral voice. The author may have made judgements about the characters or the situation in the story, and this can affect how it is told. In *The Trout*, the omniscient narrator encourages the reader to empathise with Julia: we understand how The Dark Walk is both scary and thrilling for her, and her motivation for freeing the trout is made clear to us.

About The Author

Seán Ó Faoláin (1900 – 1991)

Seán Ó Faoláin is one of Ireland's most celebrated short story writers. He was born in Cork City as John Francis Whelan.

Ó Faoláin was profoundly affected by the 1916 Easter Rising. He was at first opposed to the rebellion but he became militant after the British forces executed the Rising's leaders. He learnt Irish, changed his name to its Irish version and fought against the British in the War of Independence. During the Civil War, he fought on the Republican side. However, Ó Faoláin said he avoided extreme violence, 'To have cast me for the role of a gunman would have been like casting me as a bull-fighter.'

He devoted the rest of his life to writing and lecturing. He taught in both Britain and America. Ó Faoláin was most famous for his short stories and novels but he also wrote literary criticism, travel books and biographies.

He was a member of Aosdána, a group of artists who are recognised for their exceptional contribution to the arts. On occasion, a member may be given the title of Saoi (literally meaning 'wise one') in recognition of outstanding achievement. Only seven Aosdána members may hold this title at one time. Ó Faoláin was awarded the title in 1986, 5 years before he died.

Fiction

Superman and Paula Brown's New Snowsuit by Sylvia Plath

The year the war began I was in the fifth grade at the Annie F. Warren Grammar School in Winthrop, and that was the winter I won the prize for drawing the best Civil Defense signs. That was also the winter of Paula Brown's new snowsuit, and even now, thirteen years later, I can recall the changing colors of those days, clear and definite patterns seen through a kaleidoscope.

I lived on the bay side of town, on Johnson Avenue, opposite the Logan Airport, and before I went to bed each night, I used to kneel by the west window of my room and look over to the lights of Boston that blazed and blinked far off across the darkening water. The sunset flaunted its pink flag above the airport, and the sound of waves was lost in the perpetual droning of the planes. I marveled at the moving beacons on the runway and watched, until it grew completely dark, the flashing red and green lights that rose and set in the sky like shooting stars. The airport was my Mecca, my Jerusalem. All night I dreamed of flying.

Those were the days of my technicolor dreams. Mother believed that I should have an enormous amount of sleep, and so I was never really tired when I went to bed. This was the best time of the day, when I could lie in the vague twilight, drifting off to sleep, making up dreams inside my head the way they should go. My flying dreams were believable as a landscape by Dalí, so real that I would awake with a sudden shock, a breathless sense of having tumbled like Icarus from the sky and caught myself on the soft bed just in time.

These nightly adventures in space began when Superman started invading my dreams and teaching me how to fly. He used to come roaring by in his shining blue suit with his cape whistling in the wind, looking remarkably like my Uncle Frank, who was living with Mother and me. In the magic whirring of his cape I could hear the wings of a hundred seagulls, the motors of a thousand planes.

I was not the only worshiper of Superman in our block. David Sterling, a pale, bookish boy who lived down the street, shared my love for the sheer poetry of flight. Before supper every night, we listened to Superman together on the radio, and during the day we made up our own adventures on the way to school.

The Annie F. Warren Grammar School was a red brick building, set back from the main highway on a black tar street, surrounded by barren gravel playgrounds. Out by the parking lot David and I found a perfect alcove for our Superman dramas. The dingy back entrance to the school was deep set in a long passageway which was an excellent place for surprise captures and sudden rescues.

During recess, David and I came into our own. We ignored the boys playing baseball on the gravel court and the girls giggling at dodge-ball in the dell. Our Superman games made us outlaws, yet gave us a sense of windy superiority. We even found a stand-in for a villain in Sheldon Fein, the sallow mamma's boy on our block who was left out of the boys' games because he cried whenever anybody tagged him and always managed to fall down and skin his fat knees.

At this time my Uncle Frank was living with us while waiting to be drafted, and I was sure that he bore an extraordinary resemblance to Superman incognito. David couldn't see his likeness as clearly as I did, but he admitted that Uncle Frank was the strongest man he had ever known, and could do lots of tricks like making caramels disappear under napkins and walking on his hands.

That same winter, war was declared, and I remember sitting by the radio with Mother and Uncle Frank and feeling a queer foreboding in the air. Their voices were low and serious, and their talk was of planes and German bombs. Uncle Frank said something about Germans in America being put in prison for the duration, and Mother kept saying over and over again about Daddy: 'I'm only glad Otto didn't live to see this; I'm only glad Otto didn't live to see it come to this.'

In school we began to draw Civil Defense signs, and that was when I beat Jimmy Lane in our block for the fifth-grade prize. Every now and then we would practice an air raid. The fire bell would ring and we would take up our coats and pencils and file down the creaking stairs to the basement, where we sat in special corners according to our color tags, and put the pencils between our teeth so the bombs wouldn't make us bite our tongues by mistake. Some of the little children in the lower grades would cry because it was dark in the cellar, with only the bare ceiling lights on the cold black stone.

The threat of war was seeping in everywhere. At recess, Sheldon became a Nazi and borrowed a goose step from the movies, but his Uncle Macy was really over in Germany, and Mrs. Fein began to grow thin and pale because she heard that Macy was a prisoner and then nothing more.

The winter dragged on, with a wet east wind coming always from the ocean, and the snow melting before there was enough for coasting. One Friday afternoon, just before Christmas, Paula Brown gave her annual birthday party, and I was invited because it was for all the children on our block. Paula lived across from Jimmy Lane on Somerset Terrace, and nobody on our block really liked her, because she was bossy and stuck up, with pale skin and long red pigtails and watery blue eyes.

She met us at the door of her house in a white organdy dress, her red hair tied up in sausage curls with a satin bow. Before we could sit down at the table for birthday cake and ice cream, she had to show us all her presents. There were a great many because it was both her birthday and Christmas time too.

Paula's favorite present was a new snowsuit, and she tried it on for us. The snowsuit was powder blue and came in a silver box from Sweden, she said. The front of the jacket was all embroidered with pink and white roses and bluebirds, and the leggings had embroidered straps. She even had a little white angora beret and angora mittens to go with it.

After dessert we were all driven to the movies by Jimmy Lane's father to see the late afternoon show as a special treat. Mother had found out that the main feature was *Snow White* before she would let me go, but she hadn't realized that there was a war picture playing with it.

After I went to bed that night, as soon as I closed my eyes, the prison camp sprang to life in my mind. No matter how hard I thought of Superman before I went to sleep, no crusading blue figure came roaring down in heavenly anger to smash the yellow men who invaded my dreams. When I woke up in the morning, my sheets were damp with sweat.

Saturday was bitterly cold, and the skies were gray and blurred with the threat of snow. I was dallying home from the store that afternoon, curling up my chilled fingers in my mittens, when I saw a couple of kids playing Chinese tag out in front of Paula Brown's house.

Paula stopped in the middle of the game to eye me coldly. 'We need someone else,' she said. 'Want to play?' She tagged me on the ankle then, and I hopped around and finally caught Sheldon Fein as he was bending down to fasten one of his furlined overshoes. An early thaw had melted away the snow in the street, and the tarred pavement was gritted with sand left from the snow trucks. In front of Paula's house somebody's car had left a glittering black stain of oil slick.

We went running about in the street, retreating to the hard, brown lawns when the one who was 'It' came too close. Jimmy Lane came out of his house and stood watching us for a short while, and then joined in. Every time he was 'It,' he chased Paula in her powder blue snowsuit, and she screamed shrilly and looked around at him with her wide, watery eyes, and he always managed to catch her.

Only one time she forgot to look where she was going, and as Jimmy reached out to tag her, she slid into the oil slick. We all froze when she went down on her side as if we were playing statues. No one said a word, and for a minute there was only the sound of the plane across the bay. The dull, green light of later afternoon came closing down on us, cold and final as a window blind.

Paula's snowsuit was smeared wet and black with oil along the side. Her angora mittens were dripping like black cat's fur. Slowly, she sat up and looked at us standing around her, as if searching for something. Then, suddenly, her eyes fixed on me.

'You,' she said deliberately, pointing at me, 'you pushed me.'

There was another second of silence, and then Jimmy Lane turned on me. 'You did it,' he taunted. 'You did it.'

Sheldon and Paula and Jimmy and the rest of them faced me with a strange joy flickering in the back of their eyes. 'You did it, you pushed her,' they said.

And even when I shouted 'I did not!' they were all moving in on me, chanting in a chorus, 'Yes, you did, yes, you did, we saw you.' In the well of faces moving toward me I saw no help, and I began to wonder if Jimmy had pushed Paula, or if she had fallen by herself, and I was not sure. I wasn't sure at all.

I started walking past them, walking home, determined not to run, but when I had left them behind me, I felt the sharp thud of a snowball on my left shoulder, and another. I picked up a faster stride and rounded the corner by Kellys'. There was my dark brown shingled house ahead of me, and inside, Mother and Uncle Frank, home on furlough. I began to run in the cold, raw evening toward the bright squares of light in the windows that were home.

Uncle Frank met me at the door. 'How's my favourite trooper?' he asked, and he swung me so high in the air that my head grazed the ceiling. There was a big love in his voice that drowned out the shouting which still echoed in my ears.

'I'm fine,' I lied, and he taught me some jujitsu in the living room until Mother called us for supper.

Candles were set on the white linen tablecloth, and miniature flames flickered in the silver and the glasses. I could see another room reflected beyond the dark dining-room window where the people laughed and talked in a secure web of light, held together by its indestructible brilliance.

All at once the doorbell rang, and Mother rose to answer it. I could hear David Sterling's high, clear voice in the hall. There was a cold draft from the open doorway, but he and Mother kept on talking, and he did not come in. When Mother came back to the table, her face was sad. 'Why didn't you tell me?' she said. 'Why didn't you tell me that you pushed Paula in the mud and spoiled her new snowsuit?'

A mouthful of chocolate pudding blocked my throat, thick and bitter. I had to wash it down with milk. Finally, I said, 'I didn't do it.'

But the words came out like hard, dry little seeds, hollow and insincere. I tried again. 'I didn't do it. Jimmy Lane did it.'

'Of course we'll believe you,' Mother said slowly, 'but the whole neighborhood is talking about it. Mrs. Sterling heard the story from Mrs. Fein and sent David over to say we should buy Paula a new snowsuit. I can't understand it.'

'I didn't do it,' I repeated, and the blood beat in my ears like a slack drum. I pushed my chair away from the table, not looking at Uncle Frank or Mother sitting there, solemn and sorrowful in the candlelight.

The staircase to the second floor was dark, but I went down the long hall to my room without turning on the light switch and shut the door. A small unripe moon was shafting squares of greenish light along the floor and the windowpanes were fringed with frost.

I threw myself fiercely down on my bed and lay there, dry-eyed and burning. After a while I heard Uncle Frank coming up the stairs and knocking on my door. When I didn't answer, he walked in and sat down on my bed. I could see his strong shoulders bulk against the moonlight, but in the shadows his face was featureless.

'Tell me, honey,' he said very softly, 'tell me. You don't have to be afraid. We'll understand. Only tell me what really happened. You have never had to hide anything from me, you know that. Only tell me how it really happened.'

'I told you,' I said. 'I told you what happened, and I can't make it any different. Not even for you I can't make it any different.'

He sighed then and got up to go away. 'Okay, honey,' he said at the door. 'Okay, but we'll pay for another snowsuit anyway just to make everybody happy, and ten years from now no one will ever know the difference.'

The door shut behind him and I could hear his footsteps growing fainter as he walked off down the hall. I lay there alone in bed, feeling the black shadow creeping up the underside of the world like a flood tide. The silver airplanes and the blue capes all dissolved and vanished, wiped away like the crude drawings of a child in colored chalk from the colossal blackboard of the dark. That was the year the war began, and the real world, and the difference.

Glossary

Dalí: Salvador Dalí, a Spanish painter famous for his surrealist (dreamlike) paintings.

Icarus: a boy from Greek mythology who escaped a labyrinth using wings of wax and feathers. Despite his father's warnings, Icarus flew too close to the sun. His wings melted and he drowned in the sea.

furlough: a holiday or leave from military service

Questions

Exploring *Superman and Paula Brown's New Snowsuit*

1. In your own words, explain what happened to Paula Brown's new snowsuit.
2. Describe the narrator's attitude towards her Uncle Frank. Refer to the story in your answer.
3. Do you feel that the child's mother and uncle handled the problem of Paula Brown's snowsuit well? Explain your answer.
4. The narrator refers to the conversation between her mother and Mr Sterling at the front door. Write the dialogue for this conversation as you imagine it.
5. How does Sylvia Plath convey the narrator's frustration at being falsely accused?
6. In your opinion, what kind of person is the narrator of this story?
7. What point do you think the narrator is making in the final paragraph when she says: 'The silver airplanes and the blue capes all dissolved and vanished, wiped away like the crude drawings of a child in colored chalk from the colossal blackboard of the dark'?
8. Do you think it is significant that the story is set against the backdrop of World War II? Explain your answer.
9. Explain each of the following sentences in your own words.
   (a) 'I can recall the changing colors of those days, clear and definite patterns seen through a kaleidoscope.'
   (b) 'In the magic whirring of his cape I could hear the wings of a hundred seagulls, the motors of a thousand planes.'
   (c) 'But the words came out like hard, dry little seeds, hollow and insincere.'
   (d) 'That was the year the war began, and the real world, and the difference.'
10. (a) The narrator refers to colour and light a number of times in this story. Find five examples of this.
    (b) How do the references to colour and light change in the second half of the story?
    (c) Why do you think Sylvia Plath chose to refer to colour and light in this way?

Writers' Workshop

Imagine you are Paula Brown. Write a diary entry for the day your snowsuit was ruined.

Language Lesson: Feature of Fiction – First Person Narrative

A first person narrative is a story told from the perspective of one of the characters. This encourages the reader to feel very close to the narrator and to consider the character's point of view. In this story, Sylvia Plath writes in the first person: 'The year the war began I was in the fifth grade'; 'I lay there alone in bed, feeling the black shadow creeping up the underside of the world'; 'I lied.'

In a first person narrative, often the reader will empathise with the character, feeling sorry for them if something bad happens and celebrating if the character overcomes an obstacle. In Plath's story, the reader feels concern for the narrator when Paula Brown accuses her of ruining the snowsuit, and just like the narrator, the reader feels frustrated when the mother and uncle decide to buy Paula a new one.

About The Author

Sylvia Plath (1932 – 1963)

Sylvia Plath was born in Massachusetts in America in 1932. Her father died when she was only eight and this experience left a lasting impression on her.

In her early twenties, Plath won a short-story competition which allowed her to work as an editor of *Mademoiselle* magazine for a summer in New York. However, after she returned home she suffered a severe bout of depression, attempted suicide and was admitted to a mental institution where she received electric shock therapy. Much of this experience inspired her semi-autobiographical novel *The Bell Jar.*

Plath seemed to recover well and eventually won a scholarship to Cambridge University in England where she met the poet Ted Hughes in early 1956. Their attraction to each other was immediate and passionate; they were married in June the same year.

Plath's collection of poems, *Colossus,* was published in 1960 and within two years she had given birth to two children: Frieda and Nicholas. The same year her son was born, Hughes left Plath for Assia Wevill with whom he had been having an affair. During the winter of 1962, Plath suffered a deep depression but wrote most of the poems for her collection of poetry, *Ariel*. Her only novel, *The Bell Jar,* was published the following year.

Throughout her life Plath had suffered from bouts of depression. Sadly, during the winter of 1963, she felt unable to cope and committed suicide. She was thirty years old.

She was buried in West Yorkshire under the name 'Sylvia Plath Hughes'. Some of Plath's fans blamed Ted Hughes for her suicide and admirers of her work defaced her gravestone by chiselling off the name 'Hughes'. The stone has been repaired a number of times.

After her death, Plath's book *Ariel* was published by Ted Hughes. It was acclaimed by critics and cemented Plath's place as a great poet.

Fiction

The Tell-Tale Heart by Edgar Allan Poe

TRUE! – nervous – very, very dreadfully nervous I had been and am; but why *will* you say that I am mad? The disease had sharpened my senses – not destroyed – not dulled them. Above all was the sense of hearing acute. I heard all things in the heaven and in the earth. I heard many things in hell. How, then, am I mad? Hearken! and observe how healthily – how calmly, I can tell you the whole story.

It is impossible to say how first the idea entered my brain; but, once conceived, it haunted me day and night. Object there was none. Passion there was none. I loved the old man. He had never wronged me. He had never given me insult. For his gold I had no desire. I think it was his eye! yes, it was this! One of his eyes resembled that of a vulture – a pale blue eye with a film over it. Whenever it fell upon me my blood ran cold; and so by degrees – very gradually – I made up my mind to take the life of the old man, and thus rid myself of the eye for ever.

Now this is the point. You fancy me mad. Madmen know nothing. But you should have seen *me*. You should have seen how wisely I proceeded – with what caution – with what foresight – with what dissimulation I went to work! I was never kinder to the old man than during the whole week before I killed him. And every night, about midnight, I turned the latch of his door and opened it – oh, so gently! And then, when I had made an opening sufficient for my head, I put in a dark lantern all closed, closed so that no light shone out, and then I thrust in my head. Oh, you would have laughed to see how cunningly I thrust it in! I moved it slowly – very, very slowly, so that I might not disturb the old man's sleep. It took me an hour to place my whole head within the opening so far that I could see him as he lay upon his bed. Ha! – would a madman have been so wise as this? And then when my head was well in the room I undid the lantern cautiously – oh, so cautiously – cautiously (for the hinges creaked), I undid it just so much that a single thin ray fell upon the vulture eye. And this I did for seven long nights – every night just at midnight – but I found the eye always closed, and so it was impossible to do the work, for it was not the old man who vexed me but his Evil Eye. And every morning, when the day broke, I went boldly into the chamber and spoke courageously to him, calling him by name in a hearty tone, and inquiring how he had passed the night. So you see he would have been a very profound old man, indeed, to suspect that every night, just at twelve, I looked in upon him while he slept.

Upon the eighth night I was more than usually cautious in opening the door. A watch's minute hand moves more quickly than did mine. Never before that night had I *felt* the extent of my own powers – of my sagacity. I could scarcely contain my feelings of triumph. To think that there I was, opening the door little by little, and he not even to dream of my secret deeds or thoughts. I fairly chuckled at the idea; and perhaps he heard me – for he moved on the bed suddenly as if startled. Now you may think that I drew back – but no. His room was as black as pitch with the thick darkness (for the shutters were close fastened through fear of robbers), and so I knew that he could not see the opening of the door, and I kept pushing it on steadily, steadily.

I had my head in, and was about to open the lantern, when my thumb slipped upon the tin fastening, and the old man sprang up in the bed, crying out, 'Who's there?'

I kept quite still and said nothing. For a whole hour I did not move a muscle, and in the meantime I did not hear him lie down. He was still sitting up in the bed, listening – just as I have done night after night hearkening to the death watches in the wall.

Presently, I heard a slight groan, and I knew it was the groan of mortal terror. It was not a groan of pain or of grief – oh, no! – it was the low stifled sound that arises from the bottom of the soul when overcharged with awe. I knew the sound well. Many a night, just at midnight, when all the world slept, it has welled up from my own bosom, deepening, with its dreadful echo, the terrors that distracted me. I say I knew it well. I knew what the old man felt, and pitied him although I chuckled at heart. I knew that he had been lying awake ever since the first slight noise when he had turned in the bed. His fears had been ever since growing upon him. He had been trying to fancy them causeless, but could not. He had been saying to himself, 'It is nothing but the wind in the chimney – it is only a mouse crossing the floor,' or, 'It is merely a cricket which has made a single chirp.' Yes he had been trying to comfort himself with these suppositions; but he had found all in vain. *All in vain*; because Death, in approaching him, had stalked with his black shadow before him, and enveloped the victim. And it was the mournful influence of the unperceived shadow that caused him to feel – although he neither saw nor heard – to *feel* the presence of my head within the room.

When I had waited a long time, very patiently, without hearing him lie down, I resolved to open a little – a very, very little crevice in the lantern. So I opened it – you cannot imagine how stealthily, stealthily – until, at length a single dim ray, like the thread of the spider, shot out from the crevice and fell upon the vulture eye.

It was open – wide, wide open – and I grew furious as I gazed upon it. I saw it with perfect distinctness – all a dull blue, with a hideous veil over it that chilled the very marrow in my bones; but I could see nothing else of the old man's face or person, for I had directed the ray, as if by instinct, precisely upon the damned spot.

And now have I not told you that what you mistake for madness is but over-acuteness of the senses? – now, I say, there came to my ears a low, dull, quick sound, such as a watch makes when enveloped in cotton. I knew *that* sound well too. It was the beating of the old man's heart. It increased my fury, as the beating of a drum stimulates the soldier into courage.

But even yet I refrained and kept still. I scarcely breathed. I held the lantern motionless. I tried how steadily I could maintain the ray upon the eye. Meantime the hellish tattoo of the heart increased. It grew quicker and quicker, and louder and louder, every instant. The old man's terror *must* have been extreme! It grew louder, I say, louder every moment! – do you mark me well? I have told you that I am nervous: so I am. And now at the dead hour of the night, amid the dreadful silence of that old house, so strange a noise as this excited me to uncontrollable terror. Yet, for some minutes longer, I refrained and stood still. But the beating grew louder, louder! I thought the heart must burst. And now a new anxiety seized me – the sound would be heard by a neighbour! The old man's hour had come! With a loud yell I threw open the lantern and leaped into the room. He shrieked once – once only. In an instant I dragged him to the floor, and pulled the heavy bed over him. I then smiled gaily, to find the deed so far done. But, for many minutes, the heart beat on with a muffled sound. This, however, did not vex me; it would not be heard through the wall. At length it ceased. The old man was dead. I removed the bed and examined the corpse. Yes, he was stone, stone dead. I placed my hand upon the heart and held it there many minutes. There was no pulsation. He was stone dead. His eye would trouble me no more.

If still you think me mad, you will think so no longer when I describe the wise precautions I took for the concealment of the body. The night waned, and I worked hastily, but in silence. First of all I dismembered the corpse. I cut off the head and the arms and the legs.

I then took up three planks from the flooring of the chamber, and deposited all between the scantlings. I then replaced the boards so cleverly, so cunningly, that no human eye – not even *his* – could have detected anything wrong. There was nothing to wash out – no stain of any kind – no blood-spot whatever. I had been too wary for that. A tub had caught all – ha! ha!

When I had made an end of these labours, it was four o'clock – still dark as midnight. As the bell sounded the hour, there came a knocking at the street door. I went down to open it with a light heart, – for what had I *now* to fear? There entered three men, who introduced themselves, with perfect suavity, as officers of the police. A shriek had been heard by a neighbour during the night; suspicion of foul play had been aroused; information had been lodged at the police office, and they (the officers) had been deputed to search the premises.

I smiled – for *what* had I to fear? I bade the gentlemen welcome. The shriek, I said, was my own in a dream. The old man, I mentioned, was absent in the country. I took my visitors all over the house. I bade them search – search *well*. I led them, at length, to *his* chamber. I showed them his treasures, secure, undisturbed. In the enthusiasm of my confidence, I brought chairs into the room, and desired them *here* to rest from their fatigues, while I myself, in the wild audacity of my perfect triumph, placed my own seat upon the very spot beneath which reposed the corpse of the victim.

The officers were satisfied. My manner had convinced them. I was singularly at ease. They sat, and while I answered cheerily, they chatted of familiar things. But, ere long, I felt myself getting pale and wished them gone. My head ached, and I fancied a ringing in my ears; but still they sat, and still chatted. The ringing became more distinct – it continued and became more distinct. I talked more freely to get rid of the feeling; but it continued and gained definitiveness – until, at length, I found that the noise was *not* within my ears.

No doubt I now grew very pale; but I talked more fluently, and with a heightened voice. Yet the sound increased – and what could I do? It was a *low, dull, quick sound – much such a sound as a watch makes when enveloped in cotton*. I gasped for breath – and yet the officers heard it not. I talked more quickly – more vehemently; but the noise steadily increased. I arose and argued about trifles, in a high key and with violent gesticulations; but the noise steadily increased. Why *would* they not be gone? I paced the floor to and fro with heavy strides, as if excited to fury by the observations of the men – but the noise steadily increased. O God! what *could* I do? I foamed – I raved – I swore! I swung the chair upon which I had been sitting, and grated it upon the boards, but the noise arose over all and continually increased. It grew louder – louder – *louder!* And still the men chatted pleasantly, and smiled. Was it possible they heard not? Almighty God! – no, no? They heard! – they suspected! – they *knew!* – they were making a mockery of my horror! – this I thought, and this I think. But anything was better than this agony! Anything was more tolerable than this derision! I could bear those hypocritical smiles no longer! I felt that I must scream or die! – and now – again! hark! louder! louder! louder! *louder!* —

'Villains!' I shrieked, 'dissemble no more! I admit the deed! – tear up the planks! – here, here! – it is the beating of his hideous heart!'

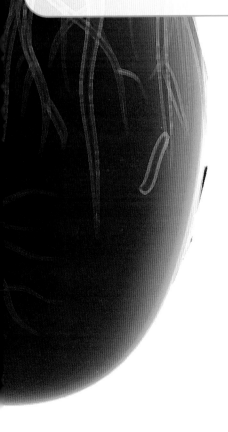

Questions
Exploring *The Tell-Tale Heart*

1. According to the speaker, why did he decide to murder the old man?
2. Why did it take eight days for the speaker to finally commit the murder?
3. (a) The speaker in the story repeatedly insists that he is sane. Find two instances of this.
   (b) Do you believe the narrator when he describes himself as sane? Explain your answer.
4. How does Edgar Allan Poe create tension in this story?
5. (a) Poe uses repetition throughout this story. Find three examples of repetition.
   (b) What effect does the use of repetition have on the reader?
6. (a) Towards the end of the story the narrator complains of a loud noise. Where does he believe the noise is coming from?
   (b) What do you think is the source of the noise?
7. Do you think *The Tell-Tale Heart* is a fitting title for the story? Explain your viewpoint with reference to the story.
8. Using a dictionary, match the following words from the story with their definitions:

1. Dissimulation	a. Covered; wrapped in
2. Vexed	b. Foresight; wisdom
3. Profound	c. Animated gestures
4. Sagacity	d. Having deep insight or intelligence
5. Suppositions	e. Bothered; annoyed; irritated
6. Enveloped	f. Concealment; disguise
7. Waned	g. Passionately; acted with great insistence or enthusiasm
8. Reposed	h. Decreased in power or intensity
9. Vehemently	i. Something that is supposed or presumed
10. Gesticulations	j. Lying in death; at rest

Writers' Workshop
1. Imagine you are one of the police officers in the story. Write the police report you would submit about the case.
2. *The Tell-Tale Heart* explores the darker side of humanity. Write your own dark tale using the following sentence in your story: 'Slowly but surely the man rose from the shadowed corner where he lay.'

Language Lesson: Feature of Fiction – The Unreliable Narrator
First person narratives often offer an interesting point of view. When the narrator is a character in the story, the reader needs to be aware that they are hearing only one side of the story. A first-person narrator may have feelings and prejudices that affect the telling of the story. If the narrator is untrustworthy, they may be referred to as an 'unreliable narrator'.

In *The Tell-Tale Heart*, the narrator is clearly mad despite the fact that he repeatedly insists on his sanity. This madness is reflected in the manner in which the story is told. As a result, the narrator often sounds hysterical and paranoid. Because the narrator is unreliable, the reader is encouraged to question the facts as they are presented. The narrator's insanity allows Edgar Allan Poe to write in a unique and interesting way.

About The Author

Edgar Allan Poe (1809 – 1849)

Edgar Allan Poe was the second child of two actors. His father abandoned the family before Poe was two years old; a year later Poe's mother died from tuberculosis (TB). Poe was raised by the wealthy Allan family from Virginia in the USA but he was never formally adopted.

Poe drank heavily throughout his life and built up huge gambling debts. He fought with his foster father, John Allan, about money and eventually joined the army.

After John Allan disowned him, Poe was dismissed from military service for disobedience. Although it was very difficult to earn a living as an author, Poe scraped by, sometimes working as an editor as well as writing his own material. He married his thirteen-year-old cousin, Virginia Clemm. After struggling as a writer for years, he finally started to earn recognition for his short stories.

Poe is often credited with writing the first detective story, *The Murders in the Rue Morgue.* His stories deal with dark subject-matter and horrifying themes.

His wife died from TB, 12 years after they were married. Poe became a broken man and began drinking very heavily.

His mysterious death is a source of intrigue. On the day he died, he was found injured on the streets of Baltimore and described by the man who found him as 'in great distress, and … in need of immediate assistance'. Oddly, Poe was not wearing his own clothes and kept repeating the name 'Reynolds'. He was too incoherent to explain what had happened to him. All of Poe's medical records and his death certificate have been lost. However, many believe that his death was the result of 'cooping'. This practice occurred on an election day when 'cooping gangs' grabbed unwilling people off the street, 'cooped' them up in a room and force-fed them alcohol or drugs to make them compliant. The kidnapped men were then taken to polling stations and made to vote for a particular candidate. Often their clothes were changed so they could vote a number of times under a different name. If somebody refused to cooperate they were beaten or even killed. However, it is not certain if these were the exact circumstances of Poe's death.

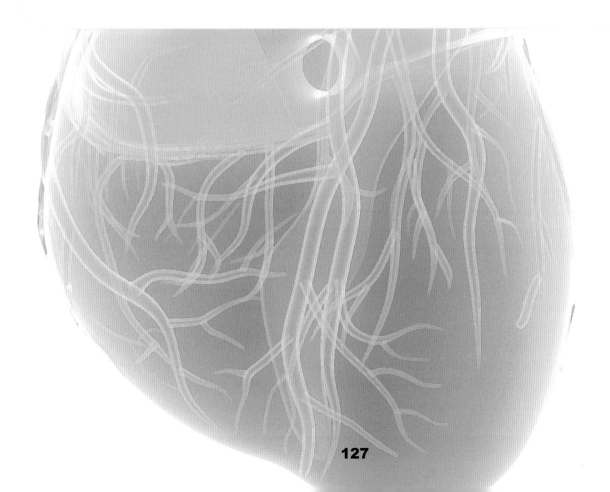

Fiction

Korea by John McGahern

'You saw an execution then too, didn't you?' I asked my father, and he started to tell as he rowed. He'd been captured in an ambush in late 1919, and they were shooting prisoners in Mountjoy as reprisals at that time. He thought it was he who'd be next, for after a few days they moved him to the cell next to the prison yard. He could see out through the bars. No rap to prepare himself came to the door that night, and at daybreak he saw the two prisoners they'd decided to shoot being marched out: a man in his early thirties, and what was little more than a boy, sixteen or seventeen, and he was weeping. They blindfolded the boy, but the man refused the blindfold. When the officer shouted, the boy clicked to attention, but the man stayed as he was, chewing very slowly. He had his hands in his pockets.

'Take your hands out of your pockets,' the officer shouted again, irritation in the voice.

The man slowly shook his head.

'It's a bit too late now in the day for that,' he said.

The officer then ordered them to fire, and as the volley rang, the boy tore at his tunic over the heart, as if to pluck out the bullets, and the buttons of the tunic began to fly into the air before he pitched forward on his face.

The other heeled quietly over on his back: it must have been because of the hands in the pockets.

The officer dispatched the boy with one shot from the revolver as he lay face downward, but he pumped five bullets in rapid succession into the man, as if to pay him back for not coming to attention.

'When I was on my honeymoon years after, it was May, and we took the tram up the hill of Howth from Sutton Cross,' my father said as he rested on the oars. 'We sat on top in the open on the wooden seats with the rail around that made it like a small ship. The sea was below, and smell of the sea and furze-bloom all about, and then I looked down and saw the furze pods bursting, and the way they burst in all directions seemed shocking like the buttons when he started to tear at his tunic. I couldn't get it out of my mind all day. It destroyed the day.'

'It's a wonder their hands weren't tied?' I asked him as he rowed between the black navigation pan and the red where the river flowed into Oakport.

'I suppose it was because they were considered soldiers.'

'Do you think the boy stood to attention because he felt that he might still get off if he obeyed the rules?'

'Sounds a bit highfalutin' to me. Comes from going to school too long,' he said aggressively, and I was silent. It was new to me to hear him talk about his own life at all. Before, if I asked him about the war, he'd draw fingers across his eyes as if to tear a spider web away, but it was my last summer with him on the river, and it seemed to make him want to talk, to give of himself before it ended.

Hand over hand I drew in the line that throbbed with fish; there were two miles of line, a hook on a lead line every three yards. The licence allowed us a thousand hooks, but we used more. We were the last to fish this freshwater for a living.

As the eels came in over the side I cut them loose with a knife into a wire cage, where they slid over each other in their own oil, the twisted eel hook in their mouths. The other fish – pike choked on hooked perch they'd tried to swallow, bream, roach – I slid up the floorboards towards the bow of the boat. We'd sell them in the village or give them away. The hooks that hadn't been taken I cleaned and stuck in rows round the side of the wooden box. I let the line fall in its centre. After a mile he took my place in the stern and I rowed. People hadn't woken yet, and the early morning cold and mist were on the river. Outside of the slow ripple of the oars and the threshing of the fish on the line beaded with running drops of water as it came in, the river was dead silent, except for the occasional lowing of cattle on the banks.

'Have you any idea what you'll do after this summer?' he asked.

'No. I'll wait and see what comes up,' I answered.

'How do you mean *what comes up*?'

'Whatever result I get in the exam. If the result is good, I'll have choices. If it's not, there won't be choices. I'll have to take what I can get.'

'How good do you think they'll be?'

'I think they'll be all right, but there's no use counting chickens, is there?'

'No,' he said, but there was something calculating in the face; it made me watchful of him as I rowed the last stretch of the line. The day had come, the distant noises of the farms and the first flies on the river, by the time we'd lifted the large wire cage out of the bulrushes, emptied in the morning's catch of eels, and sunk it again.

'We'll have enough for a consignment tomorrow,' he said.

Each week we sent the live eels to Billingsgate in London.

'But say, say even if you do well, you wouldn't think of throwing this country up altogether and going to America?' he said, the words fumbled for as I pushed the boat out of the bulrushes after sinking the cage of eels, using the oar as a pole, the mud rising a dirty yellow between the stems.

'Why America?'

'Well, it's the land of opportunity, isn't it, a big, expanding country? There's no room for ambition in this poky place. All there's room for is to make holes in pints of porter.'

I was wary of the big words. They were not in his own voice.

'Who'd pay the fare?'

'We'd manage that. We'd scrape it together somehow.'

'Why should you scrape for me to go to America if I can get a job here?'

'I feel I'd be giving you a chance I never got. I fought for this country. And now they want to take away even the licence to fish. Will you think about it anyhow?'

'I'll think about it,' I answered.

Through the day he trimmed the brows of ridges in the potato field while I replaced hooks on the line and dug worms, pain of doing things for the last time as well as the boredom the knowledge brings that soon there'll be no need to do them, that they could be discarded almost now. The guilt of leaving came: I was discarding his life to assume my own, a man to row the boat would eat into the decreasing profits of the fishing, and it was even not certain he'd get renewal of his licence. The tourist board had opposed the last application. They said we impoverished the coarse fishing for tourists – the tourists who came every summer from Liverpool and Birmingham in increasing numbers to sit in aluminium deck-chairs on the riverbank and fish with rods. The fields we had would be a bare living without the fishing.

I saw him stretch across the wall in conversation with the cattle-dealer Farrell as I came round to put the worms where we stored them in clay in the darkness of the lavatory. Farrell leaned on the bar of his bicycle on the road. I passed into the lavatory thinking they were talking about the price of cattle, but as I emptied the worms into the box, the word *Moran* came, and I carefully opened the door to listen. It was my father's voice. He was excited.

'I know. I heard the exact sum. They got ten thousand dollars when Luke was killed. Every American soldier's life is insured to the tune of ten thousand dollars.'

'I heard they get two hundred and fifty dollars a month each for Michael and Sam while they're serving,' he went on.

'They're buying cattle left and right,' Farrell's voice came as I closed the door and stood in the darkness, in the smell of shit and piss and the warm fleshy smell of worms crawling in too little clay.

The shock I felt was the shock I was to feel later when I made some social blunder, the splintering of a self-esteem and the need to crawl into a lavatory to think.

Luke Moran's body had come from Korea in a leaden casket, had crossed the stone bridge to the slow funeral bell with the big cars from the embassy behind, the coffin draped in the Stars and Stripes. Shots had been fired above the grave before they threw in the clay. There were photos of his decorations being presented to his family by a military attaché.

He'd scrape the fare, I'd be conscripted there, each month he'd get so many dollars while I served, and he'd get ten thousand if I was killed.

In the darkness of the lavatory between the boxes of crawling worms before we set the night line for the eels I knew my youth had ended.

I rowed as he let out the night line, his fingers baiting each twisted hook so beautifully that it seemed a single movement. The dark was closing from the shadow of Oakport to Nutley's boathouse, bats made ugly whirls overhead, the wings of duck shirred as they curved down into the bay.

'Have you thought about what I said about going to America?' he asked, without lifting his eyes from the hooks and the box of worms.

'I have.'

The oars dipped in the water without splash, the hole whirling wider in the calm as it slipped past him on the stern seat.

'Have you decided to take the chance, then?'

'No. I'm not going.'

'You won't be able to say I didn't give you the chance when you come to nothing in this fool of a country. It'll be your own funeral.'

'It'll be my own funeral,' I answered, and asked after a long silence, 'As you grow older, do you find your own days in the war and jails coming much back to you?'

'I do. And I don't want to talk about them. Talking about the execution disturbed me no end, those cursed buttons bursting into the air. And the most I think is that if I'd conducted my own wars, and let the fool of a country fend for itself, I'd be much better off today. I don't want to talk about it.'

I knew this silence was fixed for ever as I rowed in silence till he asked, 'Do you think, will it be much good tonight?'

'It's too calm,' I answered.

'Unless the night wind gets up,' he said anxiously.

'Unless a night wind,' I repeated.

As the boat moved through the calm water and the line slipped through his fingers over the side I'd never felt so close to him before, not even when he'd carried me on his shoulders above the laughing crowd to the Final. Each move he made I watched as closely as if I too had to prepare myself to murder.

Questions

Exploring *Korea*

1. **(a)** Which memory of the War of Independence does the father tell his son about?
   (b) How did this memory affect his father's honeymoon?
2. **(a)** What reasons does the father give his son to encourage him to emigrate?
   (b) What is the real reason he wants his son to go to America?
3. In your opinion, what kind of man is the father?
4. After overhearing his father's conversation with Farrell, the narrator says, 'I knew my youth had ended.' What do you think he means by this?
5. Comment on the story's final paragraph. Do you find it strange, believable, saddening? What point do you think the author is making?
6. Comment on McGahern's style of writing in this story.
7. Read the biography of John McGahern below. Do you think there is a connection between *Korea* and McGahern's life? Explain your answer.

Writers' Workshop

Imagine the narrator of the story decides to confront his father. Write the scene that takes place.

About The Author

John McGahern (1934 – 2006)

John McGahern, the son of a Garda sergeant and a school teacher, was born in County Leitrim. For the early years of his life he lived on the family farm with his mother and six siblings. His father lived at the police barracks in Roscommon. When McGahern was ten, his mother died from cancer and the family moved to the police barracks in Roscommon.

His father was physically abusive; McGahern recalls seeing his sister being beaten senseless by a spade. The children were kept close to starvation. Every month, McGahern's father would line the family up, read the grocery bill and scold them for the amount they ate. He took to feeding them cow's heads in order to save money.

McGahern's father wanted him to leave school and learn a trade. However, McGahern was determined to receive an education. He used to cycle seven miles a day to attend secondary school. McGahern learned a love of books from a Protestant neighbour who allowed McGahern to borrow from his library.

McGahern was a clever child; he won scholarships to secondary school and university. He became a primary school teacher and started to publish novels and short stories.

His second novel, *The Dark*, caused a lot of controversy because of its sexual content and was heavily criticised by the Catholic Church. The novel was banned in Ireland. During the controversy, McGahern was dismissed from his teaching post. This was due to the furore surrounding his novel, but also, as he was told later, because he had married a 'foreign woman' (Finnish theatre director, Annikki Laaksi).

For the rest of his life McGahern wrote novels, plays, short stories and he published a memoir. He worked part time on his farm, spending a couple of hours each day writing. Occasionally he taught in universities. McGahern received huge critical success during his lifetime; he won numerous awards and is considered one of Ireland's greatest writers. He died from cancer in 2006 and was survived by his second wife, the American photographer, Madeline Green.

The Conger Eel by Liam O'Flaherty

He was eight feet long. At the centre of his back he was two feet in circumference. Slipping sinuously along the bottom of the sea at a gigantic pace, his black, mysterious body glistened and twirled like a wisp in a foaming cataract. His little eyes, stationed wide apart in his flat-boned, broad skull, searched the ocean for food. He coursed ravenously for miles along the base of the range of cliffs. He searched fruitlessly, except for three baby pollocks which he swallowed in one mouthful without arresting his progress. He was very hungry.

Then he turned by a sharp promontory and entered a cliff-bound harbour where the sea was dark and silent, shaded by the concave cliffs. Savagely he looked ahead into the dark waters. Then instantaneously he flicked his tail, rippling his body like a twisted screw, and shot forward. His long, thin, single whisker, hanging from his lower snout like a label tag, jerked back under his belly. His glassy eyes rested ferociously on minute white spots that scurried about in the sea a long distance ahead. The conger eel had sighted his prey. There was a school of mackerel a mile away.

He came upon them headlong, in a flash. He rose out of the deep from beneath their white bellies, and gripped one mackerel in his wide-open jaws ere his snout met the surface. Then, as if in a swoon, his body went limp, and tumbling over and over, convulsing like a crushed worm, he sank lower and lower until at last he had swallowed the fish. Then immediately he straightened out and flicked his tail, ready to pursue his prey afresh.

The school of mackerel, when the dread monster had appeared among them, were swimming just beneath the surface of the sea. When the eel rushed up they had hurled themselves clean out of the water with the sound of innumerable grains of sand being shaken in an immense sieve. The thousand blue and white bodies flashed and shimmered in the sun for three moments, and then they disappeared, leaving a large patch of the dark water convulsing turbulently. Ten thousand little fins cut the surface of the sea as the mackerel set off in headlong flight. Their white bellies were no longer visible. They plunged down into the depths of the sea, where their blue-black sides and backs, the colour of the sea, hid them from their enemy. The eel surged about in immense figures of eight; but he had lost them.

Half hungry, half satisfied, he roamed about for half an hour, a demented giant of the deep, travelling restlessly at an incredible speed. Then at last his little eyes again sighted his prey. Little white spots again hung like faded drops of brine in the sea ahead of him. He rushed thither. He opened his jaws as the spots assumed shape, and they loomed up close to his eyes. But just as he attempted to gobble the nearest one, he felt a savage impact. Then something hard and yet intangible pressed against his head and then down along his back. He leaped and turned somersault. The hard, gripping material completely enveloped him. He was in a net. While on all sides of him mackerel wriggled gasping in the meshes.

The eel paused for two seconds amazed and terrified. Then all around him he saw a web of black strands hanging miraculously in the water, everywhere, while mackerel with heaving gills stood rigid in the web, some with their tails and heads both caught and their bodies curved in an arch, others encompassed many times in the uneven folds, others girdled firmly below the gills with a single black thread. Glittering, they eddied back and forth with the stream of the sea, a mass of fish being strangled in the deep.

Then the eel began to struggle fiercely to escape. He hurtled hither and thither, swinging his long slippery body backwards and forwards, ripping with his snout, surging forward suddenly at full speed, churning the water. He ripped and tore the net, cutting great long gashes in it. But the more he cut and ripped the more deeply enmeshed did he become. He did not release himself, but he released some of the mackerel. They fell from the torn meshes, stiff and crippled, downwards, sinking like dead things.

Then suddenly one after another they seemed to wake from sleep, shook their tails, and darted away, while the giant eel was gathering coil upon coil of the net about his slippery body. Then, at last, exhausted and half strangled, he lay still, heaving.

Presently he felt himself being hauled up in the net. The net crowded around him more, so that the little gleaming mackerel, imprisoned with him, rubbed his sides and lay soft and flabby against him, all hauled up in the net with him. He lay still. He reached the surface and gasped, but he made no movement. Then he was hauled heavily into a boat, and fell with a thud into the bottom.

The two fishermen in the boat began to curse violently when they saw the monstrous eel that had torn their net and ruined their catch of mackerel. The old man on the oars in the bow called out: 'Free him and kill him, the whore.' The young man who was hauling in the net looked in terror at the slippery monster that lay between his feet, with its little eyes looking up cunningly, as if it were human. He almost trembled as he picked up the net and began to undo the coils. 'Slash it with your knife,' yelled the old man, 'before he does more harm.' The young man picked up his knife from the gunwale where it was stuck, and cut the net, freeing the eel. The eel, with a sudden and amazing movement, glided up the bottom of the boat, so that he stretched full length.

Then he doubled back, rocking the boat as he beat the sides with his whirling tail, his belly flopping in the water that lay in the bottom. The two men screamed, both crying: 'Kill him, or he'll drown us.' 'Strike him on the nable.' They both reached for the short, thick stick that hung from a peg amidships. The young man grabbed it, bent down, and struck at the eel. 'Hit him on the nable!' cried the old man; 'catch him, catch him, and turn him over.'

They both bent down, pawing at the eel, cursing and panting, while the boat rocked ominously and the huge conger eel glided around and around at an amazing speed. Their hands clawed his sides, slipping over them like skates on ice. They gripped him with their knees, they stood on him, they tried to lie on him, but in their confusion they could not catch him.

Then at last the young man lifted him in his arms, holding him in the middle, gripping him as if he were trying to crush him to death. He staggered upwards. 'Now strike him on the nable!' he yelled to the old man. But suddenly he staggered backwards. The boat rocked. He dropped the eel with an oath, reaching out with his hands to steady himself. The eel's head fell over the canted gunwale. His snout dipped into the sea. With an immense shiver he glided away, straight down, down to the depths, down like an arrow, until he reached the dark, weed-covered rocks at the bottom.

Then stretching out to his full length he coursed in a wide arc to his enormous lair, far away in the silent depths.

Questions

Exploring *The Conger Eel*

1. In your own words, describe what happens to the eel in this story.
2. How do the fishermen react to the eel that lands in their boat?
3. **(a)** Find two phrases that depict the eel as powerful and menacing.
   (b) Find two phrases that portray the eel as mysterious.
4. Do you feel sympathy for the conger eel? Why/why not?
5. Liam O'Flaherty uses a number of interesting verbs to describe the behaviour of the animals and men in the story. List five such verbs used in this text.
6. **(a)** Find three examples of vivid descriptive writing in this story that stood out for you.
   (b) Explain why you found these lines striking.
7. Where do you feel the climax of the story occurs? Explain your answer.
8. 'There is little difference between animals and men in Liam O'Flaherty's stories.' Comment on this statement in relation to *The Conger Eel*.
9. Which of the comments below do you feel best suits the story? Explain your answer with reference to the text.
   ▶ *For O'Flaherty, life is a battle in which only the fittest survive.*
   ▶ *It is his ability to capture the moment that makes Liam O'Flaherty's writing so impressive.*
   ▶ *Liam O'Flaherty simultaneously displays the cruelty and vulnerability of the natural world.*
10. Did you like or dislike this story? Explain your answer.

Writers' Workshop

Imagine you are one of the fishermen on the boat. Write a first-person account of the incident with the conger eel.

Language Lesson: Feature of Fiction – Structure

There is no formula for writing the perfect short story. Writers often experiment and are always free to break literary conventions. However, many successful stories – like *The Conger Eel* – are built around a five-part structure. This structure works as follows:

Introduction – This introduces the characters and the situation they find themselves in. The introduction of *The Conger Eel* establishes the character of the monstrous eel and the reader learns about his hunger.

Conflict – In this second stage, the character encounters a problem or difficulty. In this story, the eel finds himself caught in the fishermen's net.

Climax – This is a moment of great emotional intensity. It is the turning point of the story where the character's fate is about to change for better or worse. In this story, the climax is reached as the eel slides around the boat and the fishermen try to kill him.

Resolution – In this fourth stage, the problem faced by the character is resolved. In *The Conger Eel*, the eel escapes from the clutches of the fisherman.

Conclusion – The story concludes and there is an emotional release for the reader. This moment occurs in O'Flaherty's story as the eel swims away into the dark.

Although you are free to structure your own stories in any way you wish, it is interesting to note how many stories roughly adopt this type of structure.

About The Author

Liam O'Flaherty (1896 – 1984)

'I was born on a windswept rock and hate the soft growth of sun-baked lands where there is no frost in men's bones.' This is how Liam O'Flaherty described his birth on Inishmore, the largest of the Aran Islands.

O'Flaherty attended a number of schools before joining the British Army when he was seventeen. He fought in World War I in which he was injured and suffered shell shock. He recovered in England and then Dublin before travelling the world.

O'Flaherty became involved in politics and co-founded the Communist Party of Ireland. In 1922, shortly after the founding of the Irish Free State, O'Flaherty and a group of 200 unemployed workers took control of the Rotunda Concert Hall in Dublin to protest against high unemployment. Crowds gathered outside and fired shots over the building. After holding out for four days, the protestors finally fled shortly before the building was overrun by the Free State Army. While standing on O'Connell Street afterwards, he overheard a woman saying, 'Did you hear that bloody murderer Liam O'Flaherty is killed, thanks be to God.' He fled to London with a pistol strapped to his back.

He then travelled around America and Europe. He published novels and numerous short stories. Many of his works, such as *The Informer,* were turned into acclaimed movies by his cousin, the Hollywood film director John Ford.

O'Flaherty separated from his wife in 1932 and then suffered a nervous breakdown reportedly caused by writer's block. Happily he met his lifelong partner, Kitty Harding Tailer, a year later. He finally settled in Dublin where he lived for the rest of his life.

Bicycles, Muscles, Cigarettes
by Raymond Carver

It had been two days since Evan Hamilton had stopped smoking, and it seemed to him everything he'd said and thought for the two days somehow suggested cigarettes. He looked at his hands under the kitchen light. He sniffed his knuckles and his fingers.

'I can smell it,' he said.

'I know. It's as if it sweats out of you,' Ann Hamilton said. 'For three days after I stopped I could smell it on me. Even when I got out of the bath. It was disgusting.' She was putting plates on the table for dinner. 'I'm so sorry, dear. I know what you're going through. But, if it's any consolation, the second day is always the hardest. The third day is hard, too, of course, but from then on, if you can stay with it that long, you're over the hump. But I'm so happy you're serious about quitting, I can't tell you.' She touched his arm. 'Now, if you'll just call Roger, we'll eat.'

Hamilton opened the front door. It was already dark. It was early in November and the days were short and cool. An older boy he had never seen before was sitting on a small, well equipped bicycle in the driveway. The boy leaned forward just off the seat, the toes of his shoes touching the pavement and keeping him upright.

'You Mr Hamilton?' the boy said.

'Yes, I am,' Hamilton said. 'What is it? Is it Roger?'

'I guess Roger is down at my house talking to my mother. Kip is there and this boy named Gary Berman. It is about my brother's bike. I don't know for sure,' the boy said, twisting the handle grips, 'but my mother asked me to come and get you. One of Roger's parents.'

'But he's all right?' Hamilton said. 'Yes, of course, I'll be right with you.'

He went into the house to put his shoes on.

'Did you find him?' Ann Hamilton said.

'He's in some kind of jam,' Hamilton answered. 'Over a bicycle. Some boy – I didn't catch his name – is outside. He wants one of us to go back with him to his house.'

'Is he all right?' Ann Hamilton said and took her apron off.

'Sure, he's all right.' Hamilton looked at her and shook his head. 'It sounds like it's just a childish argument, and the boy's mother is getting herself involved.'

'Do you want me to go?' Ann Hamilton asked.

He thought for a minute. 'Yes, I'd rather you went, but I'll go. Just hold dinner until we're back. We shouldn't be long.'

'I don't like his being out after dark,' Ann Hamilton said. 'I don't like it.'

The boy was sitting on his bicycle and working the handbrake now.

'How far?' Hamilton said as they started down the sidewalk.

'Over in Arbuckle Court,' the boy answered, and when Hamilton looked at him, the boy added, 'Not far. About two blocks from here.'

'What seems to be the trouble?' Hamilton asked.

'I don't know for sure. I don't understand all of it. He and Kip and this Gary Berman are supposed to have used my brother's bike while we were on vacation, and I guess they wrecked it. On purpose. But I don't know. Anyway, that's what they're talking about. My brother can't find his bike and they had it last, Kip and Roger. My mom is trying to find out where it's at.'

'I know Kip,' Hamilton said. 'Who's this other boy?'

'Gary Berman. I guess he's new in the neighborhood. His dad is coming as soon as he gets home.'

They turned a corner. The boy pushed himself along, keeping just slightly ahead. Hamilton saw an orchard, and then they turned another corner onto a dead-end street. He hadn't known of the existence of this street and was sure he would not recognize any of the people who lived here. He looked around him at the unfamiliar houses and was struck with the range of his son's personal life.

The boy turned into a driveway and got off the bicycle and leaned it against the house. When the boy opened the front door, Hamilton followed him through the living room and into the kitchen, where he saw his son sitting on one side of a table along with Kip Hollister and another boy. Hamilton looked closely at Roger and then he turned to the stout, dark-haired woman at the head of the table.

'You're Roger's father?' the woman said to him.

'Yes, my name is Evan Hamilton. Good evening.'

'I'm Mrs Miller, Gilbert's mother,' she said. 'Sorry to ask you over here, but we have a problem.'

Hamilton sat down in a chair at the other end of the table and looked around. A boy of nine or ten, the boy whose bicycle was missing, Hamilton supposed, sat next to the woman. Another boy, fourteen or so, sat on the draining board, legs dangling, and watched another boy who was talking on the telephone. Grinning slyly at something that had just been said to him over the line, the boy reached over to the sink with a cigarette. Hamilton heard the sound of the cigarette sputting out in a glass of water. The boy who had brought him leaned against the refrigerator and crossed his arms.

'Did you get one of Kip's parents?' the woman said to the boy.

'His sister said they were shopping. I went to Gary Berman's and his father will be here in a few minutes. I left the address.'

'Mr Hamilton,' the woman said, 'I'll tell you what happened. We were on vacation last month and Kip wanted to borrow Gilbert's bike so that Roger could help him with Kip's paper route. I guess Roger's bike had a flat tire or something. Well, as it turns out –'

'Gary was choking me, Dad,' Roger said.

'What?' Hamilton said, looking at his son carefully.

'He was choking me. I got the marks.' His son pulled down the collar of his T-shirt to show his neck.

'They were out in the garage,' the woman continued. 'I didn't know what they were doing until Curt, my oldest, went out to see.'

'He started it!' Gary Berman said to Hamilton. 'He called me a jerk.' Gary Berman looked toward the front door.

'I think my bike cost about sixty dollars, you guys,' the boy named Gilbert said. 'You can pay me for it. '

'You keep out of this, Gilbert,' the woman said to him.

Hamilton took a breath. 'Go on,' he said.

'Well, as it turns out, Kip and Roger used Gilbert's bike to help Kip deliver his papers, and then the two of them, and Gary too, they say, took turns rolling it.'

'What do you mean "rolling it"?' Hamilton said.

'Rolling it,' the woman said. 'Sending it down the street with a push and letting it fall over. Then, mind you – and they just admitted this a few minutes ago – Kip and Roger took it up to the school and threw it against a goalpost.'

'Is that true, Roger?' Hamilton said, looking at his son again.

'Part of it's true, Dad,' Roger said, looking down and rubbing his finger over the table. 'But we only rolled it once. Kip did it, then Gary, and then I did it.'

'Once is too much,' Hamilton said. 'Once is one too many times, Roger. I'm surprised and disappointed in you. And you too, Kip,' Hamilton said.

'But you see,' the woman said, 'someone's fibbing tonight or else not telling all he knows, for the fact is the bike's still missing.' The older boys in the kitchen laughed and kidded with the boy who still talked on the telephone.

'We don't know where the bike is, Mrs Miller,' the boy named Kip said. 'We told you already. The last time we saw it was when me and Roger took it to my house after we had it at school. I mean, that was the next to last time. The very last time was when I took it back here the next morning and parked it behind the house.' He shook his head. 'We don't know where it is,' the boy said.

'Sixty dollars,' the boy named Gilbert said to the boy named Kip. 'You can pay me off like five dollars a week.'

'Gilbert, I'm warning you,' the woman said. 'You see, *they* claim,' the woman went on, frowning now, 'it disappeared from *here*, from behind the house. But how can we believe them when they haven't been all that truthful this evening?'

'We've told the truth,' Roger said. 'Everything.'

Gilbert leaned back in his chair and shook his head at Hamilton's son.

The doorbell sounded and the boy on the draining board jumped down and went into the living room.

A stiff-shouldered man with a crew haircut and sharp gray eyes entered the kitchen without speaking. He glanced at the woman and moved over behind Gary Berman's chair.

'You must be Mr Berman?' the woman said. 'Happy to meet you. I'm Gilbert's mother, and this is Mr Hamilton, Roger's father. '

The man inclined his head at Hamilton but did not offer his hand.

'What's all this about?' Berman said to his son.

The boys at the table began to speak at once.

'Quiet down!' Berman said. 'I'm talking to Gary. You'll get your turn.'

The boy began his account of the affair. His father listened closely, now and then narrowing his eyes to study the other two boys.

When Gary Berman had finished, the woman said, 'I'd like to get to the bottom of this. I'm not accusing any one of them, you understand, Mr Hamilton, Mr Berman – I'd just like to get to the bottom of this.' She looked steadily at Roger and Kip, who were shaking their heads at Gary Berman.

'It's not true, Gary,' Roger said.

'Dad, can I talk to you in private?' Gary Berman said.

'Let's go,' the man said, and they walked into the living room.

Hamilton watched them go. He had the feeling he should stop them, this secrecy. His palms were wet, and he reached to his shirt pocket for a cigarette. Then, breathing deeply, he passed the back of his hand under his nose and said, 'Roger, do you know any more about this, other than what you've already said? Do you know where Gilbert's bike is?'

'No, I don't,' the boy said. 'I swear it.'

'When was the last time you saw the bicycle?' Hamilton said.

'When we brought it home from school and left it at Kip's house.'

'Kip,' Hamilton said, 'do you know where Gilbert's bicycle is now?'

'I swear I don't, either,' the boy answered. 'I brought it back the next morning after we had it at school and I parked it behind the garage.'

'I thought you said you left it behind the *house*,' the woman said quickly.

'I mean the house! That's what I meant,' the boy said.

'Did you come back here some other day to ride it?' she asked, leaning forward.

'No, I didn't,' Kip answered.

'Kip?' she said.

'I didn't! I don't know where it is!' the boy shouted.

The woman raised her shoulders and let them drop. 'How do you know who or what to believe?' she said to Hamilton. 'All I know is, Gilbert's missing a bicycle.'

Gary Berman and his father returned to the kitchen.

'It was Roger's idea to roll it,' Gary Berman said.

'It was yours!' Roger said, coming out of his chair. 'You wanted to! Then you wanted to take it to the orchard and strip it!'

'You shut up!' Berman said to Roger. 'You can speak when spoken to, young man, not before. Gary, I'll handle this – I'm dragged out at night because of a couple of roughnecks! Now if either of you,' Berman said, looking first at Kip and then Roger, 'know where this kid's bicycle is, I'd advise you to start talking.'

'I think you're getting out of line,' Hamilton said.

'What?' Berman said, his forehead darkening. 'And I think you'd do better to mind your own business!'

'Let's go, Roger,' Hamilton said, standing up. 'Kip, you come now or stay.' He turned to the woman. 'I don't know what else we can do tonight. I intend to talk this over more with Roger, but if there is a question of restitution I feel since Roger did help manhandle the bike, he can pay a third if it comes to that. '

'I don't know what to say,' the woman replied, following Hamilton through the living room. 'I'll talk to Gilbert's father – he's out of town now. We'll see. It's probably one of those things finally, but I'll talk to his father.'

Hamilton moved to one side so that the boys could pass ahead of him onto the porch, and from behind him he heard Gary Berman say, 'He called me a jerk, Dad.'

'He did, did he?' Hamilton heard Berman say. 'Well, he's the jerk. He looks like a jerk.'

Hamilton turned and said, 'I think you're seriously out of line here tonight, Mr Berman. Why don't you get control of yourself?'

'And I told you I think you should keep out of it!' Berman said.

'You get home, Roger,' Hamilton said, moistening his lips.

'I mean it,' he said, 'get going!' Roger and Kip moved out to the sidewalk. Hamilton stood in the doorway and looked at Berman, who was crossing the living room with his son.

'Mr Hamilton,' the woman began nervously but did not finish.

'What do you want?' Berman said to him. 'Watch out now, get out of my way!' Berman brushed Hamilton's shoulder and Hamilton stepped off the porch into some prickly cracking bushes. He couldn't believe it was happening. He moved out of the bushes and lunged at the man where he stood on the porch. They fell heavily onto the lawn. They rolled on the lawn, Hamilton wrestling Berman onto his back and coming down hard with his knees on the man's biceps. He had Berman by the collar now and began to pound his head against the lawn while the woman cried, 'God almighty, someone stop them! For God's sake, someone call the police!'

Hamilton stopped.

Berman looked up at him and said, 'Get off me.'

'Are you all right?' the woman called to the men as they separated. 'For God's sake,' she said. She looked at the men, who stood a few feet apart, backs to each other, breathing hard. The older boys had crowded onto the porch to watch; now that it was over, they waited, watching the men, and then they began feinting and punching each other on the arms and ribs.

'You boys get back in the house,' the woman said. 'I never thought I'd see,' she said and put her hand on her breast.

Hamilton was sweating and his lungs burned when he tried to take a deep breath. There was a ball of something in his throat so that he couldn't swallow for a minute. He started walking, his son and the boy named Kip at his sides. He heard car doors slam, an engine start. Headlights swept over him as he walked.

Roger sobbed once, and Hamilton put his arm around the boy's shoulders.

'I better get home,' Kip said and began to cry. 'My dad'll be looking for me,' and the boy ran.

'I'm sorry,' Hamilton said. 'I'm sorry you had to see something like that,' Hamilton said to his son.
They kept walking and when they reached their block, Hamilton took his arm away.
'What if he'd picked up a knife, Dad? Or a club?'
'He wouldn't have done anything like that,' Hamilton said.
'But what if he had?' his son said.
'It's hard to say what people will do when they're angry,' Hamilton said.
They started up the walk to their door. His heart moved when Hamilton saw the lighted windows.
'Let me feel your muscle,' his son said.
'Not now,' Hamilton said. 'You just go in now and have your dinner and hurry up to bed. Tell your mother I'm all right and I'm going to sit on the porch for a few minutes.'
The boy rocked from one foot to the other and looked at his father, and then he dashed into the house and began calling, 'Mom! Mom!'

* * * *

He sat on the porch and leaned against the garage wall and stretched his legs. The sweat had dried on his forehead. He felt clammy under his clothes. He had once seen his father – a pale, slow-talking man with slumped shoulders – in something like this. It was a bad one, and both men had been hurt. It had happened in a café. The other man was a farmhand. Hamilton had loved his father and could recall many things about him. But now he recalled his father's one fistfight as if it were all there was to the man.
He was still sitting on the porch when his wife came out.
'Dear God,' she said and took his head in her hands. 'Come in and shower and then have something to eat and tell me about it. Everything is still warm. Roger has gone to bed.'
But he heard his son calling him.
'He's still awake,' she said.
'I'll be down in a minute,' Hamilton said. 'Then maybe we should have a drink.'
She shook her head. 'I really don't believe any of this yet.'
He went into the boy's room and sat down at the foot of the bed.
'It's pretty late and you're still up, so I'll say good night,' Hamilton said.
'Good night,' the boy said, hands behind his neck, elbows jutting.
He was in his pajamas and had a warm fresh smell about him that Hamilton breathed deeply. He patted his son through the covers.
'You take it easy from now on. Stay away from that part of the neighborhood, and don't let me ever hear of you damaging a bicycle or any other personal property. Is that clear?' Hamilton said.
The boy nodded. He took his hands from behind his neck and began picking at something on the bedspread.
'Okay, then,' Hamilton said, 'I'll say good night.'
He moved to kiss his son, but the boy began talking.
'Dad, was Grandfather strong like you? When he was your age, I mean, you know, and you –'
'And I was nine years old? Is that what you mean? Yes, I guess he was,' Hamilton said.
'Sometimes I can hardly remember him,' the boy said. 'I don't want to forget him or anything, you know? You know what I mean, Dad?'
When Hamilton did not answer at once, the boy went on. 'When you were young, was it like it is with you and me? Did you love him more than me? Or just the same?' The boy said this abruptly. He moved his feet under the covers and looked away. When Hamilton still did not answer, the boy said, 'Did he smoke? I think I remember a pipe or something.'
'He started smoking a pipe before he died, that's true,' Hamilton said. 'He used to smoke cigarettes a long time ago and then he'd get depressed with something or other and quit, but later he'd change

brands and start in again. Let me show you something,' Hamilton said. 'Smell the back of my hand.' The boy took the hand in his, sniffed it, and said, 'I guess I don't smell anything, Dad. What is it?'

Hamilton sniffed the hand and then the fingers. 'Now I can't smell anything, either,' he said. 'It was there before, but now it's gone.' Maybe it was scared out of me, he thought. 'I wanted to show you something. All right, it's late now. You better go to sleep,' Hamilton said.

The boy rolled onto his side and watched his father walk to the door and watched him put his hand to the switch. And then the boy said, 'Dad? You'll think I'm pretty crazy, but I wish I'd known you when you were little. I mean, about as old as I am right now. I don't know how to say it, but I'm lonesome about it. It's like – it's like I miss you already if I think about it now. That's pretty crazy, isn't it? Anyway, please leave the door open.'

Hamilton left the door open, and then he thought better of it and closed it halfway.

Questions
Exploring *Muscles, Bicycles, Cigarettes*

1. Explain why Hamilton was asked to call to Mrs Miller's house.
2. Do you think it is significant to the story that Hamilton had recently given up cigarettes? Explain your viewpoint.
3. What kind of man do you think Mr Berman is? Refer to the story in your answer.
4. Mrs Miller says her husband is 'out of town'. Write the dialogue that you imagine takes place between Mrs Miller and her husband when he returns from his trip.
5. Do you think Hamilton is a good father? Explain your viewpoint.
6. **(a)** Why do you think Roger asks Hamilton if he can feel his muscle?
   (b) Why do you think Hamilton puts him off?
7. Towards the end of the story, Roger says 'I wish I'd known you when you were little. I mean, about as old as I am right now. I don't know how to say it, but I'm lonesome about it. It's like – it's like I miss you'. What do you think the boy is trying to communicate to his father when he says this?
8. What evidence from the story reveals that the writer is American?
9. How would you describe Raymond Carver's style of writing. Choose examples from the story to support your ideas.
10. Choose another title for this story. Explain why you chose this title.

Writers' Workshop
Write a short story that features an argument between two characters.

Language Lesson: Feature of Fiction – Suspense

Suspense is an important element in fiction. Suspense creates the sense that something important is about to happen; this keeps the reader excited and interested in the story.

From the beginning of *Muscles, Bicycles, Cigarettes,* the reader is made to feel a sense of anxiety and unease. Hamilton is tense as he battles his cravings for cigarettes. This contributes to the reader's feeling that something is going to go wrong for the character.

Hamilton's initial mistrust of Mr Berman contributes to the story's suspense. This is furthered by small but significant details in the story such as the disagreement between the boys and Berman's arrogant manner. The secret conversation between Berman and his son, and Hamilton's argument with Berman adds to the mounting suspense. When Berman shouts at Hamilton's son, the room becomes very tense. The reader can't help but feel that something bad is about to happen. The situation finally explodes into a fist fight on the lawn.

A story's conclusion usually releases the tension that has built up, and the outcome brings relief for the reader. In *Muscles, Bicycles, Cigarettes,* the tension is released after the fight. The tender moment between Hamilton and his son at the end of the story contrasts with the earlier tension and suspense. This final moment of unity and understanding is made to seem all the more special after the suspense and violence of the earlier events.

About The Author

Raymond Carver (1938 – 1988)

Raymond Carver is one of America's most celebrated short story writers. Carver held a number of low-paid manual jobs throughout his life and had to make time and space to do his writing. In California he worked as a night janitor in a hospital; he would complete all his cleaning duties in an hour and write short stories for the rest of the shift.

He would sometimes drive to a car park and sit and do his writing there, 'I'd just go out and sit in the car in the parking lot, just to be away from the kids and the turmoil and confusion in the house. That was my office.'

Poverty was a feature of Carver's life; he twice filed for bankruptcy. As he started to achieve success as a writer he found better paid jobs in editing and eventually lecturing.

Carver struggled with alcoholism which affected his work; at one point he stopped writing altogether. He was hospitalised three times because of alcohol. Eventually, he entered a treatment centre, stopped drinking and returned to writing.

He married the poet Tess Gallagher six weeks before he passed away from cancer. He was fifty.

Controversy surrounds the influence of Carver's editor Gordon Lish. Some commentators feel that Lish edited the work too heavily, stripping down the stories to achieve the minimal style for which Carver is famous. In some cases up to 78% of Carver's words were cut. Although Carver was grateful for the success Lish's editing brought him, he felt that the lifeblood of the stories had been drained away. In 2010, 22 years after his death, the pre-edited, original versions of some of Carver's stories were published in a collection called *Beginners.*

The Story of an Hour by Kate Chopin

Knowing that Mrs. Mallard was afflicted with a heart trouble, great care was taken to break to her as gently as possible the news of her husband's death.

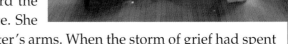

It was her sister Josephine who told her, in broken sentences; veiled hints that revealed in half concealing. Her husband's friend Richards was there, too, near her. It was he who had been in the newspaper office when intelligence of the railroad disaster was received, with Brently Mallard's name leading the list of 'killed.' He had only taken the time to assure himself of its truth by a second telegram, and had hastened to forestall any less careful, less tender friend in bearing the sad message.

She did not hear the story as many women have heard the same, with a paralyzed inability to accept its significance. She wept at once, with sudden, wild abandonment, in her sister's arms. When the storm of grief had spent itself she went away to her room alone. She would have no one follow her.

There stood, facing the open window, a comfortable, roomy armchair. Into this she sank, pressed down by a physical exhaustion that haunted her body and seemed to reach into her soul.

She could see in the open square before her house the tops of trees that were all aquiver with the new spring life. The delicious breath of rain was in the air. In the street below a peddler was crying his wares. The notes of a distant song which some one was singing reached her faintly, and countless sparrows were twittering in the eaves.

There were patches of blue sky showing here and there through the clouds that had met and piled one above the other in the west facing her window.

She sat with her head thrown back upon the cushion of the chair, quite motionless, except when a sob came up into her throat and shook her, as a child who has cried itself to sleep continues to sob in its dreams.

She was young, with a fair, calm face, whose lines bespoke repression and even a certain strength. But now there was a dull stare in her eyes, whose gaze was fixed away off yonder on one of those patches of blue sky. It was not a glance of reflection, but rather indicated a suspension of intelligent thought.

There was something coming to her and she was waiting for it, fearfully. What was it? She did not know; it was too subtle and elusive to name. But she felt it, creeping out of the sky, reaching toward her through the sounds, the scents, the color that filled the air.

Now her bosom rose and fell tumultuously. She was beginning to recognize this thing that was approaching to possess her, and she was striving to beat it back with her will – as powerless as her two white slender hands would have been. When she abandoned herself a little whispered word escaped her slightly parted lips. She said it over and over under her breath: 'free, free, free!' The vacant stare and the look of terror that had followed it went from her eyes. They stayed keen and bright. Her pulses beat fast, and the coursing blood warmed and relaxed every inch of her body.

She did not stop to ask if it were or were not a monstrous joy that held her. A clear and exalted perception enabled her to dismiss the suggestion as trivial. She knew that she would weep again when she saw the kind, tender hands folded in death; the face that had never looked save with love upon her, fixed and gray and dead. But she saw beyond that bitter moment a long procession of years to come that would belong to her absolutely. And she opened and spread her arms out to them in welcome.

There would be no one to live for during those coming years; she would live for herself. There would be no powerful will bending hers in that blind persistence with which men and women believe they have a right to impose a private will upon a fellow-creature. A kind intention or a cruel intention made the act seem no less a crime as she looked upon it in that brief moment of illumination.

And yet she had loved him – sometimes. Often she had not. What did it matter! What could love, the unsolved mystery, count for in face of this possession of self-assertion which she suddenly recognized as the strongest impulse of her being!

'Free! Body and soul free!' she kept whispering.

Josephine was kneeling before the closed door with her lips to the keyhole, imploring for admission. 'Louise, open the door! I beg, open the door – you will make yourself ill. What are you doing, Louise? For heaven's sake open the door.'

'Go away. I am not making myself ill.' No; she was drinking in a very elixir of life through that open window.

Her fancy was running riot along those days ahead of her. Spring days, and summer days, and all sorts of days that would be her own. She breathed a quick prayer that life might be long. It was only yesterday she had thought with a shudder that life might be long.

She arose at length and opened the door to her sister's importunities. There was a feverish triumph in her eyes, and she carried herself unwittingly like a goddess of Victory. She clasped her sister's waist, and together they descended the stairs. Richards stood waiting for them at the bottom.

Some one was opening the front door with a latchkey. It was Brently Mallard who entered, a little travel-stained, composedly carrying his grip-sack and umbrella. He had been far from the scene of accident, and did not even know there had been one. He stood amazed at Josephine's piercing cry; at Richards' quick motion to screen him from the view of his wife.

But Richards was too late.

When the doctors came they said she had died of heart disease – of the joy that kills.

Questions

Exploring *The Story of an Hour*

1. (a) Describe Mrs. Mallard's initial reaction to the news that her husband has died.
    (b) How do her feelings about the situation change?
2. When Mrs. Mallard realises she is free to live on her own, her emotions are described as a 'monstrous joy'. What do you think is meant by this phrase?
3. What kind of relationship do you think Mrs. Mallard had with her husband?
4. The first sentence of the story informs the reader that 'Mrs. Mallard was afflicted with a heart trouble'. Explain the relevance of this sentence in the context of the story.
5. (a) In your own words, describe Mrs. Mallard's view from the window.
    (b) Do you think these details reflect her thoughts? Explain your viewpoint.
6. The narrator describes Mrs. Mallard as 'young, with a fair, calm face'. Are you surprised by this description? Explain your answer.
7. Describe the character of Josephine as she is presented in the story.
8. (a) How do the doctors explain Mrs. Mallard's death?
    (b) Do you agree with their assessment? Explain your viewpoint making reference to the story.
9. What do you think is Kate Chopin's view of marriage? Refer to the story in your response.

Writers' Workshop

Imagine Mrs. Mallard wrote in her diary when she locked herself in her room. Write the diary entry she would have composed.

Language Lesson: Feature of Fiction – Character

An interesting character is a vital part of any good story. *The Story of an Hour* revolves around the thoughts and feelings of its central character, the intriguing Mrs. Mallard.

A reader comes to know a character through their:

- **Physical appearance** – an author may signpost a character's personality by how they look. For example, many villains are given a physical abnormality to make them appear more monstrous. In *The Story of an Hour,* Mrs. Mallard is shown to be young and pretty. This encourages sympathy from the reader.

- **Behaviour** – what a character says or does clearly establishes the kind of individual he/she is. How a character speaks can also be revealing. A character may show the capacity to change or develop; this gives a character greater depth. Mrs. Mallard's shock at the news of her husband's death shows that she is genuinely upset. When she locks herself in her room, the reader learns that she is a private person who wishes to face the situation independently.

- **Thoughts** – the author may give the reader insight into what a character is thinking. A character's motivation or ambition is an important part of who he/she is. What is most intriguing about Mrs. Mallard is how she grows to see her husband's death as an opportunity and guiltily welcomes the change in her life.

- **Treatment at the hands of other characters** – how other personalities in the story behave around a character reveals much to the reader. The concern afforded Mrs. Mallard by the other characters shows that she is much loved by her friends and relatives.

About The Author

Kate Chopin (1850 – 1904)

Kate Chopin was born Katherine O'Flaherty in St Louis, USA to an Irish father and a mother of French extraction. She benefitted from the influence of many strong female figures in her life who taught her to be independent and fearless. Her father was a successful businessman and she enjoyed a comfortable upbringing.

At the age of twenty, she married Oscar Chopin and moved to New Orleans. She had six children. Twelve years later her husband died. His business had been unsuccessful and Chopin was left with a large debt. For two years she tried to run her husband's businesses. During this time she reportedly had a number of romantic affairs, including one with a married man.

She returned to her family home in St Louis where money was not a problem. Her mother died a year later. All of this emotional turmoil left Chopin in a state of depression. She was advised by a doctor to try writing as an outlet for her energy and emotions. Chopin eagerly began to write novels, stories and articles and achieved modest success. However, some of her work was ahead of its time and many critics saw it as immoral. Some commentators claim her work was even banned in certain institutions.

She died as a result of a brain haemorrhage at the age of fifty-three.

Chopin's work increased in popularity after her death. She helped pioneer the vision of an independent female character and her writing has proved to be particularly inspirational for generations of female writers.

The Destructors by Graham Greene

1

It was on the eve of August Bank Holiday that the latest recruit became the leader of the Wormsley Common gang. No one was surprised except Mike, but Mike at the age of nine was surprised by everything. 'If you don't shut your mouth,' somebody once said to him, 'you'll get a frog down it.' After that Mike had kept his teeth tightly clamped except when the surprise was too great.

The new recruit had been with the gang since the beginning of the summer holidays, and there were possibilities about his brooding silence that all recognized. He never wasted a word even to tell his name until that was required of him by the rules. When he said 'Trevor' it was a statement of fact, not as it would have been with the others a statement of shame or defiance. Nor did anyone laugh except Mike, who finding himself without support and meeting the dark gaze of the newcomer opened his mouth and was quiet again. There was every reason why T., as he was afterward referred to, should have been an object of mockery – there was his name (and they substituted the initial because otherwise they had no excuse not to laugh at it), the fact that his father, a former architect and present clerk, had 'come down in the world' and that his mother considered herself better than the neighbours. What but an odd quality of danger, of the unpredictable, established him in the gang without any ignoble ceremony of initiation?

The gang met every morning in an impromptu car-park, the site of the last bomb of the first blitz. The leader, who was known as Blackie, claimed to have heard it fall, and no one was precise enough in his dates to point out that he would have been one year old and fast asleep on the down platform of Wormsley Common Underground Station. On one side of the car-park leaned the first occupied house, No. 3, of the shattered Northwood Terrace – literally leaned, for it had suffered from the blast of the bomb and the side walls were supported on wooden struts. A smaller bomb and some incendiaries had fallen beyond, so that the house stuck up like a jagged tooth and carried on the further wall relics of its neighbour, a dado, the remains of a fireplace. T., whose words were almost confined to voting 'Yes' or 'No' to the plan of operations proposed each day by Blackie, once startled the whole gang by saying broodingly, 'Wren built that house, father says.'

'Who's Wren?'

'The man who built St. Paul's.'

'Who cares?' Blackie said. 'It's only Old Misery's.'

Old Misery – whose real name was Thomas – had once been a builder and decorator. He lived alone in the crippled house, doing for himself: once a week you could see him coming back across the common with bread and vegetables, and once as the boys played in the car-park he put his head over the smashed wall of his garden and looked at them.

'Been to the lav,' one of the boys said, for it was common knowledge that since the bombs fell something had gone wrong with the pipes of the house and Old Misery was too mean to spend money on the property. He could do the redecorating himself at cost price, but he had never learned plumbing. The loo was a wooden shed at the bottom of the narrow garden with a star-shaped hole in the door: It had escaped the blast which had smashed the house next door and sucked out the window frames of No. 3.

The next time the gang became aware of Mr. Thomas was more surprising. Blackie, Mike, and a thin yellow boy, who for some reason was called by his surname Summers, met him on the common coming back from the market. Mr. Thomas stopped them. He said glumly, 'You belong to the lot that play in the car-park?'

Mike was about to answer when Blackie stopped him. As the leader he had responsibilities. 'Suppose we are?' he said ambiguously.

'I got some chocolates,' Mr. Thomas said. 'Don't like 'em myself. Here you are. Not enough to go round, I don't suppose. There never is,' he added with sombre conviction. He handed over three packets of Smarties.

The gang were puzzled and perturbed by this action and tried to explain it away. 'Bet someone dropped them and he picked 'em up,' somebody suggested.

'Pinched 'em and then got in a bleeding funk,' another thought aloud.

'It's a bribe,' Summers said. 'He wants us to stop bouncing balls on his wall.'

'We'll show him we don't take bribes,' Blackie said, and they sacrificed the whole morning to the game of bouncing that only Mike was young enough to enjoy. There was no sign from Mr. Thomas.

Next day T. astonished them all. He was late at the rendezvous, and the voting for that day's exploit took place without him. At Blackie's suggestion the gang was to disperse in pairs, take buses at random, and see how many free rides could be snatched from unwary conductors (the operation was to be carried out in pairs to avoid cheating). They were drawing lots for their companions when T. arrived.

'Where you been, T.?' Blackie asked. 'You can't vote now. You know the rules.'

'I've been there,' T. said. He looked at the ground, as though he had thoughts to hide.

'Where?'

'At Old Misery's.' Mike's mouth opened and then hurriedly closed again with a click. He had remembered the frog.

'At Old Misery's?' Blackie said. There was nothing in the rules against it, but he had a sensation that T. was treading on dangerous ground. He asked hopefully, 'Did you break in?'

'No. I rang the bell.'

'And what did you say?'

'I said I wanted to see his house.'

'What did he do?'

'He showed it me.'

'Pinch anything?'

'No.'

'What did you do it for then?'

The gang had gathered round: it was as though an impromptu court were about to form and try some case of deviation. T. said, 'It's a beautiful house,' and still watching the ground, meeting no one's eyes, he licked his lips first one way, then the other.

'What do you mean, a beautiful house?' Blackie asked with scorn.

'It's got a staircase two hundred years old like a corkscrew. Nothing holds it up.'

'What do you mean, nothing holds it up. Does it float?'

'It's to do with opposite forces, Old Misery said.'

'What else?'

'There's panelling.'

'Like in the Blue Boar?'

'Two hundred years old.'

'Is Old Misery two hundred years old?'

Mike laughed suddenly and then was quiet again. The meeting was in a serious mood. For the first time since T. had strolled into the car-park on the first day of the holidays his position was in danger. It only needed a single use of his real name and the gang would be at his heels.

'What did you do it for?' Blackie asked. He was just, he had no jealousy, he was anxious to retain T. in the gang if he could. It was the word 'beautiful' that worried him – that belonged to a class world that you could still see parodied at the Wormsley Common Empire by a man wearing a top hat and a monocle, with a haw-haw accent. He was tempted to say, 'My dear Trevor, old chap,' and unleash his hell hounds. 'If you'd broken in,' he said sadly – that indeed would have been an exploit worthy of the gang.

'This was better,' T. said. 'I found out things.' He continued to stare at his feet, not meeting anybody's eye, as though he were absorbed in some dream he was unwilling – or ashamed – to share.

'What things?'

'Old Misery's going to be away all tomorrow and Bank Holiday.'

Blackie said with relief, 'You mean we could break in?'

'And pinch things?' somebody asked.

Blackie said, 'Nobody's going to pinch things. Breaking in – that's good enough, isn't it? We don't want any court stuff.'

'I don't want to pinch anything,' T. said. 'I've got a better idea.'

'What is it?'

T. raised his eyes, as grey and disturbed as the drab August day. 'We'll pull it down,' he said. 'We'll destroy it.'

Blackie gave a single hoot of laughter and then, like Mike, fell quiet, daunted by the serious implacable gaze. 'What'd the police be doing all the time?' he said.

'They'd never know. We'd do it from inside. I've found a way in.' He said with a sort of intensity, 'We'd be like worms, don't you see, in an apple. When we came out again there'd be nothing there, no staircase, no panels, nothing but just walls, and then we'd make the walls fall down – somehow.'

'We'd go to jug,' Blackie said.

'Who's to prove? And anyway we wouldn't have pinched anything.' He added without the smallest flicker of glee, 'There wouldn't be anything to pinch after we'd finished.'

'I've never heard of going to prison for breaking things,' Summers said.

'There wouldn't be time,' Blackie said. 'I've seen housebreakers at work.'

'There are twelve of us,' T. said. 'We'd organize.'

'None of us know how…'

'I know,' T. said. He looked across at Blackie. 'Have you got a better plan?'

'Today,' Mike said tactlessly, 'we're pinching free rides…'

'Free rides,' T. said. 'You can stand down, Blackie, if you'd rather…'

'The gang's got to vote.'

'Put it up then.'

Blackie said uneasily, 'It's proposed that tomorrow and Monday we destroy Old Misery's house.'

'Here, here,' said a fat boy called Joe.

'Who's in favour?'

T. said, 'It's carried.'

'How do we start?' Summers asked.

'He'll tell you,' Blackie said. It was the end of his leadership. He went away to the back of the car-park and began to kick a stone, dribbling it this way and that. There was only one old Morris in the park, for few cars were left there except lorries: without an attendant there was no safety. He took a flying kick at the car and scraped a little paint off the rear mudguard. Beyond, paying no more attention to him than to a stranger, the gang had gathered round T.; Blackie was dimly aware of the fickleness of favour. He thought of going home, of never returning, of letting them all discover the hollowness of T.'s leadership, but suppose after all what T. proposed was possible – nothing like it had ever been done before. The fame of the Wormsley Common car-park gang would surely reach around London. There would be headlines in the papers. Even the grown-up gangs who ran the betting at the all-in wrestling and the barrow-boys would hear with respect of how Old Misery's house had been destroyed. Driven by the pure, simple, and altruistic ambition of fame for the gang, Blackie came back to where T. stood in the shadow of Misery's wall.

T. was giving his orders with decision: it was as though this plan had been with him all his life, pondered through the seasons, now in his fifteenth year crystallized with the pain of puberty. 'You,' he said to Mike, 'bring some big nails, the biggest you can find, and a hammer. Anyone else who can better bring a hammer and a screwdriver. We'll need plenty of them. Chisels too. We can't have too many chisels. Can anybody bring a saw?'

'I can,' Mike said.

'Not a child's saw,' T. said. 'A real saw.'

Blackie realized he had raised his hand like any ordinary member of the gang.

'Right, you bring one, Blackie. But now there's a difficulty. We want a hacksaw.'

'What's a hacksaw?' someone asked.

'You can get 'em at Woolworth's,' Summers said.

The fat boy called Joe said gloomily, 'I knew it would end in a collection.'

'I'll get one myself,' T. said. 'I don't want your money. But I can't buy a sledge-hammer.'

Blackie said, 'They are working on No. 15. I know where they'll leave their stuff for Bank Holiday.'

'Then that's all,' T. said. 'We meet here at nine sharp.'

'I've got to go to church,' Mike said.

'Come over the wall and whistle. We'll let you in.'

2

On Sunday morning all were punctual except Blackie, even Mike. Mike had had a stroke of luck. His mother felt ill, his father was tired after Saturday night, and he was told to go to church alone with many warnings of what would happen if he strayed. Blackie had had difficulty in smuggling out the saw, and then in finding the sledge-hammer at the back of No. 15. He approached the house from a lane at the rear of the garden, for fear of the policeman's beat along the main road. The tired evergreens kept off a stormy sun: another wet Bank Holiday was being prepared over the Atlantic, beginning in swirls of dust under the trees. Blackie climbed the wall into Misery's garden.

There was no sign of anybody anywhere. The lav stood like a tomb in a neglected graveyard. The curtains were drawn. The house slept. Blackie lumbered nearer with the saw and the sledgehammer. Perhaps after all nobody had turned up: the plan had been a wild invention: they had woken wiser. But when he came close to the back door he could hear a confusion of sound, hardly louder than a hive in swarm: a clickety-clack, a bang bang, a scraping, a creaking, a sudden painful crack. He thought: it's true, and whistled.

They opened the back door to him and he came in. He had at once the impression of organization, very different from the old happy-go-lucky ways under his leadership. For a while he wandered up and down stairs looking for T. Nobody addressed him: he had a sense of great urgency, and already he could begin to see the plan. The interior of the house was being carefully demolished without touching the outer walls. Summers with hammer and chisel was ripping out the skirting-boards in the ground floor dining room: he had already smashed the panels of the door. In the same room Joe was heaving up the parquet blocks, exposing the soft wood floorboards over the cellar. Coils of wire came out of the damaged skirting and Mike sat happily on the floor, clipping the wires.

On the curved stairs two of the gang were working hard with an inadequate child's saw on the banisters – when they saw Blackie's big saw they signalled for it wordlessly. When he next saw them a quarter of the banisters had been dropped into the hall. He found T. at last in the bathroom – he sat moodily in the least cared-for room in the house, listening to the sounds coming up from below.

'You've really done it,' Blackie said with awe. 'What's going to happen?'

'We've only just begun,' T. said. He looked at the sledge-hammer and gave his instructions. 'You stay here and break the bath and the washbasin. Don't bother about the pipes. They come later.'

Mike appeared at the door. 'I've finished the wire, T.,' he said.

'Good. You've just got to go wandering round now. The kitchen's in the basement. Smash all the china and glass and bottles you can lay hold of. Don't turn on the taps – we don't want a flood – yet. Then go into all the rooms and turn out drawers. If they are locked get one of the others to break them open. Tear up any papers you find and smash all the ornaments. Better take a carving knife with you from the kitchen. The bedroom's opposite here. Open the pillows and tear up the sheets. That's enough for the moment. And you, Blackie, when you've finished in here crack the plaster in the passage up with your sledge-hammer.'

'What are you going to do?' Blackie asked.

'I'm looking for something special,' T. said.

It was nearly lunchtime before Blackie had finished and went in search of T. Chaos had advanced. The kitchen was a shambles of broken glass and china. The dining room was stripped of parquet, the skirting was up, the door had been taken off its hinges, and the destroyers had moved up a floor. Streaks of light came in through the closed shutters where they worked with the seriousness of creators – and destruction after all is a form of creation. A kind of imagination had seen this house as it had now become.

Mike said, 'I've got to go home for dinner.'

'Who else?' T. asked, but all the others on one excuse or another had brought provisions with them.

They squatted in the ruins of the room and swapped unwanted sandwiches. Half an hour for lunch and they were at work again. By the time Mike returned, they were on the top floor, and by six the superficial damage was completed. The doors were all off, all the skirtings raised, the furniture pillaged and ripped and smashed – no one could have slept in the house except on a bed of broken plaster. T. gave his orders – eight o'clock next morning – and to escape notice they climbed singly over the garden wall, into the car-park. Only Blackie and T. were left; the light had nearly gone, and when they touched a switch, nothing worked – Mike had done his job thoroughly.

'Did you find anything special?' Blackie asked.

T. nodded. 'Come over here,' he said, 'and look.' Out of both pockets he drew bundles of pound notes. 'Old Misery's savings,' he said. 'Mike ripped out the mattress, but he missed them.'

'What are you going to do? Share them?'

'We aren't thieves,' T. said. 'Nobody's going to steal anything from this house. I kept these for you and me – a celebration.' He knelt down on the floor and counted them out – there were seventy in all. 'We'll burn them,' he said, 'one by one,' and taking it in turns they held a note upward and lit the top corner, so that the flame burnt slowly toward their fingers. The grey ash floated above them and fell on their heads like age. 'I'd like to see Old Misery's face when we are through,' T. said.

'You hate him a lot?' Blackie asked.

'Of course I don't hate him,' T. said. 'There'd be no fun if I hated him.' The last burning note illuminated his brooding face. 'All this hate and love,' he said, 'it's soft, it's hooey. There's only things, Blackie,' and he looked round the room crowded with the unfamiliar shadows of half things, broken things, former things. 'I'll race you home, Blackie,' he said.

3

Next morning the serious destruction started. Two were missing – Mike and another boy, whose parents were off to Southend and Brighton in spite of the slow warm drops that had begun to fall and the rumble of thunder in the estuary like the first guns of the old blitz. 'We've got to hurry,' T. said.

Summers was restive. 'Haven't we done enough?' he said. 'I've been given a bob for slot machines. This is like work.'

'We've hardly started,' T. said. 'Why, there's all the floors left, and the stairs. We haven't taken out a single window. You voted like the others. We are going to *destroy* this house. There won't be anything left when we've finished.'

They began again on the first floor picking up the top floorboards next the outer wall, leaving the joists exposed. Then they sawed through the joists and retreated into the hall, as what was left of the floor heeled and sank. They had learned with practice, and the second floor collapsed more easily. By the evening an odd exhilaration seized them as they looked down the great hollow of the house. They ran risks and made mistakes: when they thought of the windows it was too late to reach them. 'Cor,' Joe said, and dropped a penny down into the dry rubble-filled well. It cracked and span among the broken glass.

'Why did we start this?' Summers asked with astonishment; T. was already on the ground, digging at the rubble, clearing a space along the outer wall. 'Turn on the taps,' he said. 'It's too dark for anyone to see now, and in the morning it won't matter.' The water overtook them on the stairs and fell through the floorless rooms.

It was then they heard Mike's whistle at the back. 'Something's wrong,' Blackie said. They could hear his urgent breathing as they unlocked the door.

'The bogies?' Summers asked.

'Old Misery,' Mike said. 'He's on his way.' He put his head between his knees and retched. 'Ran all the way,' he said with pride.

'But why?' T. said. 'He told me…' He protested with the fury of the child he had never been, 'It isn't fair.'

'He was down at Southend,' Mike said, 'and he was on the train coming back. Said it was too cold and wet.' He paused and gazed at the water. 'My, you've had a storm here. Is the roof leaking?'

'How long will he be?'

'Five minutes. I gave Ma the slip and ran.'

'We better clear,' Summers said. 'We've done enough, anyway.'

'Oh, no, we haven't. Anybody could do this – ' 'this' was the shattered hollowed house with nothing left but the walls. Yet walls could be preserved. Façades were valuable. They could build inside again more beautifully than before. This could again be a home. He said angrily, 'We've got to finish. Don't move. Let me think.'

'There's no time,' a boy said.

'There's got to be a way,' T. said. 'We couldn't have got this far…'

'We've done a lot,' Blackie said.

'No. No, we haven't. Somebody watch the front.'

'We can't do any more.'

'He may come in at the back.'

'Watch the back too.' T. began to plead. 'Just give me a minute and I'll fix it. I swear I'll fix it.' But his authority had gone with his ambiguity. He was only one of the gang. 'Please,' he said.

'Please,' Summers mimicked him, and then suddenly struck home with the fatal name. 'Run along home, Trevor.'

T. stood with his back to the rubble like a boxer knocked groggy against the ropes. He had no words as his dreams shook and slid. Then Blackie acted before the gang had time to laugh, pushing Summers backward. 'I'll watch the front, T.,' he said, and cautiously he opened the shutters of the hall. The grey wet common stretched ahead, and the lamps gleamed in the puddles. 'Someone's coming, T. No, it's not him. What's your plan, T.?'

'Tell Mike to go out to the lav and hide close beside it. When he hears me whistle he's got to count ten and start to shout.'

'Shout what?'

'Oh, "Help," anything.'

'You hear, Mike,' Blackie said. He was the leader again. He took a quick look between the shutters. 'He's coming, T.'

'Quick, Mike. The lav. Stay here, Blackie, all of you, till I yell.'

'Where are you going, T.?'

'Don't worry. I'll see to this. I said I would, didn't I?'

Old Misery came limping off the common. He had mud on his shoes and he stopped to scrape them on the pavement's edge. He didn't want to soil his house, which stood jagged and dark between the bomb sites, saved so narrowly, as he believed, from destruction. Even the fanlight had been left unbroken by the bomb's blast. Somewhere somebody whistled. Old Misery looked sharply round. He didn't trust whistles. A child was shouting: it seemed to come from his own garden. Then a boy ran into the road from the car-park. 'Mr. Thomas,' he called, 'Mr. Thomas.'

'What is it?'

'I'm terribly sorry, Mr. Thomas. One of us got taken short, and we thought you wouldn't mind, and now he can't get out.'

'What do you mean, boy?'

'He's got stuck in your lav.'

'He'd no business…Haven't I seen you before?'

'You showed me your house.'

'So I did. So I did. That doesn't give you the right to…'

'Do hurry, Mr. Thomas. He'll suffocate.'

'Nonsense. He can't suffocate. Wait till I put my bag in.'

'I'll carry your bag.'

'Oh, no, you don't. I carry my own.'

'This way, Mr. Thomas.'

'I can't get in the garden that way. I've got to go through the house.'

'But you can get in the garden this way, Mr. Thomas. We often do.'

'You often do?' He followed the boy with a scandalized fascination. 'When? What right…?'

'Do you see…? the wall's low.'

'I'm not going to climb walls into my own garden. It's absurd.'

'This is how we do it. One foot here, one foot there, and over.' The boy's face peered down, an arm shot out, and Mr. Thomas found his bag taken and deposited on the other side of the wall.

'Give me back my bag,' Mr. Thomas said. From the loo a boy yelled and yelled. 'I'll call the police.'

'Your bag's all right, Mr. Thomas. Look. One foot there. On your right. Now just above. To your left.' Mr. Thomas climbed over his own garden wall. 'Here's your bag, Mr. Thomas.'

'I'll have the wall built up,' Mr. Thomas said. 'I'll not have you boys coming over here, using my loo.' He stumbled on the path, but the boy caught his elbow and supported him. 'Thank you, thank you, my boy,' he murmured automatically. Somebody shouted again through the dark. 'I'm coming, I'm coming,' Mr. Thomas called. He said to the boy beside him, 'I'm not unreasonable. Been a boy myself. As long as things are done regular. I don't mind you playing round the place Saturday mornings. Sometimes I like company. Only it's got to be regular. One of you asks leave and I say Yes. Sometimes I'll say No.

152

Won't feel like it. And you come in at the front door and out at the back. No garden walls.'

'Do get him out, Mr. Thomas.'

'He won't come to any harm in my loo,' Mr. Thomas said, stumbling slowly down the garden. 'Oh, my rheumatics,' he said. 'Always get 'em on Bank Holiday. I've got to go careful. There's loose stones here. Give me your hand. Do you know what my horoscope said yesterday? "Abstain from any dealings in first half of week. Danger of serious crash." That might be on this path,' Mr. Thomas said. 'They speak in parables and double meanings.' He paused at the door of the loo. 'What's the matter in there?' he called. There was no reply.

'Perhaps he's fainted,' the boy said.

'Not in my loo. Here, you, come out,' Mr. Thomas said, and giving a great jerk at the door he nearly fell on his back when it swung easily open. A hand first supported him and then pushed him hard. His head hit the opposite wall and he sat heavily down. His bag hit his feet. A hand whipped the key out of the lock and the door slammed. 'Let me out,' he called, and heard the key turn in the lock. 'A serious crash,' he thought, and felt dithery and confused and old.

A voice spoke to him softly through the star-shaped hole in the door. 'Don't worry, Mr. Thomas,' it said, 'we won't hurt you, not if you stay quiet.'

Mr. Thomas put his head between his hands and pondered. He had noticed that there was only one lorry in the car-park, and he felt certain that the driver would not come for it before the morning. Nobody could hear him from the road in front, and the lane at the back was seldom used. Anyone who passed there would be hurrying home and would not pause for what they would certainly take to be drunken cries. And if he did call 'Help,' who, on a lonely Bank Holiday evening, would have the courage to investigate? Mr. Thomas sat on the loo and pondered with the wisdom of age.

After a while it seemed to him that there were sounds in the silence – they were faint and came from the direction of his house. He stood up and peered through the ventilation-hole – between the cracks in one of the shutters he saw a light, not the light of a lamp, but the wavering light that a candle might give. Then he thought he heard the sound of hammering and scraping and chipping. He thought of burglars – perhaps they had employed the boy as a scout, but why should burglars engage in what sounded more and more like a stealthy form of carpentry? Mr. Thomas let out an experimental yell, but nobody answered. The noise could not even have reached his enemies.

4

Mike had gone home to bed, but the rest stayed. The question of leadership no longer concerned the gang. With nails, chisels, screwdrivers, anything that was sharp and penetrating they moved around the inner walls worrying at the mortar between the bricks. They started too high, and it was Blackie who hit on the damp course and realized the work could be halved if they weakened the joints immediately above. It was a long, tiring, unamusing job, but at last it was finished. The gutted house stood there balanced on a few inches of mortar between the damp course and the bricks.

There remained the most dangerous task of all, out in the open at the edge of the bomb site. Summers was sent to watch the road for passers by, and Mr. Thomas, sitting on the loo, heard clearly now the sound of sawing. It no longer came from his house, and that a little reassured him. He felt less concerned. Perhaps the other noises too had no significance.

A voice spoke to him through the hole. 'Mr. Thomas.'

'Let me out,' Mr. Thomas said sternly.

'Here's a blanket,' the voice said, and a long grey sausage was worked through the hole and fell in swathes over Mr. Thomas's head.

'There's nothing personal,' the voice said. 'We want you to be comfortable tonight.'

'Tonight,' Mr. Thomas repeated incredulously.

'Catch,' the voice said. 'Penny buns – we've buttered them, and sausage-rolls. We don't want you to starve, Mr. Thomas.'

Mr. Thomas pleaded desperately. 'A joke's a joke, boy. Let me out and I won't say a thing. I've got rheumatics. I got to sleep comfortable.'

'You wouldn't be comfortable, not in your house, you wouldn't. Not now.'

'What do you mean, boy?' But the footsteps receded. There was only the silence of night: no sound of sawing. Mr. Thomas tried one more yell, but he was daunted and rebuked by the silence – a long way off an owl hooted and made away again on its muffled flight through the soundless world.

At seven next morning the driver came to fetch his lorry. He climbed into the seat and tried to start the engine. He was vaguely aware of a voice shouting, but it didn't concern him. At last the engine responded and he backed the lorry until it touched the great wooden shore that supported Mr. Thomas's house. That way he could drive right out and down the street without reversing. The lorry moved forward, was momentarily checked as though something were pulling it from behind, and then went on to the sound of a long rumbling crash. The driver was astonished to see bricks bouncing ahead of him, while stones hit the roof of his cab. He put on his brakes. When he climbed out the whole landscape had suddenly altered. There was no house beside the car-park, only a hill of rubble. He went round and examined the back of his car for damage, and found a rope tied there that was still twisted at the other end round part of a wooden strut.

The driver again became aware of somebody shouting. It came from the wooden erection which was the nearest thing to a house in that desolation of broken brick. The driver climbed the smashed wall and unlocked the door. Mr. Thomas came out of the loo. He was wearing a grey blanket to which flakes of pastry adhered. He gave a sobbing cry. 'My house,' he said. 'Where's my house?'

'Search me,' the driver said. His eye lit on the remains of a bath and what had once been a dresser and he began to laugh. There wasn't anything left anywhere.

'How dare you laugh,' Mr. Thomas said. 'It was my house. My house.'

'I'm sorry,' the driver said, making heroic efforts, but when he remembered the sudden check to his lorry, the crash of bricks falling, he became convulsed again. One moment the house had stood there with such dignity between the bomb sites like a man in a top hat, and then, bang, crash, there wasn't anything left – not anything. He said, 'I'm sorry. I can't help it, Mr. Thomas. There's nothing personal, but you got to admit it's funny.'

Questions

Exploring *The Destructors*

1. Why do the gang have so much time to get up to mischief?
2. Why was Old Misery's toilet located at the bottom of the garden?
3. In your words, retell the moment when T. became the leader of the Wormsley Common Gang.
4. Describe Old Misery's house as it is portrayed by T.
5. Explain how the gang destroyed Old Misery's house.
6. **(a)** Describe the setting of Graham Greene's *The Destructors*.
   (b) Comment on how the setting contributes to the atmosphere or mood of the story.
7. Explain how the following elements of the story are ironic*:
   (a) T.'s father's previous occupation
   (b) The house's survival of the Blitz
   (c) Old Misery's former occupation
   (d) Old Misery's horoscope
8. Why do you think T. and the gang destroyed Old Misery's house?
9. What is your impression of T.? Refer to the story to support your view.
10. What theme or issue do you think Graham Greene is exploring in this story? Refer to the text in your response.
11. Comment on the meaning of the following lines from the story: 'they worked with the seriousness of creators – and destruction after all is a form of creation. A kind of imagination had seen this house as it had now become.'
12. Do you think children in real life are capable of this kind of cruelty? Explain your viewpoint.
13. Using a dictionary, match the following words from the story with their definitions.

1.	Ignoble	a.	Troubled or bothered
2.	Sombre	b.	Violently shaken as with laughter or in a spasm
3.	Perturbed		
4.	Impromptu	c.	Done without preparation; off the cuff
5.	Implacable	d.	Gloomy; serious
6.	Altruistic	e.	Outward appearance; shallow
7.	Superficial	f.	Not to be fazed; undeterred
8.	Pillaged	g.	Overcome with fear; disheartened
9.	Daunted	h.	Plundered; robbed ruthlessly
10.	Convulsed	i.	Unselfishly
		j.	Lowly; dishonourable; degraded

*Irony is when a stated idea is the opposite of reality or when an idea seems out of place with reality. **For example:** Old Misery used to build and decorate houses (idea) but now his is being destroyed (reality). Dramatic irony is when a situation is understood by the reader but not the character. The examples in this question (Question 7) are all ironic or dramatically ironic.

Writers' Workshop

Write an article for a newspaper expressing your views on vandalism or graffiti.

Language Lesson: Feature of Fiction – Setting

The setting of a story is the time, place and culture where the action takes place. It serves as a backdrop that adds to the mood and helps to create an atmosphere in the story. It can also affect the plot and reflect a story's theme. The idea of 'setting' can be explored under the following headings:

Time – <u>when</u> a story takes place helps to shape the action. There may be an important historical event that has an effect on the story. Equally, if a story takes place during a particular season, the mood and atmosphere are affected. *The Destructors* is set against the backdrop of World War II. The Blitz was a period of the war when London and other towns in Britain were severely damaged by German bombing campaigns. This creates a bleak vision of the world and an air of violence and destruction.

Place – <u>where</u> a story is set is of vital importance. The story's landscape will add to both the plot and the atmosphere. *The Destructors* is set in the aftermath of a destructive bombing campaign. Greene uses words like 'shattered', 'suffered' and 'smashed' to set the scene, along with vivid images of ruined buildings: 'the house stuck up like a jagged tooth'. The vision of destroyed buildings connects with the act of vandalism at the heart of the story.

Society – a setting is more than just the physical aspects of a fictional world, it is also the <u>people</u> who inhabit the place. When considering the 'social setting' it is important to consider the three following points: (a) the values of the society, (b) the economic and social circumstances and (c) the people's traditions, attitudes and beliefs. In Graham Greene's story, the boys' outlook seems shaped by the devastation and ruin caused by the war. Considering how the boys annihilate Old Misery's house, this obliterated landscape seems fitting to the story. The backdrop of greater destruction and violence suggests a comparison between the boys' behaviour and the adult world.

Activity

Film Comparison

The Destructors is referred to in Richard Kelly's film *Donnie Darko*. The subject matter of Graham Greene's story is also echoed in the film. Watch *Donnie Darko* and explore the parallels it has with *The Destructors*.

About The Author

Graham Greene (1904 – 1991)

Graham Greene was born in Hertfordshire in England. His early life was beset by bullying and depression. His father was the headmaster of the school Greene attended and this made life difficult for him. After a number of suicide attempts, Greene left school and wrote to his parents to say that he would not return. As a result he underwent psychotherapy at the age of fifteen. His therapist encouraged Greene to write as a way of dealing with his unhappiness.

After college, he found work editing magazines and newspapers and writing book reviews. He was converted to Catholicism by his soon-to-be wife, Vivien Dayrell-Browning. This faith is an important feature of his early work.

Greene initially struggled to succeed as a writer. A number of early novels sold poorly. It wasn't until he published the novel *Stamboul Train* in 1932 that he found success as an author. He went on to publish a number of hugely popular works such as *Brighton Rock*, *The Heart of the Matter* and *Our Man in Havana*. Many of his stories have been turned into films: the Internet Movie Database (IMDb) lists 66 films based on Greene's stories.

Throughout his life, Greene travelled widely, visiting exotic locations such as Cuba, Kenya, Haiti and Vietnam. During World War II, he worked for the MI6 Secret Intelligence Services. This allowed him to see more of the world and gave him material for his novels. Politically, Greene associated with a variety of interesting figures such as Fidel Castro, the president of Cuba.

He lived his last years in Switzerland where he was friends with Charlie Chaplin. He died of leukaemia at the age of 86.

Project
Text Report

Task
- Write a text report on a novel you have studied independently.

Project Guidelines

Your report should contain all of the following:

❋ **A short biography of the writer** – Where is the writer from? Has his/her life been interesting, unusual or controversial? Has the author won any major awards?

❋ **A character study** – Choose one character from the novel that you found interesting. Write about the character's personality, outlook on life, attitude, ability to deal with problems and the degree of success they achieve in the story.

❋ **Key moments** – Choose two important episodes or moments from the novel. For each key moment, describe what happened and explain why you felt this scene was important. An episode may be important because it is a turning point in the plot, reveals something about the characters, contributes to your understanding of the theme or is exciting or entertaining.

❋ **Theme** – Write about the theme of your novel. Think about the message the author is trying to convey or the issue that is being explored.

❋ **Cultural Context / Social Setting** – Describe the world of the novel. Is it a place where characters enjoy freedom or are there obstacles in their way? What are the values of the society in the novel? Is the world portrayed in a positive or negative light? You may want to consider some of the following ideas about society: gender roles, religion, wealth/poverty, power, freedom, race.

❋ **Personal Response** – Did you enjoy the novel? Explain what you liked or disliked about the book. Did you find any features of the novel particularly interesting or enjoyable? Who would you recommend the novel to, if anyone?

Mechanics:
Colons and Semi-Colons

Colons

Like commas and full stops, colons encourage the reader to pause. They are also used to introduce the next part of a sentence.

Colons are used to:
⇨ announce the next part of a sentence
   This much was obvious: the woman was completely insane.

⇨ introduce a list
   He loved only three things in this world: his wife, his child and when they both went out for the day.

⇨ introduce a quote
   As Dylan Thomas writes: 'Old age should burn and rave at close of day.'

⇨ introduce an explanation, definition or a qualification.
   Space: the final frontier.
   Z: the last letter in the alphabet.

⇨ divide a main title from a subtitle
   Barking Mad: Man Imitates Dog in Court Today

⇨ separate characters' names from dialogue in a drama script.
   MACBETH: Is this a dagger which I see before me...?

Practising Colons

Rewrite these sentences inserting colons in the correct places.
1. Despite her bad temper and ill patience, she had one good quality her generosity.
2. Oscar Wilde's dying words still amuse today 'Either that wallpaper goes, or I do.'
3. Capricorn the sign of the goat.
4. Poetry The Packsack of Invisible Keepsakes
5. Juliet O Romeo, Romeo, Wherefore art thou Romeo?
6. There are four things one should never forget when going to the airport passport, tickets, money and more money.
7. His reason for robbing the bank was quite straightforward he wanted the money.
8. Have some sympathy for the most commonly misused and abused punctuation marks colons, semi-colons, apostrophes and exclamations marks.

Semi-Colons

Like colons, semi-colons indicate a pause in a sentence. Semi-colons can often be replaced by a full stop or a comma. However, semi-colons can help to make a piece of writing clearer and avoid confusion.

Semi-colons are used:

(a) instead of a full stop. This occurs when two sentences are closely related.

I remember when he used to eat six hamburgers a day; now he's running marathons and drinking smoothies.

Here a full stop could be used instead of a semi-colon:

I remember when he used to eat six hamburgers a day. Now he's running marathons and drinking smoothies.

However, because the two ideas are closely related, a semi-colon works better.

In the following examples, we can see how the relationship between two ideas is stronger using a semi-colon rather than a full stop.

I told my boss I was quitting. I hope he knows I was joking.

I told my boss I was quitting; I hope he knows I was joking.

(b) to separate phrases in a list. When writing lists, semi-colons sometimes prove more useful than commas.

Look at how the following list is confusing without semi-colons.

He tried to contact his girlfriend in every possible way: on Twitter, the microblogging site, by poking her on Facebook, by texting her, using his new iPhone, by calling her land line, and even (shock horror), by visiting her home. After a week, he started to get the feeling that she was avoiding him.

The meaning becomes much clearer when semi-colons are introduced:

He tried to contact his girlfriend in every possible way: on Twitter, the microblogging site; by poking her on Facebook; by texting her, using his new iPhone; by calling her land line; and even (shock horror), by visiting her home. After a week, he started to get the feeling that she was avoiding him.

Practising Semi-Colons

1. **Join these pairs of sentences together by replacing the full stops with semi-colons.**
   (a) She had tried bungy jumping, sky-diving and white-water rafting. Now she was planning to take up base-jumping.
   (b) Emma didn't want to be parted from the new puppy. That night the dog slept at the foot of the little girl's bed.
   (c) The roof had collapsed in the storm. The plaster on the walls was swollen with rain water, and ducks quacked in the living room.

2. **Rewrite this sentence replacing the unnecessary commas with semi-colons.**
   They had toured the world: Japan, where they got food poisoning, New York, where they were mugged, Bali, where they ran out of money, and even found themselves in Dublin, where it rained the entire time.

5 Drama: Life with the Dull Bits Cut Out

> What is drama, after all, but life with the dull bits cut out.

Alfred Hitchcock, British film director

www.CartoonStock.com

Terraces by Willy Russell

Introduction

Terraces was originally written as a short film for television. The playwright, Willy Russell, later adapted it for the stage. The play depicts a close-knit working-class community in Britain, united by their support for their local football team. Their enthusiasm creates a subculture in which individuals are pressurised into conforming to the expectations of the whole community. The play looks at 'mob mentality' and the struggle between the individual and society.

The Cast

EDDY	MICHAEL	FIRST WOMAN
JOEY	BILLY	SECOND WOMAN
JOHN	JOAN	BARMAID
SUSAN	JOYCE	YOUNGSTER
DANNY	SHOPKEEPER	

Scene 1

A local pub on a Saturday night: noisy, smoky and brash. The women sit drinking at the tables. The men argue loudly at the bar. Everyone is in competition with the jukebox.

EDDY: An' the ball ... now listen, listen ... Tommy Wingfield picked it up at the half way line. He goes thunderin' past the defence ... just like a rocket.

[*The women laugh*]

JOEY [*Supporting EDDY*]: 'Ey, don't laugh ... that's just what he was like, a rocket.

EDDY: A bloody wizard! But what do their defenders do when they see they can't beat him with skill?

JOHN: Swines!

EDDY: They hack him down, don't they! [*There is a respectful pause*] But does Tommy worry about a bit of violence? No, he's up in a flash, the ball still at his feet an' then he lets go ... Wham! D' y' know, his foot moved so fast it was blurred. The ball leaves it like a missile off a launchin' pad. It goes straight past the goaly, into the back of the net, breaks the net, busts right through the back terrace wall, demolishes a bus, puts a hole in the church steeple, kills fourteen pigeons an' guess what?

JOYCE: What, Eddy?

EDDY [*slamming down his pint*]: It was friggin' offside!

Scene 2

DANNY'S house, the same night. MICHAEL, his son, is doing a crossword in the paper. DANNY is reading a novel.

SUSAN:	Are we goin', Danny?
DANNY [*absent*]:	Mm?
SUSAN:	Are we goin' down there or not?
MICHAEL:	Dad ... what's a [*reading*] a 'Historical gang' beginnin' with M... three letters?
DANNY: [*looking up, puzzled*]:	A what? Here ... let's have a look.
MICHAEL:	A historical gang.
DANNY [*getting up and looking at the paper*]:	Historical! Hysterical ... you nutter!
MICHAEL:	Oh yeh.
DANNY:	Mob it is ... mob! Historical!
SUSAN:	Are we goin'?
DANNY:	D' y' fancy it?
MICHAEL:	Dad ... what's a ten letter word that means 'one who always agrees'?
DANNY:	Who's supposed to be doin' this crossword?
MICHAEL:	Me. But you're helpin' me with it.
DANNY:	What's it begin with?
MICHAEL:	I think I've got the first three letters. I think it starts with CON.
DANNY:	Well can't y' work it out?
MICHAEL:	No!
DANNY:	'Conformist', isn't it?
MICHAEL:	Is it?
DANNY:	Yes.
SUSAN:	I thought y'd want to go down to the Grapes so you could celebrate gettin' through to the final.
DANNY:	That's not celebratin'. It's just drinkin' for the sake of it an' going over every last detail a thousand times. You don't need to celebrate a game of football. The enjoyment's in watchin' the game.
SUSAN:	You're a real killjoy, you are. Other fellers would be overjoyed if their team got through to the final.
DANNY:	I *am* overjoyed. I just can't see much point in goin' over it again an' again. Eddy an' that lot, they're like a television panel. They go on about it so much I think they enjoy talkin' about the game more than they enjoy the game itself.
SUSAN:	So we're not goin' out?
DANNY:	I didn't say that. Do you want to go out, love?
SUSAN:	Well, it is Saturday night.
DANNY:	Yes, but do you want to go out?
SUSAN:	Yes. Yes!
DANNY:	Well get your coat on. If you want to go out, we'll go out.
SUSAN:	Well why didn't you say that in the first place? Come on. I bet it's a riot down there tonight!

Scene 3

The pub again, heavy with a sense of occasion. The club doesn't reach the final every season.

JOHN:	Well, what I think, Eddy, is that this street should show its support for the team.
JOEY:	What are you on about? There's not a family in this street that doesn't support the team.
JOHN:	Yes, but what I'm talkin' about is showing support. It's all right supporting the team in silence but we must be seen to support them.
EDDY:	John's right. It's a great achievement and it must be treated as such. To some people it might just be a game of football, a team, but to me it's a game of ... of ... life!
JOHN:	Hear hear! A game of life ... I like that, Ed.
JOEY:	Well look, why don't we put pictures of the team in all the windows?
EDDY:	No ... ! That's what y' do at election time. What we're talkin' about is somethin' serious!
JOEY:	Well, what do we do then?
EDDY:	I don't know but it's gotta be something big, y' know, a bit of a splash with all the street involved, even the women.
JOHN:	Let's all have a think about it.
	[*They all go into earnest thought as DANNY and his wife enter. The women call out to SUSAN and make way for her to sit with them. DANNY comes across to EDDY and co.*]
DANNY:	All right? Celebration pints all round, is it?
EDDY:	What a victory though, Danny, eh, eh?
JOHN and JOEY:	All right, Danny!
DANNY:	Four pints an' a vodka an' lime, Jose.
EDDY:	Danny, listen, we're tryin' to see if we can sort out some way in which the street can show its support for the lads.
JOHN:	Come on Danny, surely you can think of somethin', with an imagination like yours.
JOEY:	Got any ideas, Danny?
DANNY [*Handing SUSAN'S drink across*]:	Yeh. Go 'n watch the team when they're playin' in the final! [*Lifting his pint*] Cheers!
EDDY [*Lifting his pint*]:	Hold on, Danny. [*He stops drinking*] Hold on. [*Raps on the bar*] 'Ey. Let's have a bit of order! [*Supporting shouts of Quiet, Shush*] I propose a toast. A toast to the glorious lads in yellow who today created ... history. To the lads! [*Everyone reverent: To the lads.*] An' what about a cheer? [*EDDY starts it and everyone joins in. The bubble of conversation blows up again*] No, what I'm talkin' about, Danny, is whippin' up some, y' know, some real interest like.
DANNY:	Y' don't need t' do that.
JOHN:	Why not? It'd be good, Danny.

DANNY:	To me it's the game that's important, John. Y' don't want to be gettin' into all these daft things like pictures in windows an' slogans. It's a game, not something else, not something you go out and paint the streets for.
EDDY [*Grasping him and it*]:	That's it! That's it! The whole bloody street, every inch of it in the team's colour!
JOHN:	Yellow!
JOEY:	'Ey, yeh! A yellow street! Brilliant, Danny.
DANNY [*laughing*]:	Get lost! I didn't mean ...
EDDY:	We're on. That's it! Right. [*Eddy bangs on the bar for order. He gets it*] Is everyone listenin'?
DANNY:	Eddy ... listen ...
EDDY:	Right. Now everyone here tonight knows that today our own team, this street's team, got through to the final. [*There's a thundering cheer*] Well look, we've been talking and we think that this street should show its support for the glorious efforts of our noble lads. [*Everyone cheers wildly*]
JOHN [*shouting*]:	Well, what are we goin' to do, Ed?
EDDY:	I'll tell you. I'll tell all of you. [*Pause*] Is everyone agreed? [*Shouts of agreement*] Right. Billy . . . where's Billy? [*A head pops up from the crowd*]
BILLY:	Here, Eddy.
EDDY:	Billy ... have y' got any yellow paint in the shop?
BILLY:	I've got gallons of it. It's been there for years.
EDDY:	Will y' open the shop tomorrow? So we can buy it?
BILLY:	Buy it? Y' won't buy it. For somethin' like this y' can have it for free. [*A spontaneous cheer for BILLY. The pub talk, excited, starts up again*]
JOYCE:	Don't tell me. Don't tell me that at long last I'm gettin' me house painted! Ohhh, I can't believe it.
SUSAN:	What a laugh, eh? Trust your Eddy. He's a case.
JOAN:	I'll bet we get reporters around. An' the telly.
JOYCE:	Oh God ... I'll have to get me hair done!
JOAN:	Our street could become famous, couldn't it?
SUSAN:	Do you really think the telly people will come?
JOYCE:	Well they wouldn't miss something like this, would they? I mean, it's important, isn't it?

Looking at Drama: Setting

Terraces is set in a working-class neighbourhood, somewhere in Britain in the 1970s. However, the play's themes of conformity and individualism are timeless.

All the action in this play takes place in the pub, Danny's house or on the street. This gives the audience a window into a small, contained environment and contributes to the sense of claustrophobia in Danny's world. The limited number of locations also makes it easier to stage the play.

Scene 4

DANNY'S house. Early next morning. The curtains are drawn. SUSAN brings in a cup of tea from the kitchen and puts it by DANNY'S side.

SUSAN:	Joyce reckons the telly cameras might turn up when it's done.
DANNY:	Eh?
SUSAN:	When the street's painted. [*She laughs*] 'Ey ... they might even interview some of us. Don't y' fancy seein' me on telly, Danny?
DANNY:	Don't be soft. The street won't get painted. Well our house won't, anyway!
SUSAN:	And why not?
DANNY:	Come on. It's just stupid.
SUSAN:	Why?
DANNY:	Come on ... it is.
SUSAN:	Why aren't we havin' our house painted?
DANNY:	Because I don't want it painted.
SUSAN:	Well you bloody misery!
DANNY [*laughing*]:	Agh ... come on.
SUSAN:	Everyone else is painting their house! Why aren't we?
DANNY:	Everyone *won't* be paintin' their houses. If I'd thought they were serious in there I'd have said something. They'll all have forgotten it by now. [*SUSAN peers through a chink in the curtains, then opens them triumphantly. EDDY is revealed up a ladder, painting his house*]
SUSAN:	Oh yes. 'They'll all have forgotten it by now.'
DANNY:	Mmm?
SUSAN:	Look.
DANNY:	What?
SUSAN:	Come and have a look. [*DANNY gets up and sees EDDY at work*]
DANNY:	The bloody nutter!
SUSAN:	Why is he?
DANNY:	He's round the bend. Nobody else will do it. He'll be embarrassed out of his mind. The only yellow house in the street. The Lone Canary.
SUSAN:	How will his be the only one? Everyone's doin' it.
DANNY:	You mean everyone said they'd do it. What they said they'll do and what they *will* do are two different things. [*MICHAEL comes rushing in. Excited, breathless*]
MICHAEL:	Dad ... Dad ... When are we paintin' our house? Dad, can I help y'? Everyone in the street's doin' it.
DANNY:	Listen, Michael, Eddy Wills is not everyone.
MICHAEL:	I know. But John Cameron's dad's doin' his house down the other end of the street. An' Peter Wilksy's, an' Morgan's, an' they said all the street's gonna be yellow.
SUSAN [*smug*]:	Satisfied! [*DANNY stretches out of window to see further down the street. SUSAN leans out too, and calls to EDDY*]
SUSAN:	Let's have a look, Eddy! Ahhh. It's lookin' lovely, Ed! Just what we need in this street, Eddy, a bit more community spirit.

EDDY [*shouting over*]:	Look at them, they're all gettin' stuck in now. Where's that feller of yours? Come on, Sue, kick him out of bed an' get him movin'.
SUSAN [*shutting window*]:	Come on, Danny, let's get the ladders. Come on, I'll help you.
MICHAEL:	An' me, Dad … an' me.
SUSAN [*rushing around looking for brushes*]:	I've told you. You fellers should have done something like this years ago. Women wouldn't moan about football if they were included a bit more often. Come on.
DANNY:	Do you want the house painting yellow?
SUSAN:	Well everyone's doin' it.
DANNY:	I didn't ask you that. Do you want the house painting yellow?
SUSAN:	Danny! I want the house painting like the rest of the street and if the colour they've chosen is yellow then I'll have my house yellow!
DANNY:	Would you have it painted yellow if nobody else was doin' the same?
MICHAEL:	Ah come on, Dad!
SUSAN [*becoming exasperated*]:	Of course I wouldn't. I don't even like yellow!
DANNY:	Good. Because I'm not going to paint this house yellow.
SUSAN:	And why not?
DANNY:	Because I don't want to!
MICHAEL:	Ah 'ey, Dad!
SUSAN:	*You* don't want to? What do you mean, you don't want to! It's not up to you. The street's decided ….
DANNY:	Yes! An' *I've* decided I don't want my house painting.
MICHAEL:	Ah that's rotten!
SUSAN [*becoming heated*]:	I thought you supported the team.
DANNY:	And will painting my house increase my support? When kids go daubing paint over bus shelters, scrawling the team's name on a wall, does that mean greater support? I support my team all right, but that's got nothing to do with painting a house. [*Pause. SUSAN glares at him*]
MICHAEL:	All right then. OK. I'll go an' help Wilksy paint his house!
DANNY:	Michael!
SUSAN:	Go on. You go, Michael love. You go an' help Mr Wilks. [*He storms out. To DANNY*] You make me sick!
DANNY [*disgustedly*]:	Agh this is ridiculous!
SUSAN [*tidying up*]:	Yes … I know.
DANNY:	Why in the name of God does it have to cause this sort of feeling in the house?
SUSAN:	Well it doesn't, does it?
DANNY:	Meaning what?
SUSAN:	Meaning when you come to your senses, we'll start bein' civil again. Why do you begrudge your own child a bit of pleasure?
DANNY:	It's got nothing to do with begrudging pleasure and you know it!
SUSAN:	Oh no I don't. It's all very simple, Danny. You stop being high and mighty. Paint the house, and things can get back to normal. [*DANNY looks at her, turns, and goes out*]

Questions

Exploring *Terraces*, Scenes 1 – 4

1. What event is the street celebrating?
2. What plan is decided upon in the pub to mark the occasion?
3. Describe the character of Eddy as he is presented in the first four scenes.
4. **(a)** Why does Danny refuse to paint his house yellow?
   (b) Do you think he is being unreasonable? Explain your answer.
5. **(a)** What argument does Susan make in favour of painting the house?
   (b) Do you agree with her? Why/why not?
6. **(a)** Look back at Scene 2. Michael asks his father to help him with the crossword; which two words is he looking for?
   (b) From what you've read of the play, do you think these two words are relevant to the play's plot and theme? Explain your answer.

Looking at Drama: Stage Directions

Stage directions are instructions given to actors, directors and producers by the playwright. They are usually enclosed in square brackets and explain how a stage should look and how a character should behave or speak. For example, Willy Russell establishes the opening scene with the following stage direction: [*A local pub on a Saturday night: noisy, smoky and brash*]. He also explains how the actors should behave and speak: [*looking up, puzzled*], [*laughing*].

Some playwrights give detailed stage directions, while some like to leave decisions to the director and actors by including few stage directions.

Scene 5

The pub. Lunchtime. EDDY, JOHN and JOEY sit exhausted, beaming, paint-splattered, with pints in hand.

EDDY:	What a response!
JOHN:	It was a great idea, Ed.
EDDY:	It'll all be done inside the week.
JOHN:	Every house ... yellow!
JOEY:	Have y' heard when the cameras are comin', Eddy?
EDDY:	What cameras?
JOHN:	What cameras? The television cameras of course.
EDDY:	What? They're gonna put us on telly?
JOHN:	Well think about it. There's not many streets as devoted as ours. Oh yes, the cameras will be here, Eddy. I mean, it's a phenomenon, this.
EDDY:	'Ey ... it bloody is, isn't it? [*Thinks*] I'll have to get me suit pressed!
JOEY:	Think they'll interview y' then, Eddy?
EDDY:	Well it stands to reason, doesn't it? I mean for God's sake – if the cameramen are here they'll want to interview the architect of the idea, won't they?
JOEY:	I thought it was Danny's idea.
EDDY:	Yes, *Danny* thought of it. But without braggin', I did put flesh and bones on it, didn't I?
JOEY:	That's true, Eddy.
JOHN:	Oh it is ... it is.
EDDY [*thinking*]:	I wonder who'll be doing the interviewing then?
JOEY:	I hope it's someone from the sports side.
JOHN:	We don't want any of them Robin Days around here.
EDDY:	I wonder if it'll be Frank, y' know, Frank Bough.
JOEY:	He's a good lad, Frank.
JOHN:	Our Muriel was sayin' she hopes it's Russell Harty who comes to interview.
EDDY:	Yeh, well that's women for y', isn't it? No ... it'll be a sportin' man they send. [*DANNY enters, crosses to the bar, and orders a pint. He can hear the comments of the others*]
EDDY:	I see some people still observe the Sabbath round here.
JOEY:	Just got up have y', Danny? [*DANNY collects his pint and goes across to join them*]
DANNY:	All right.
JOHN:	I hope you've noticed the work that's been done while you've been sleepin'.
EDDY:	Better get y' finger out, Danny. Frank Bough's comin' y' know, Dan.
JOEY:	An' Robin Day.
EDDY:	Keep this quiet, Danny, but, er, I've heard they might be devotin' a whole programme to it.
DANNY:	Listen, Eddy, I think y'd better know. I've got no intention of paintin' my house.
EDDY [*pause, puzzled*]:	What d' y' mean?
DANNY:	What I say. I'm not painting my house. [*There is a silence in which they all look at him*] Look, lads. It's quite simple – I don't want to paint my house! Now can we just leave it there? [*Pause*] Come on, let's talk about somethin' else.
EDDY [*stunned*]:	Somethin' else!

JOEY:	What's wrong with y', Danny?
DANNY:	Nothing's wrong with me, Joe. But I don't want to paint my house.
JOHN:	And why not?
DANNY:	No reason, John. I just don't want to.
EDDY:	But Danny, Danny, is it a question of what you want?
DANNY:	It is my house. It's my decision.
JOHN:	But you live in a community, Danny. You've got to think of others as well.
DANNY:	I've thought of others, John, an' if my house remains unpainted it won't hurt one insect, animal or human being.
EDDY:	How do you know you won't be hurtin' anyone?
JOEY:	Frank Bough won't like it.
EDDY:	Now come on, Danny lad. Let's stop arsin' round! [*He puts his hand in his pocket and produces a fiver*] Here, Joey. Go an' get a few whiskies in.
DANNY:	Listen, Eddy …
EDDY [*laughing*]:	You're a case, you are, Danny. Always were a bit of the awkward one. A bit different. 'Ey, John, I'll bet he was an awkward bugger when he was a kid, eh? [*JOHN and EDDY laugh*]
DANNY:	Eddy, y' can laugh, buy whisky for me, bring in a troupe of dancin' girls if you like, but I won't be paintin' my house.
EDDY [*the laughter fading*]:	People won't like it, y' know, Danny. [*DANNY shrugs*]
JOHN:	Why try to be the odd one out, Danny?
DANNY:	I'm not trying to be anythin', John. [*He sighs*] I just don't want … to … paint … my house. [*JOEY arrives with the whiskey and places a glass down in front of each man*] All right? So can we just forget it now? Eh? [*DANNY leans forward to pick up his drink. A hand covers the top of the glass before DANNY'S can reach it*]
EDDY:	No way, Danny!
DANNY:	What's up?
EDDY:	If a feller doesn't want to join in with me, all right. That's OK. But if he's not with me in all things, he's not with me at all.
DANNY:	For Christ's sake, hasn't this gone far enough? Stop bein' stupid!
EDDY:	It's not me that's bein' stupid, Danny. [*Pause*] Now, are y' gonna drink with me?
DANNY [*pause. He looks at the glass*]:	I'll drink with you, Eddy.
EDDY [*beginning to remove his hand*]:	Good lad, good lad.
DANNY:	But I won't paint my house!
EDDY [*his hand shooting back to the glass*]:	Well y' won't drink with me either! [*They look at each other. DANNY suddenly gets up*]
DANNY:	Y' can stick your friggin' drink! [*DANNY heads for the pub door*]
EDDY [*shouting after him*]:	It's up to you, lad. This drink'll still be here at closing time. It's up to you!

Scene 6

DANNY'S house. DANNY is late home. He has been wandering the streets, sorting out his thoughts. Now it is past closing time, and he knows that the drink EDDY placed on the table as a symbol of togetherness is no longer there to be consumed.

DANNY:	Any tea made, love? [*Silence*] Susan ... any tea? [*Pause*] We're not still carryin' this stupid thing on, are we?
SUSAN:	If you want tea you know where the pot is. [*She studies the TV screen with unusual intensity. DANNY looks at her, then goes to the kitchen. There's a knock on the door, and EDDY puts his head round tentatively. JOEY, JOHN and several others are behind him*]
EDDY:	All right, Sue love, can we have a word with Danny?
SUSAN:	Come on in, Ed. He's in the kitchen. [*The men stream in. Not a mob: more a deputation*]
SUSAN:	Danny! Eddy's here! [*Pause. There is no response*]
EDDY:	Listen, Danny ... we've been talkin'.
DANNY [*From the kitchen, making tea*]:	Have you?
JOHN:	We've been a bit rash, Danny. [*DANNY comes to the door*]
DANNY:	Well I'm glad you've realised it, John.
EDDY:	Look, Dan. I mean, OK. You don't wanna be bothered paintin' the house. So what we've done, Danny, is a few of the lads an' meself have agreed that we'll do it for y'.
	SUSAN [*From the back of the group*] Ah ... now that's what I call real friendship, Eddy.
EDDY [*Making to go. Others follow*]:	So we'll get the paint and get stuck in tomorrow, Danny. OK? An' we'll forget about today. All right?
DANNY:	[*Following them to the door*]: Eddy.
EDDY:	What's that, Dan?
DANNY:	You lay one hand, one finger on an inch of my brickwork an' I'll have the coppers round here before you can move!
SUSAN:	Danny!
EDDY:	Danny lad! We're offerin' to do you a favour.
JOEY:	We'll even paint it back to the normal colour when the final's over.
DANNY:	No thanks. [*Pause*]
EDDY:	I wouldn't push it *too* far, Danny.
DANNY:	I'm not pushing it at all.
JOHN:	Listen, mate. We came round here to make things OK between us. Now if you're gonna start bein' unreasonable ...
DANNY [*Closing door after them*]:	Ta-rar, lads.
EDDY [*Wedging his foot in door*]:	I'm warnin' you. You'd better bloody grow up. Or you'll be sorry. [*DANNY closes the door*]
SUSAN:	You're warped! Did you know that? Warped, that's what you are. They're your friends.

DANNY: No! Friends will let you be yourself!
[*He walks past her and back into the kitchen*]

Exploring *Terraces*, Scenes 5 – 6

7. **(a)** What 'news' does Joey report to the others?
   (b) Do you feel that this news will create more pressure for Danny? Explain your answer.
8. How does Eddy place pressure on Danny in these scenes?
9. Which of the following words best describes Danny: *stubborn, brave, independent, killjoy, unreasonable*? Refer to the text in your response.
10. **(a)** How does Susan treat Danny in these scenes?
    (b) Do you feel she is being unfair? Explain your answer.
11. Comment on the relationship between the sexes in the play. Do you feel that men and women in *Terraces* see each other as equals? Refer to the text in your answer.

Scene 7

A general shop. Next day. JOYCE and other women are waiting to be served. SUSAN enters.

JOYCE:	We're just sayin', Sue. The telly people are coming, you know.
FIRST WOMAN:	When's that feller of yours goin' to get started?
SHOPKEEPER:	Russell Harty's comin', isn't he?
JOYCE:	An' Hughie Greene. Oh' they're all comin'.
SUSAN:	He'll do it. Don't worry.
SECOND WOMAN:	I heard someone sayin' that Harold Wilson's openin' a school near here on Friday.
JOYCE:	Go 'way. An' they're bringin' him to see the street?
SECOND WOMAN:	Well they didn't exactly say ….
JOYCE:	I know … but he will come, won't he? I mean he always goes to see the interesting things. [*Pause*] Harold Wilson comin' to our street! You'll have to get your feller movin', Sue.

Scene 8

It is evening. DANNY is walking along on the way back from work. Even more houses are painted now. The street is taking an overall yellow look. He walks past JOEY'S door. JOEY is just putting his key in.

JOEY [*Whispering nervously*]:	Danny. 'Ey, Danny.
DANNY [*Stopping*]:	What?
JOEY [*Checking to make sure he's not being watched*]:	Come here. I don't wanna be seen. Listen, I don't think they're gonna be comin' till tomorrow, the telly people.
DANNY:	Yeh. Well?
JOEY:	Listen, Danny. I'm tryin' to help you. I shouldn't even be seen talkin' to you, mate. What I'm sayin', Danny, is … you've still got time. Y' could get it painted by tonight. [*DANNY turns and walks away*]

Scene 9

DANNY'S house. In the living room stand three gallon tins of yellow paint and a large brush. DANNY can't miss them. SUSAN is sitting in the armchair.

DANNY: What's that?

SUSAN: Paint.

DANNY: I can see that. What's it for?

SUSAN: You're going to paint this house, Danny.

DANNY: Oh am I?

SUSAN: I'm not going to be humiliated any longer. It's all right for you. You don't get it. You're out at work all day. But I have to live here, in this street. All day, people goin' on at me, makin' me feel small. Well I'm not puttin' up with it any more, Danny. I'm not bein' humiliated again.

DANNY: You don't have to be humiliated. Stand by me and there'll be no humiliation.

SUSAN [*Bouncing out of the chair*]: I'm not arguin' with y', Danny. I've had enough of bein' the reject. Now listen, I'm givin' you a warnin', Danny: either you paint this house tonight ... or I'm gettin' out!

DANNY: Don't be so stupid!

SUSAN: Stupid! You call me stupid?

DANNY: Yes. You're acting like a child.

[*The front door is heard opening. MICHAEL, tear stained and screaming, rushes in, DANNY tries to take him, but he runs to his mother*]

SUSAN: Michael ... Michael ... what's wrong?

MICHAEL [*Between sobs*]: They won't …they won't … play with me …they all said ... an' everyone in school …they all said … [*Breaking down*]

SUSAN: Said what, love? What did they say?

MICHAEL: Said our house ... is a ... a house for freaks! [*Breaks down*]

SUSAN [*Screaming at DANNY*]: See! See what you and your stupid bloody ways have done! [*She puts her arms around the child and leads him to the door*] Don't cry, love. Don't cry. You're right. It is a freak's house. Look, there's the freak ... y' father! He's the one who's turned it into a house for rejects. Well he'd better do somethin' about it quick or, else he'll be the only one livin' here!

[*They exit, leaving DANNY alone in the room. DANNY looks at the paint, sighs, and takes off his coat. He goes into the hall, and returns wearing overalls, and carrying a paint brush in one hand and step ladders in the other. He is about to add a gallon of paint to his load when there is a loud bang on the door. A note comes through the letter box. DANNY bends down and picks it up*]

DANNY [*Reading*]: 'This is a warning! Paint – or find somewhere else to live!' [*DANNY screws the note up. He opens the front door and steps out into the street. He places three cans of paint on to the pavement. He stands looking at the houses opposite. All yellow. There is a deliberate 'Western' atmosphere building up*]

DANNY [*Shouting at houses*]: Are you all watching? All listening? Are y'? [*Laughs*] Come on ... come out and have a look. [*Pause*] Where are y'? Come on ... come on out! [*Pause*] See... look...the paint's here. Come on, you can come out.
[*Slowly front doors begin to open*]
Come on ... all of y' ... COME ON!
[*Neighbours begin to emerge*]
See ... look ... there's the paint. It's yellow, see. Right? [*Pause*] Now someone wants me to paint my house, eh?

EDDY [*Shouting across*]: I'm glad you've seen some sense, Danny.

DANNY: Sense? Oh yes, I've seen sense. [*He stands and surveys the onlookers*] I've seen sense all right. You all want me to paint the house, do y'?

EDDY: Good lad, Danny.

JOHN: Good man ... good man.

DANNY: Watch just watch. [*He slowly bends and prises open one of the calls. He lifts it*]

EDDY [*To a neighbour*]: I knew he'd see sense in the end. [*He turns back to look at DANNY.
DANNY is pouring the paint down the grid*]

DANNY: Well that's my answer. That's what I say to you. And just in case you didn't hear me – [*He quickly prises open another can and hurls the paint across the road*] Can you hear my answer now? Can y'? [*He shouts loud and clear*] All I wanted to do was leave my house. That's all. [*He grabs the third and final can. Behind DANNY, SUSAN and MICHAEL emerge from the house. It is obvious that they are leaving*]
Go on ... Yes ... you go. Go and join your friends. [*He watches as they cross the street and are comforted and taken in by JOYCE*]

EDDY [*Shouting across*]: I always thought there was somethin' about you, mate, an' now I know what it is: they build places for people like you – asylums!
[*DANNY rushes forward and grabs the paint brush. He swings and scoops up paint with it, hurling it all along the street. It is a gesture of total and frustrated anger. There are screams as people try to get out of the way of the flying paint.
DANNY, his anger momentarily spent, stands glaring and breathing very hard*]

Scene 10

The pub. EDDY, his cronies and others are drinking at the bar.

BARMAID: Well I know one thing, he'll never get served in this pub again.

JOHN [*Shaking his head*]: I just couldn't get over it. I thought he was just being a bit stubborn. But did y' see him with that paint? Did y' see him though?

EDDY: He's dangerous if y' ask me.

BARMAID: Who would have thought. I mean, livin' in this street so long and no one would have guessed we had someone like that in the midst of us.

EDDY: He bloody well worms his way into our friendship. Drinks with us, laughs with us, goes out with us ... an' all the time he's pretendin' he's normal.

JOHN: He's not normal. He's a sick man. Sick in the mind.

JOEY: Yeh, an', for God's sake, there's half the cameras of the world gonna be beamin' in on us tomorrow.

BARMAID: Not now. No. They won't come here.

EDDY: Why won't they?

BARMAID: They'll go to Wingfield Street. They've copied us, haven't they?

EDDY: Y' what?

BARMAID: All the Wingfield Street end are makin' arrangements to do their street up in the team's colours.

EDDY: But the cameras won't cover them. We were the originals.

JOHN: The originals, yes. But Wingfield Street is gonna' be completely yellow, Eddy. Not just almost yellow, yellow with a dark blob in the middle.

BARMAID: That's why they'll get all the attention in Wingfield Street.

EDDY: Oh no they won't!

JOEY: They will, Eddy. If there's a part of our street not painted they'll go and ...

EDDY: Yes. But there's not gonna be a part of our street that isn't painted! [*Rallying*] We're not gonna let one feller, one diminished feller, put the boot in on us are we? Eh? Someone should've told Danny Harris that this country is ruled by majorities. We've got no time for the oddballs and queerheads here. I'm bloody sick of the awkward ones, I am – the left-handers and backward walkers. I'm up to here with the awkwardites an' them who think they can do what they like while the rest of us just have to stand by. It's the likes of Danny Harris who've given this country a bad name, who've pulled it down into the muck an' slime. Most of us just get on with things in a quiet an' orderly fashion while the screwballs like him fling spanners in the works. [*Pause*] Well if he doesn't wanna fit in it's his hard luck. We'll have to make him fit in.

JOEY: What'll we do, Eddy?

EDDY: Right. Listen. Tomorrow ... while he's at work ....

Scene 11

Outside DANNY'S house. JOEY is breezing along, whistling self-consciously, and glancing behind him as he goes. He carries a paint tin and brush. At DANNY'S house he opens a can of paint, and starts painting, checking that no one is watching. Satisfied, he relaxes. As he does, an upstairs window opens quietly. A bucket appears. JOEY, still relaxed, whistles while he paints. Suddenly water cascades over him. He looks up and sees DANNY in the bedroom window.

JOEY:	Bastard. You bastard, Harris!
DANNY [*Calm*]:	Come back and you'll get it again.
JOEY [*Pointing up*]:	We'll get you, Danny Harris … Don't worry … We'll get y'. [*He slopes off, angry and dripping wet*]

Questions

Exploring *Terraces*, Scenes 7 – 11

12. **(a)** How did Danny react to the threatening note?
    (b) Do you feel this was an appropriate reaction?
13. How else does the community increase the pressure on Danny?
14. Why does the barmaid think the TV cameras will film Wingfield Street instead?
15. Eddy describes Danny as an 'awkwardite'. What does he mean by this?
16. If you were Danny, would you agree to paint your house at this point? Why/why not?
17. If you were asked to direct a film version of this play, which actors would you cast in the roles of:
    (a) Danny?
    (b) Susan?
    (c) Eddy?

In the case of each, explain why you would choose this particular actor by referring to the text. You may wish to think about each actor's personality, physical appearance, previous roles, age etc.

Looking at Drama: Conflict

Drama relies on conflict in order to hold the interest of the audience. Conflict can occur in two ways:

- **Between characters** – when characters are at odds with one another, the tension between them makes for fascinating drama. In *Terraces*, the conflict between Danny and the rest of the street and between Danny and his family is captivating for the audience as they wonder who will win out in the struggle.

- **Within a character** – this is known as **internal conflict**. Often characters may be unsure or confused. This uncertainty helps to make a character more psychologically interesting. Although this isn't a central feature of the characters in *Terraces*, the actor playing Danny would need to show the internal conflict between standing by one's principles and going along with the crowd.

Scene 12

DANNY'S house. A YOUNGSTER knocks at the door. DANNY opens it.

YOUNGSTER:	You Mister Harris?
DANNY:	Yeh.
YOUNGSTER:	There's a phone call for y' in the pub.
DANNY:	Who's it from?
YOUNGSTER:	I dunno. The woman in the pub just sent me down here to tell y'.
DANNY [*Suspicious*]:	She didn't say who it was from?
YOUNGSTER:	I think it was from y' wife.
DANNY:	Me wife?
YOUNGSTER:	I think that's what she said.
DANNY [*Checking that no one is around*]:	Right. [*He comes out and closes the door*]

Scene 13

The pub. DANNY enters and walks up to the bar.

DANNY:	Someone said there's a call for me.
BARMAID:	Oh yes ... there was, Danny ... they rang off though. Said they'd call back in a few minutes. [*Pause*]
DANNY:	Was it from Sue?
BARMAID:	I don't know, erm, Danny. I didn't answer it, Phil did. Look, why don't you have a drink while you're ... What'll it be? [*She hands a pint across, and DANNY makes to pay. The Barmaid pushes the money back to him*]
BARMAID:	No ... go on, Danny ... have this one on me.
DANNY:	[*About to drink. He becomes suspicious and lowers his drink*]: How long have you been givin' away free drinks?
BARMAID [*Nervy*]:	Oh ... y' know. [*Pause*]
DANNY:	Who, erm ... who was it on the phone then ... ? [*DANNY idly goes to the window and looks out*]
BARMAID:	Erm ... I don't ... er ... I think it was Sue, Danny.
DANNY	[*Quietly walking back from window*] You think it was Sue? You lying bitch! [*He slams the pint down on the counter and runs out*]

Scene 14

Outside DANNY'S house. EDDY and JOEY are painting frantically, up a ladder.
DANNY runs up the street.
EDDY and JOEY look down in horror as they see the paint suddenly being kicked over. They shin down the ladder and run off. DANNY stands, breathing heavily; glaring, wild.

Scene 15

It is light in DANNY'S house. DANNY is asleep. He turns over, half wakes, and then, fully-waking, listens to soft sounds creeping in from outside.

He gets up, goes to window and sees a large group of men below, preparing to paint. DANNY slips into the bathroom, clips a hose pipe to the tap. He turns it on, running the water into a bucket so that he can carry the hose back to the bedroom window. He quietly raises the sash, lifts the hose, and a jet of water gushes out into the night. The nocturnal decorators scatter, shouting, shocked.

DANNY leaves the hose pipe propped so that it runs out of the window. Then he brings a chair and sits waiting. When foxes prowl the farmer must sit the long night out.

Scene 16

The pub. EDDY, JOHN and others are standing by the bar, drinking in ominous silence; drinking with a purpose.
EDDY lays down his pint and looks at the clock: It is 6.10.
JOEY rushes through the door.

EDDY: Right lads ... let's go!
JOEY: Eddy ... Eddy ... Eddy ... I've just heard Royalty's visitin' the neighbourhood tomorrow, Eddy ... what are we gonna do?
EDDY: Let's go.
JOEY [*Following*] Where, Eddy?
EDDY [*Leading the group of men*]: Just follow me.

Scene 17

Outside DANNY'S house. SUSAN is knocking at the door. DANNY opens it with extreme suspicion.

SUSAN [*Nervous, reluctant almost*]: Hya ... Danny.
DANNY: Hello!
SUSAN: Can I come in?
DANNY: Who've y' got with you?
SUSAN: For God's sake, Danny! [*DANNY peeps out, checking that all is clear*]
DANNY: All right. Come in.
[*She enters. DANNY closes the door and stands in the hall. There is an awkward silence between them*]
SUSAN: Well, aren't you going to offer me a cup of tea? [*He looks at her. Blank*] Shall I make it?
[*She goes through to the kitchen. DANNY follows her*]
DANNY: What's all this in aid of then? Have they sent you to try an' change my mind?
SUSAN [*Getting tea things ready*]: Don't you think you could have thought of Michael and me in all this, Danny? [*Pause*]
DANNY: Couldn't you have thought of me? [*Pause*] We're a family. [*Pause*] We didn't have to do what a street chose to do.
SUSAN: Where's the cups? I'll bet you haven't washed a dish, have y'? All the cups in the front room ... Go an' get a couple and I'll wash them.

[*DANNY goes through to the front room*]

DANNY [*From front room*]: Well ... what have you come here for? Are y' coming back for good?

SUSAN [*Quietly unlocking and unbolting the back door*]: I'll come back, Danny, when you see sense and paint the house. [*Pause*] You're just like a little boy over all this.

DANNY [*Appearing at kitchen door with two mugs*]: I've missed you. And Michael.

SUSAN: Danny! Go on ... before it's too late ... just say you'll paint the house. And then we'll come back.

DANNY: But can't you see? If I do that there's no point is there? There's no point in you coming back, in us being together.

SUSAN: Please, Danny ... please! Before it's too late ... please!

DANNY: What do y' mean, 'before it's too late'?

[*And in answer the back door opens. EDDY and a group of men burst in. DANNY looks at SUSAN. SUSAN looks away*]

What have y' done? What have you done?

SUSAN: I'll come back, Danny ... when it's painted. We'll be all right then, Danny. [*She goes out of the back door*]

[*The men grab DANNY, and there is a struggle as he is forced into the street outside. Someone has picked up a straight backed kitchen chair, and DANNY, forced to sit in it, is tied to it with rope. EDDY and the men begin to paint the house rapidly*]

EDDY: We're sorry it had to come to this, Danny. It hurts us more than it does you. But we hope it makes y' see sense, Danny. I want y' t' know, Danny, that when this is over, we can all go back to bein' mates. You had to be knocked back in line, Danny. But when this is over there'll be a drink waitin' for y' in the pub.

[*In no time at all DANNY'S house is yellow, like every house in the street. DANNY sits in the chair, slaughtered. Eventually he struggles up as the men pick up their tools and leave for the pub. The ropes fall loosely to the ground*]

EDDY [*Calling from the other end of the street*]: Don't forget your pint, Danny lad!

[*DANNY looks at the house. He turns away in the opposite direction*]

The End

Questions

Exploring *Terraces*, Scenes 12 – 17

13. Explain why Danny was called to the pub.
14. What measures does Danny take to stop the others painting his house.
15. Towards the end of the play, Eddy says, 'I want y' t' know, Danny, that when this is over, we can all go back to bein' mates.' Do you believe him? Why/why not?
16. In the final scene, which character do you think behaved the worst: Eddy or Susan? Explain your answer.
17. Which of the following sentences best describes your thoughts on the play? Explain your answer by referring to the text.
    * *Terraces* is a play that illustrates the power of the mob.
    * This play taught me how important it is to be yourself.
    * I disliked/liked Willy Russell's *Terraces*.
18. Imagine your school is putting on a production of *Terraces*. Describe how you would design the stage and what props you would use. You may wish to illustrate your plans for the set design.

Writers' Workshop

At the end of the play, Susan tells Danny she'll come back once the house has been painted. Write the conversation you imagine they have once she returns to the newly painted house.

About The Playwright

Willy Russell (born 1947)

Willy Russell grew up on the outskirts of Liverpool. He left school after passing only English in his O-Level exams (the equivalent of the Junior Cert). He worked as a hairdresser for a number of years and held a variety of other jobs before returning to education and becoming a teacher. Russell drew on this experience in his play *Educating Rita*. In this play, Rita, a Liverpudlian working-class hairdresser, looks to change her life by pursuing a degree in English. The play explores her relationship with her college tutor.

Willy Russell is a hugely popular playwright. His plays are regularly performed around the world. Among his best known works are: *Educating Rita*, *Our Day Out*, *Shirley Valentine* and his musical *Blood Brothers*. His work has also been successfully adapted for film.

The Good Old Days

Introduction

Monty Python was a British comedy group famous for their television show *Monty Python's Flying Circus*. Although often seen as strange and unconventional, Monty Python's comedy became hugely popular. After the success of their television programme, the group made a number of films, including *The Life of Brian* and *The Holy Grail*. The group's popularity paved the way for great innovation in comedy both on screen and in stand-up. *The Good Old Days* was written by two members of Monty Python and performed by the whole group.

[*It is sundown time at the tropical paradise. Four elderly men in tuxedos sit contemplating the sunset. A waiter pours some wine for one of them to taste.*]

JOSHUA: Very passable. Not bad at all.
[*The waiter pours the wine for the rest of them and then departs.*]

OBADIAH: Can't beat a good glass of Château de Chasselas, ey Josiah?

JOSIAH: Aye, you're right there Obadiah.

EZEKIEL: Who'd have thought… forty years ago… that we'd all be sittin' here, drinking Château de Chasselas?

JOSHUA: Aye. In those days, we were glad to have the price of a cup of tea.

OBADIAH: A cup o' *cold* tea.

EZEKIEL: Without milk or sugar.

JOSIAH: *Or* tea!

JOSHUA: Aye, and cracked cup at that.

EZEKIEL: We never had a cup. We used to have to drink out of a rolled-up newspaper.

OBADIAH: The best *we* could manage was to suck on a piece of damp cloth.

JOSIAH: But you know…we were happy in those days, although we were poor.

JOSHUA: Aye, *because* we were poor. My old Dad used to say, 'Money doesn't buy you happiness, son.'

EZEKIEL: He was right. I was happier then and I had *nothing*. We used to live in this tiny old tumbledown house, with great big holes in the roof.

OBADIAH: House? You were lucky to have a house! We used to live in one room, all twenty-six of us, no furniture. Half the floor was missing; we were all huddled together in one corner for fear of falling!

JOSIAH: You were lucky to have a room! *We* used to have to live in a corridor!

JOSHUA: Ooooh we used to *dream* of living in a corridor! That would have been a palace to us. We used to live in an old water tank on a rubbish tip. We got woken up every morning by having a load of rotting fish dumped all over us! House!? Hmph.

EZEKIEL: Well when I say 'house' … it was only a hole in the ground covered by a couple of foot of torn canvas, but it was a house to *us*.

OBADIAH: We were evicted from *our* hole in the ground. We had to go and live in a lake!

JOSIAH: You were lucky to have a lake. There were a hundred and sixty of us living in a small shoebox in the middle of the road.

JOSHUA: Cardboard box?

JOSIAH: Aye.

JOSHUA: You were lucky. We lived for three months in a brown paper bag in a septic tank. We used to have to get up at six o'clock in the morning, clean the bag, eat a crust of stale bread, work fourteen hours at the mill, day in, day out, for sixpence a week, come home, and Dad would thrash us to sleep with his belt!

OBADIAH: *Luxury!* We used to get out of the lake at three o'clock in the morning, clean it, eat a handful of hot gravel, go to work at the mill every day for tuppence a month, come home, and Dad would beat us around the head and neck with a broken bottle, *if we were lucky.*
[*Pause*]

JOSIAH: Well we had it tough. We used to have to get up out of the shoebox at twelve o'clock at night, and lick the road clean with our tongues. We had half a handful of freezing cold gravel, worked twenty-four hours a day at the mill for fourpence every six years, and when we got home, our Dad would slice us in two with a bread knife.
[*Pause*]

EZEKIEL: Right. I had to get up in the morning at ten o'clock at night, half an hour before I went to bed, eat a lump of cold poison, work twenty-nine hours a day at the mill, and pay the mill owner for permission to come to work, and when we got home, our Dad would kill us, and dance about on our graves singing 'Hallelujah.'
[*Pause*]

JOSHUA: But you try and tell the young people today that … and they won't believe ya'.

Questions

Exploring *The Good Old Days*

1. **(a)** Find three examples of exaggeration in this piece.
   (b) Why do you think the men exaggerate the details of their childhood?
2. **(a)** What are the four men doing at the start of this comedy sketch?
   (b) In what way is this ironic?*
3. **(a)** How are elderly people portrayed in *The Good Old Days*?
   (b) Do you think there is any truth to this portrayal? Explain your view.
4. Do you find this piece funny? Why/why not?
5. Imagine you were asked to direct this comedy sketch for a school production. Write down the instructions you would give your actors.

*Irony is when a stated idea is the opposite of reality or when an idea seems out of place with reality.

Watch Online

Go to Youtube and watch this comedy sketch performed by Monty Python. The performance is entitled *Four Yorkshiremen.*

Looking at Drama: Satire

Satire is a form of humorous writing that ridicules an individual or group of people by exposing their flaws or foolishness.

In *The Good Old Days* the writers satirise the nostalgic conversations that older people have about their humble beginnings. The sketch reveals theses memories to be exaggerated as each of the four speakers tries to outdo the others by describing the poverty of their childhood. This becomes increasingly ridiculous until Ezekiel declares that every night 'our Dad would kill us, and dance about on our graves'.

The comedy sketch also exposes the hypocrisy of the men who begin their conversation discussing fine wines, 'Can't beat a good glass of Château de Chasselas', but then criticise young people for their privileged upbringings: 'But you try and tell the young people today that … and they won't believe ya'.

HOMER AND APU from THE SIMPSONS (adapted)

[APU, the Kwik-E-Mart owner, notices a smell somewhere, and he sniffs over to its source: a bag of ham saying, 'Exp. Feb. 6, 1989'.]

APU: Jiminy Cricket! Wooh, expired ham. *[Scribbles over the expiry date]*
Oh, this time I have gone too far. No, no one will fall for –
HOMER: Woo hoo! Cheap meat! *[Picks it up]* Ooh, this one's open. *[Starts eating it]*

[At home on the couch, HOMER continues devouring the expired ham, but his stomach begins to rebel.]

HOMER: *[Eats ham, but his stomach groans]*
Stomach ... churning! *[Eats some more]*
Bowels ... clenching! Not much time ... must ... finish ... *[eats some more]*
[The ambulance rushes him to the hospital.]

DR HIBBERT: Well, sir, Homer's illness was either caused by ingesting spoiled food, or, heh heh, some sort of voodoo curse.
PATTY: *[HOMER's sister-in-law]*
Hey: we've just been working the eyes. *[Holds up a Homer voodoo doll with pins in the eyes]*

[Incensed, HOMER returns to the Kwik-E-Mart to have it out with APU.]

HOMER: Your old meat made me sick!
APU: Oh, I'm so sorry. *[Gets a pail of shrimp]* Please accept five pounds of frozen shrimp?
HOMER: *[Holds one up, sniffs it]* This shrimp isn't frozen! And it smells funny.
APU: OK, ten pounds.
HOMER: Woo hoo!

[Once again, the ambulance takes him to the hospital. Back at home, HOMER lies on the couch while LISA and he watch 'Bite Back with Kent Brockman'.]

KENT BROCKMAN [on TV]: Good evening. Here's an update on last week's nursing home exposé, 'Geezers in Freezers.' It turns out the rest home was adequately heated; the footage you saw was of a fur-storage facility. We've also been told to apologise for using the term 'geezer.' Now, coming up next, the case of the cantankerous old geezer.

[*Just then, HOMER's stomach groans.*]

HOMER: Oh, rancid meat attack! Stupid parasites. Is there no way I can find justice?
KENT [on TV]: If you have a consumer complaint, just call this number…
HOMER: Boring.
LISA: Dad, you should blow the whistle on the Kwik-E-Mart.

[*HOMER stares at television*]

LISA: Dad, are you listening to me?
HOMER: Shh, Lisa.

[*That night, at the channel six studios, KENT BROCKMAN talks to HOMER.*]

KENT: All right, are you willing to go undercover to nail this creep?
HOMER: No way, man. No way, man! Get yourself another patsy, man. No way am I wearing a freakin' wire!
KENT: All right, all right, all right. Would you be willing to wear a hidden camera and microphone?
HOMER: Oh, that I'll wear.

[*The next day, KENT and HOMER are inside a van labelled 'Ordinary Van' parked outside the Kwik-E-Mart.*]

KENT: We've come up with a camera so tiny it fits into this oversized novelty hat.
[*HOMER puts on the huge Stetson hat, and struggles to stand upright*]
Now, go get us some incriminating footage, and remember: you have to get in and out in ten minutes, or you'll suffer permanent neck damage.
MAN: [*Neck horribly twisted*] He's not kidding.

[*HOMER walks towards the Kwik-E-Mart doors, swaying and weaving. APU watches him, curious.*]

APU: Huh?
HOMER: Don't be alarmed, APU. Just go about your daily routine like I'm not wearing the hat.
APU: Your headgear seems to be emitting a buzzing noise, sir. Perhaps you have a bee in your bonnet?
HOMER: Bee? Aah! [*Stomps on hat, runs out*]
KENT: Homer, that hat's been with the station twenty years! He had one day left till retirement.

[*But the camera inside the hat still works. It is pointed at APU.*]

APU: Well, time to replenish the hot dog roller. La, la – oops [*drops a hot dog*] Oh, no – it is encrusted with filth [*blows it off*]. Oh well, let's sell it anyway. Now this is just between me and you … smashed hat. Hee hee –
KENT: Hot diggety-dog, we've got him, Mr. Simpson. Now let's … Mr. Simpson? [*Looks around but Homer is gone.*]
HOMER [*inside the KWIK-E-Mart*]: One hot dog, please.

Questions

Exploring *Homer and Apu*

1. Briefly explain what occurs in this extract.
2. Would you agree that Homer is portrayed as a foolish character in this extract? Refer to the text in your answer.
3. Do you find this piece funny? Why/why not?
4. Do you think it is important to have seen *The Simpsons* to appreciate this script? Explain your viewpoint.
5. The individual scenes in this extract are each very short. Why do you think this is?

Shakespearian Drama

Theatre is often represented by the image of two masks: the faces of tragedy and comedy. Shakespeare's dramas can be divided into these two broad categories.

Tragedy deals with serious issues and features a destructive or catastrophic ending. The last scene of a classical tragedy often ends in the death of many of the principal characters.

The central character in tragedy is referred to as the **hero**. The tragic hero usually has a fatal flaw such as excessive ambition, pride or jealousy that leads to his/her downfall.

Comedy, in stark contrast to tragedy, ends on a positive note. The misunderstandings, confusion and mistaken identities that characterise a comic plot are resolved in the final scene when the heroes and heroines prosper and villains are left to suffer and be mocked.

Some dramas do not fall neatly into either the category of tragedy or comedy. Plays like Shakespeare's *Merchant of Venice* are referred to as 'tragicomedies' because they contain elements of both dramatic types.

Shakespearian tragedies such as *King Lear*, *Macbeth*, *Hamlet* and *Othello* have captivated audiences and provoked discussion for centuries. You will find extracts from each of these tragedies in this chapter.

From *King Lear*, Act 1, Scene 1
by William Shakespeare (adapted)

Introduction

King Lear is one of Shakespeare's greatest tragedies. It charts King Lear's descent into madness and explores human suffering. In this first scene from the play, King Lear announces he is stepping down as king and intends to divide his land amongst his three daughters.

KING LEAR: Meantime we[1] shall express our darker purpose.
Give me the map there. Know that we have divided
In three our kingdom: and 'tis our fast intent
To shake all cares and business from our age;
Conferring them on younger strengths, while we
Unburthen'd crawl toward death.
Tell me, my daughters,–
Since now we will divest[2] us both of rule,
Interest of territory, cares of state,–
Which of you shall we say doth love us most?
That we our largest bounty[3] may extend
Where nature doth with merit challenge. Goneril,
Our eldest-born, speak first.

[1] we: Because he is royalty, King Lear uses the pronoun 'we' to refer to himself
[2] divest: get rid of
[3] bounty: generous gift

GONERIL: Sir, I love you more than words can wield the matter;
Dearer than eye-sight, space, and liberty;
Beyond what can be valued, rich or rare;
No less than life, with grace, health, beauty, honour;
As much as child e'er loved, or father found;
A love that makes breath poor, and speech unable;
Beyond all manner of so much I love you.

CORDELIA: [*Aside*] What shall Cordelia do?
Love, and be silent.

LEAR: Of all these bounds, even from this line to this,
With shadowy forests and with champains[4] rich'd,
With plenteous rivers and wide-skirted meads[5],
We make thee lady: to thine and Albany's[6] issue[7]
Be this perpetual. What says our second daughter,
Our dearest Regan, wife to Cornwall? Speak.

REGAN: Sir, I am made
Of the self-same metal that my sister is,
And prize me at her worth. In my true heart
I find she names my very deed of love;
Only she comes too short: that I profess
Myself an enemy to all other joys,
Which the most precious square of sense possesses;
And find I am alone felicitate[8]
In your dear highness' love.

CORDELIA: [*Aside*] Then poor Cordelia!
And yet not so; since, I am sure, my love's
More richer than my tongue.

KING LEAR: To thee and thine hereditary ever
Remain this ample third of our fair kingdom;
No less in space, validity, and pleasure,
Than that conferr'd on Goneril. Now, our joy,
Although the last, not least; what can you say to draw
A third more opulent[9] than your sisters? Speak.

CORDELIA: Nothing, my lord.

KING LEAR: Nothing!

CORDELIA: Nothing.

KING LEAR: Nothing will come of nothing: speak again.

CORDELIA: Unhappy that I am, I cannot heave

[4] champains rich'd: rich, fertile fields
[5] wide-skirted meads: wide meadows
[6] Albany: Goneril's husband
[7] issue: children

[8] felicitate: made happy

[9] opulent: rich

My heart into my mouth: I love your majesty
According to my bond[10]; nor more nor less.

KING LEAR: How, how, Cordelia! mend your speech a little,
Lest it may mar your fortunes.

CORDELIA: Good my lord,
You have begot[11] me, bred me, loved me: I
Return those duties back as are right fit,
Obey you, love you, and most honour you.
Why have my sisters husbands, if they say
They love you all? Haply[12], when I shall wed,
That lord whose hand must take my plight shall carry
Half my love with him, half my care and duty:
Sure, I shall never marry like my sisters,
To love my father all.

KING LEAR: But goes thy heart with this?

CORDELIA: Ay, good my lord.

KING LEAR: So young, and so untender?

CORDELIA: So young, my lord, and true.

KING LEAR: Let it be so; thy truth, then, be thy dower[13]:
For, by the sacred radiance of the sun,
The mysteries of Hecate[14], and the night;
By all the operation of the orbs[15]
From whom we do exist, and cease to be;
Here I disclaim all my paternal care,
Propinquity[16] and property of blood,
And as a stranger to my heart and me
Hold thee, from this, for ever. The barbarous Scythian[17],
Or he that makes his generation messes[18]
To gorge[19] his appetite, shall to my bosom
Be as well neighbour'd[20], pitied, and relieved,
As thou my sometime daughter.

KENT: Good my liege,–

KING LEAR: Peace, Kent!
Come not between the dragon and his wrath.
I loved her most, and thought to set my rest
On her kind nursery[21]. Hence, and avoid my sight!
So be my grave my peace, as here I give
Her father's heart from her! Cornwall and Albany,
With my two daughters' dowers digest this third:

[10] bond: duty (to her father)

[11] begot: produced; fathered
[12] Haply: perhaps

[13] dower: dowry
[14] Hecate: Goddess of the Underworld
[15] orbs: planets
[16] Propinquity: kinship; family relation
[17] Scythian: foreigners (people from Scythia)
[18] his generation messes: eats his own children
[19] gorge: to eat greedily
[20] shall to my bosom /Be as well neighbour'd: shall be as close to my heart

[21] her kind nursery: her taking care of me

Let pride, which she calls plainness[22], marry her.
I do invest you[23] jointly with my power,
Pre-eminence[24], and all the large effects
That troop with majesty[25]. Ourself, by monthly course,
With reservation of an hundred knights,
By you to be sustain'd, shall our abode
Make with you by due turns[26]. Only we still retain
The name[27], and all the additions to a king;
The sway, revenue, execution of the rest,
Beloved sons, be yours: which to confirm,
This coronet part betwixt you[28].
[*Giving the crown*]

KENT: Royal Lear,
Whom I have ever honour'd as my king,
Loved as my father, as my master follow'd,
As my great patron thought on in my prayers,–

KING LEAR: The bow is bent and drawn, make from the shaft.

KENT: Let it fall rather, though the fork invade
The region of my heart: be Kent unmannerly,
When Lear is mad. What wilt thou do, old man?
Think'st thou that duty shall have dread to speak,
When power to flattery bows? To plainness honour's bound,
When majesty stoops to folly. Reverse thy doom;
And, in thy best consideration, cheque
This hideous rashness: answer my life my judgment,
Thy youngest daughter does not love thee least;
Nor are those empty-hearted whose low sound
Reverbs no hollowness.

KING LEAR: Kent, on thy life, no more.

KENT: My life I never held but as a pawn
To wage against thy enemies; nor fear to lose it,
Thy safety being the motive.

KING LEAR: Out of my sight!

KENT: See better, Lear; and let me still remain
The true blank of thine eye.

KING LEAR: Now, by Apollo[29],–

KENT: Now, by Apollo, king,
Thou swear'st thy gods in vain.

[22] plainess: honesty
[23] invest you: provide you with
[24] pre-eminence: distinguishment; superiority
[25] the large effects /that troop with majesty: the privileges of being king
[26] Lear intends to stay in each daughter's house, rotating monthly
[27] name: title (of king)
[28] This coronet part betwixt you: split this crown between you

[29] Apollo: God of the Sun

KING LEAR: O, vassal![30] miscreant![31]
           [Laying his hand on his sword]

ALBANY and
CORNWALL: Dear sir, forbear.

KENT: Do: Kill thy physician, and the fee bestow
         Upon thy foul disease.[32] Revoke[33] thy doom;
         Or, whilst I can vent clamour from my throat,
         I'll tell thee thou dost evil.

KING LEAR: Hear me, recreant![34]
         On thine allegiance, hear me!
         Since thou hast sought to make us break our vow,
         Which we durst never yet, and with strain'd pride
         To come between our sentence and our power,
         Which nor our nature nor our place can bear,
         Our potency made good, take thy reward.
         Five days we do allot thee[35], for provision
         To shield thee from diseases of the world;
         And on the sixth to turn thy hated back
         Upon our kingdom: if, on the tenth day following,
         Thy banish'd trunk[36] be found in our dominions,
         The moment is thy death. Away! by Jupiter[37],
         This shall not be revoked.

KENT: Fare thee well, king: sith thus thou wilt appear,
         Freedom lives hence, and banishment is here.
         [*To* CORDELIA] The gods to their dear shelter take thee, maid,
         That justly think'st, and hast most rightly said!
         [*To* REGAN *and* GONERIL] And your large speeches may your deeds approve,
         That good effects may spring from words of love.
         Thus Kent, O princes, bids you all adieu;
         He'll shape his old course in a country new.

[30] vassal: slave / lowlife
[31] miscreant: villain
[32] Kill…disease: You're killing the doctor and paying the disease.
[33] Revoke: take back
[34] recreant: traitor; coward
[35] allot thee: give you
[36] thy banish'd trunk: your banished body
[37] Jupiter: King of the gods

Exploring *King Lear*, Act 1, Scene 1

1. According to King Lear, why is he dividing his kingdom amongst his daughters and stepping down as king?
2. This scene is often referred to as 'The Love Test'. Why do you think it is given this name?
3. **(a)** How does Lear react when Cordelia refuses to flatter him?
   (b) How does he punish Cordelia?
4. How does Lear punish Kent for questioning his authority?
5. Describe King Lear's personality. Quote from the scene to support your ideas.
6. What is your view of Goneril and Regan? Refer to the extract in your answer.
7. Which of the following words best describes Cordelia's behaviour: foolish, honest or stubborn? Explain your view by referring to the text.
8. Lear acts with great fury in this scene. Find two lines that display his anger.
9. In your own words, rewrite the following lines spoken by Kent:
   (a) KENT: Thy youngest daughter does not love thee least;

   　　　　　Nor are those empty-hearted whose low sound

   　　　　　Reverbs no hollowness.

   (b) KENT: My life I never held but as a pawn

   　　　　　To wage against thy enemies; nor fear to lose it,

   　　　　　Thy safety being the motive.

   (c) KENT: Fare thee well, king: sith thus thou wilt appear,

   　　　　　Freedom lives hence, and banishment is here.
10. Which of the characters from this scene would you like to play in a school production? Refer to the scene in your answer.

Imagine you are Cordelia. Write a letter to your father the day after this scene takes place. You may wish to make peace with him, express your anger or take back what was said.

Looking at Drama: Conflict

Drama is rooted in conflict. If characters' lives were easy and they never met any challenges, there would be no play. For the drama to be a success, audiences need to see characters in disagreement, at odds with their world or troubled within themselves – this is dramatic conflict.

In this scene from *King Lear*, there is conflict between many of the characters:

❏ **Lear** and **Cordelia:** Lear wants Cordelia to flatter him but she feels that her love for her father is enough. She doesn't want to compete with her sisters for his affection.

❏ **Lear** and **Kent:** Kent is a loyal subject but he criticises Lear's behaviour. This enrages King Lear and results in Kent being banished.

❏ And, to a lesser degree: **Goneril** and **Regan:** The sisters try to outdo each other in their false flattery of their father. This is to secure a larger share of his lands.

It is this type of tension that fascinates the audience and makes for good drama.

From *Hamlet*, Act 3, Scene 1
by William Shakespeare

Introduction

This play tells the story of Prince Hamlet of Denmark. Hamlet's father is recently deceased and Hamlet is disgusted when his mother marries his uncle, Claudius. The ghost of Hamlet's father then reveals that he was murdered by Claudius, his own brother. Hamlet immediately swears to revenge his father by murdering his uncle but he agonises over this act throughout the play.

This extract is one of the most famous speeches in all of Shakespeare's work. It displays the troubled mind of the play's central character as he reflects on the nature of life and expresses his own self-disgust.

HAMLET: To be, or not to be: that is the question:
Whether 'tis nobler in the mind to suffer
The slings and arrows of outrageous fortune[1],
Or to take arms against a sea of troubles,
And by opposing end them? To die: to sleep;
No more; and by a sleep to say we end
The heart-ache and the thousand natural shocks
That flesh is heir to[2], 'tis a consummation[3]
Devoutly to be wish'd. To die, to sleep;
To sleep: perchance[4] to dream: ay, there's the rub[5];
For in that sleep of death what dreams may come
When we have shuffled off[6] this mortal coil[7],
Must give us pause: there's the respect
That makes calamity[8] of so long life;
For who would bear the whips and scorns of time,
The oppressor's wrong, the proud man's contumely[9],
The pangs of disprized[10] love, the law's delay,
The insolence of office and the spurns
That patient merit of the unworthy takes,
When he himself might his quietus[11] make
With a bare bodkin?[12] who would fardels[13] bear,
To grunt and sweat under a weary life,
But that the dread of something after death,
The undiscover'd country[14] from whose bourn
No traveller returns, puzzles the will
And makes us rather bear those ills we have
Than fly to others that we know not of?
Thus conscience does make cowards of us all;
And thus the native hue of resolution[15]
Is sicklied o'er with the pale cast of thought,
And enterprises of great pith[16] and moment
With this regard their currents turn awry[17],
And lose the name of action.

[1] outrageous fortune: bad luck
[2] shocks / That flesh is heir to: the pain our bodies experience
[3] consummation: end; death
[4] perchance: perhaps
[5] rub: problem
[6] shuffled off: gotten rid of
[7] mortal coil: troublesome life
[8] calamity: disaster
[9] contumely: taunts
[10] disprized: despised
[11] quietus: final settlement
[12] bodkin: dagger
[13] fardels: burdens
[14] i.e., the afterlife
[15] the native hue of resolution: the natural colour of decisiveness
[16] great pith: great importance; great depth
[17] turn awry: are misdirected; go wrong

Questions
Exploring *Hamlet*, Act 3, Scene 1

1. **(a)** The pictograms below each represent a phrase from the extract. Write down the correct phrase for each pictogram.
   (b) What do you think each phrase means?

A

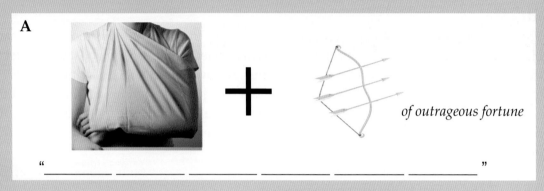

of outrageous fortune

" _____ _____ _____ _____ _____ _____ "

B

take ... *against a* ... *of troubles*

" _____ _____ _____ _____ _____ _____ _____ "

C

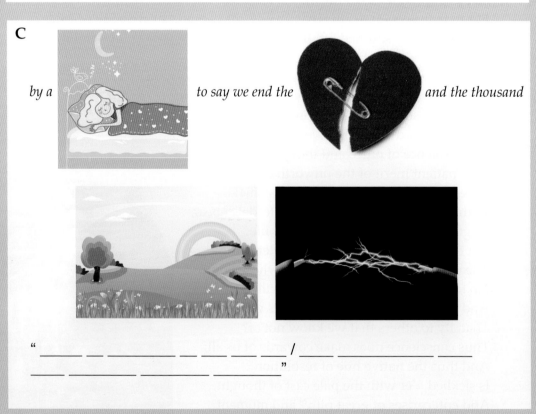

by a ... *to say we end the* ... *and the thousand*

" _____ __ _____ __ ___ ___/ ____ _____ _____
_____ _____ _____ _____ "

Exploring *Hamlet*, Act 3, Scene 1

2. Describe Hamlet's mood as he speaks in this scene. Refer to the extract in your answer.
3. What do you think Hamlet means in each of the following lines:
   (a) 'ay, there's the rub; / For in that sleep of death what dreams may come / When we have shuffled off this mortal coil'
   (b) 'the dread of something after death, / The undiscover'd country from whose bourn / No traveller returns, puzzles the will / And makes us rather bear those ills we have / Than fly to others that we know not of'
   (c) 'the native hue of resolution / Is sicklied o'er with the pale cast of thought'
4. How would you direct this scene? What directions would you give to the actor? How would you stage the scene? You may wish to refer to lighting, music, sound effects, props etc.

Writers' Workshop

Translate the extract into modern English. You may wish to use sayings and expressions from your local area.

Looking at Drama: Soliloquy

A soliloquy is a dramatic speech in which a character reveals his/her innermost thoughts to the audience. It is when a character thinks aloud on stage. Sometimes what a character says in soliloquy can be at odds with their behaviour around other characters. This is because a soliloquy is an intimate, personal moment that is only shared with the audience.

Soliloquies allow the audience insight into a character's motivations and feelings. The soliloquy allows the audience to understand a character's plans, ambition, motivation, confusion or despair. It reveals the heart of the character.

In Hamlet's soliloquy above, the audience learns how troubled his mind is. It is only when Hamlet's most private thoughts are said on stage that we can truly appreciate the depth of his despair and understand the bleakness of his view.

From *Macbeth,* Act 2, Scene 2
by William Shakespeare

Introduction

Macbeth explores the destructive nature of ambition and the suffering that comes with guilt. At the start of this dark play, Macbeth is given a prophecy by three witches that he will be king. Macbeth and his wife, Lady Macbeth, decide to murder King Duncan so that Macbeth can take the crown. They plan to frame the king's attendants for the crime. The scene below takes place just after Macbeth has committed the murder.

LADY MACBETH: That[1] which hath made them drunk hath made me bold;
    What hath quench'd them hath given me fire.
    Hark! Peace!
    It was the owl that shriek'd, the fatal bellman[2],
    Which gives the stern'st[3] good-night. He is about it:
    The doors are open; and the surfeited grooms[4]
    Do mock their charge with snores: I have drugg'd their possets[5],
    That death and nature do contend about them,
    Whether they live or die.

MACBETH: [*Within*] Who's there? what, ho!

LADY MACBETH: Alack, I am afraid they have awaked,
    And 'tis not done. The attempt and not the deed
    Confounds us. Hark! I laid their daggers ready;
    He could not miss 'em. Had he[6] not resembled
    My father as he slept, I had done't.
    [*Enter* MACBETH]
    My husband!

MACBETH: I have done the deed. Didst thou not hear a noise?

LADY MACBETH: I heard the owl scream and the crickets cry.
    Did not you speak?

MACBETH: When?

LADY MACBETH: Now.

MACBETH: As I descended?

LADY MACBETH: Ay.

MACBETH: Hark!
    Who lies i' the second chamber?

[1] i.e. wine
[2] bellman: the man who rang the bell at a funeral or execution
[3] stern'st: most stern; harshest
[4] surfeited grooms: drunk attendants
[5] possets: drinks
[6] i.e. King Duncan

LADY MACBETH: Donalbain[7].

MACBETH: This is a sorry sight.
[*Looking on his hands*]

LADY MACBETH: A foolish thought, to say a sorry sight.

MACBETH: There's one did laugh in's sleep, and one cried
'Murder!'
That they did wake each other: I stood and heard them:
But they did say their prayers, and address'd them
Again to sleep.

LADY MACBETH: There are two lodged together.

MACBETH: One cried 'God bless us!' and 'Amen' the other;
As they had seen me with these hangman's hands.
Listening their fear, I could not say 'Amen,'
When they did say 'God bless us!'

LADY MACBETH: Consider it not so deeply.

MACBETH: But wherefore could not I pronounce 'Amen'?
I had most need of blessing, and 'Amen'
Stuck in my throat.

LADY MACBETH: These deeds must not be thought
After these ways; so, it will make us mad.

MACBETH: Methought[8] I heard a voice cry 'Sleep no more!
Macbeth does murder sleep', the innocent sleep,
Sleep that knits up the ravell'd sleeve of care,
The death of each day's life, sore labour's bath,
Balm of hurt minds, great nature's second course,
Chief nourisher in life's feast,–[9]

LADY MACBETH: What do you mean?

MACBETH: Still it cried 'Sleep no more!' to all the house:
'Glamis[10] hath murder'd sleep, and therefore Cawdor[11]
Shall sleep no more; Macbeth shall sleep no more.'

LADY MACBETH: Who was it that thus cried? Why, worthy thane[12],
You do unbend your noble strength, to think
So brainsickly[13] of things. Go get some water,
And wash this filthy witness[14] from your hand.

[7] Donalbain: King Duncan's son

[8] Methought: I thought
[9] Sleep … feast: Sleep concludes the day and heals the pain experienced in life.

[10] Glamis: Macbeth is the Earl of Glamis
[11] Cawdor: Macbeth was made Earl of Cawdor after Duncan rewarded his bravery in battle
[12] thane: earl; noble lord
[13] brainsickly: madly; feverishly
[14] witness: evidence

Why did you bring these daggers from the place?
They must lie there: go carry them; and smear
The sleepy grooms with blood.

MACBETH: I'll go no more:
I am afraid to think what I have done;
Look on't again I dare not.

LADY MACBETH: Infirm of purpose![15]
Give me the daggers: the sleeping and the dead
Are but as pictures: 'tis the eye of childhood
That fears a painted devil. If he do bleed,
I'll gild[16] the faces of the grooms withal;
For it must seem their guilt.
[*Exit. Knocking within*]

[15] Infirm of purpose!: weak-willed!

[16] gild: paint

MACBETH: Whence is that knocking?
How is't with me, when every noise appals me?
What hands are here? ha! they pluck out mine eyes.
Will all great Neptune's[17] ocean wash this blood
Clean from my hand? No, this my hand will rather
The multitudinous[18] seas in incarnadine,[19]
Making the green one red.
[*Re-enter* LADY MACBETH]

[17] Neptune: God of the sea
[18] multitudinous: many.
[19] incarnadine: to dye red

LADY MACBETH: My hands are of your colour; but I shame
To wear a heart so white.
[*Knocking within*]
I hear a knocking
At the south entry: retire we to our chamber;
A little water clears us of this deed:
How easy is it, then! Your constancy
Hath left you unattended.
[*Knocking within*]
Hark! more knocking.
Get on your nightgown, lest occasion call us,
And show us to be watchers. Be not lost
So poorly in your thoughts.

MACBETH: To know my deed, 'twere best not know myself.
[*Knocking within*]
Wake Duncan with thy knocking! I would thou couldst!

Exploring *Macbeth*, Act 2, Scene 2

1. What reason does Lady Macbeth give for not murdering King Duncan herself?
2. **(a)** What did Macbeth claim he heard from the other room?
   (b) In your opinion, did Macbeth genuinely hear something or was it his imagination? Explain why you think so.
3. How do Macbeth and Lady Macbeth expect to get away with the murder?
4. **(a)** Sounds are referred to throughout this scene. Find three sounds that are mentioned by the characters or in the stage directions.
   (b) How do these sounds contribute to the mood of the scene?
5. At the beginning of the extract many of the lines are only one word long. How do these short, choppy lines add to the mood of the scene?
6. Rewrite the following lines from the play in your own words:
   (a) LADY MACBETH: These deeds must not be thought / After these ways; so, it will make us mad.
   (b) MACBETH: Will all great Neptune's ocean wash this blood / Clean from my hand? No, this my hand will rather / The multitudinous seas in incarnadine
   (c) LADY MACBETH: My hands are of your colour; but I shame / To wear a heart so white.
7. At the end of the scene Macbeth says, 'Wake Duncan with thy knocking! I would thou couldst!' How do you think Macbeth feels about the murder he has just committed?
8. Which character do you feel is stronger, Macbeth or Lady Macbeth? Give reasons for your answer.
9. Imagine you are producing a film version of this play. Which two actors would you cast in the roles of Macbeth and Lady Macbeth? Refer to the extract in your answer.
10. The murder itself takes place offstage. Why do you think Shakespeare chose to stage the scene this way?
11. How would you direct this scene? You may wish to comment on the lighting, sound effects, music, costumes, props, stage set etc. Refer to the extract throughout your answer.

Writers' Workshop

Imagine *Macbeth* is set in the modern world. Write a police report or newspaper article based on this scene.

Film Comparison

Roman Polanski's 1971 film version of *Macbeth* captures the darkness and horror of the original play. Watch his version of the scene and note the differences in his interpretation.

Looking at Drama: Atmosphere

There are many elements on stage that contribute to the dramatic atmosphere: lighting, stage set, music, body language, imagery of the language and the characters' behaviour.

In this scene from *Macbeth*, Shakespeare creates a tense, spooky atmosphere through the use of sound. The repeated knocking and the references to the sounds of crickets and owls add an eerie quality to the scene. The tension is intensified by the many short lines at the start of the scene and the visual spectacle of the characters' blood-soaked hands.

From *Othello*, Act 4, Scene 2
by William Shakespeare (adapted)

Introduction

Othello is newly married to Desdemona; they are deeply in love. However, the relationship is threatened when Iago, a subordinate of Othello, suggests that Desdemona has been unfaithful. As the play progresses, Othello becomes increasingly suspicious and jealous. Iago falsely tells Othello that Desdemona is having an affair with Cassio. Othello is driven into a jealous rage. In this extract, Othello interrogates Desdemona's maid, Emilia. He then confronts Desdemona herself. The scene paves the way for Othello's horribly tragic ending.

[*A room in the castle. Enter* OTHELLO *and* EMILIA]

OTHELLO: You have seen nothing then?

EMILIA: Nor ever heard, nor ever did suspect.

OTHELLO: Yes, you have seen Cassio and she together.

EMILIA: But then I saw no harm, and then I heard
Each syllable that breath made up between them.

OTHELLO: What, did they never whisper?

EMILIA: Never, my lord.

OTHELLO: Nor send you out o' the way?

EMILIA: Never.

OTHELLO: To fetch her fan, her gloves, her mask, nor nothing?

EMILIA: Never, my lord.

OTHELLO: That's strange.

EMILIA: I durst[1], my lord, to wager she is honest,
Lay down my soul at stake[2]: if you think other,
Remove your thought; it doth abuse your bosom[3].
If any wretch have put this in your head,
Let heaven requite it with the serpent's curse![4]
For, if she be not honest, chaste, and true,
There's no man happy; the purest of their wives
Is foul as slander.

OTHELLO: Bid her come hither: go.
[*Exit* EMILIA]
She says enough; yet she's a simple bawd[5]
That cannot say as much. This is a subtle whore,
A closet lock and key of villainous secrets
And yet she'll kneel and pray; I have seen her do't.
[*Enter* DESDEMONA *with* EMILIA]

DESDEMONA: My lord, what is your will?

OTHELLO: Pray you, chuck[6], come hither.

DESDEMONA: What is your pleasure?

OTHELLO: Let me see your eyes;
Look in my face.

DESDEMONA: What horrible fancy's this?

[1] durst: dare
[2] Lay down my soul at stake: I bet my soul on it
[3] it doth abuse your bosom: if it troubles your heart
[4] serpent's curse: the devil (represented by a serpent in the Bible)

[5] bawd: a person who maintains a brothel

[6] chuck: my little chicken (a term of affection)

OTHELLO: [*To* EMILIA] Some of your function, mistress;
            Leave procreants alone and shut the door;[7]
            Cough, or cry 'hem,' if anybody come:
            Your mystery, your mystery: nay, dispatch.
            [*Exit* EMILIA]

DESDEMONA: Upon my knees, what doth your speech import?
            I understand a fury in your words.
            But not the words.

OTHELLO: Why, what art thou?

DESDEMONA: Your wife, my lord; your true
            And loyal wife.

OTHELLO: Come, swear it, damn thyself
            Lest, being like one of heaven, the devils themselves
            Should fear to seize thee: therefore be double damned:
            Swear thou art honest.

DESDEMONA: Heaven doth truly know it.

OTHELLO: Heaven truly knows that thou art false as hell.

DESDEMONA: To whom, my lord? With whom? How am I false?

OTHELLO: O Desdemona! Away! Away! Away!

DESDEMONA: Alas the heavy day! Why do you weep?
            Am I the motive of these tears, my lord?

OTHELLO: Had it pleased heaven
            To try me with affliction; had they rained
            All kinds of sores and shames on my bare head,
            Steeped me in poverty to the very lips,
            Given to captivity me and my utmost hopes,
            I should have found in some place of my soul
            A drop of patience: but, alas, to make me
            A fixed figure for the time of scorn
            To point his slow unmoving finger at![8]
            Yet could I bear that too; well, very well:
            But there, where I have garnered up my heart,
            Where either I must live, or bear no life;
            The fountain from the which my current runs,
            Or else dries up; to be discarded thence![9]
            Or keep it as a cistern for foul toads
            To knot and gender in![10] Turn thy complexion there,
            Patience, thou young and rose-lipped cherubin,–
            Ay, there, look grim as hell![11]

DESDEMONA: I hope my noble lord esteems me honest.

OTHELLO: O, ay; as summer flies are in the shambles[12],
            That quicken even with blowing.[13] O thou weed,
            Who art so lovely fair and smell'st so sweet,[14]
            That the sense aches at thee, would thou hadst
            ne'er been born!

DESDEMONA: Alas, what ignorant sin have I committed?

OTHELLO: Was this fair paper, this most goodly book,[15]
            Made to write 'whore' upon? What committed!

[7] Here Othello is implying that Emilia is the manager of a brothel

[8] Othello sees himself as a figure that people will scorn and mock

[9] The fountain…discarded hence: The source of my children (i.e., Desdemona) has rejected me and so I will have no descendants.

[10] Or keep…gender in!: My wife has become polluted, a place where foul things breed.

[11] Turn…hell!: Even the goddess of patience would turn pale to look at this.

[12] shambles: rotting meat

[13] That quicken even with blowing: That produces maggots every time the wind blows

[14] O thou weed…sweet: You're like a weed posing as a flower.

[15] goodly book: Desdemona's face

Committed! O thou public commoner!
I should make very forges of my cheeks,
That would to cinders burn up modesty,[16]
Did I but speak thy deeds. What committed!
Heaven stops the nose at it and the moon winks,
The bawdy wind that kisses all it meets
Is hushed within the hollow mine of earth,
And will not hear it. What committed!
Impudent strumpet!

DESDEMONA: By heaven, you do me wrong.

OTHELLO: Are you not a strumpet?

DESDEMONA: No, as I am a Christian!
If to preserve this vessel[17] for my lord
From any other foul unlawful touch
Be not to be a strumpet, I am none.

OTHELLO: What, not a whore?

DESDEMONA: No, as I shall be saved.

OTHELLO: Is't possible?

DESDEMONA: O, heaven forgive us!

OTHELLO: I cry you mercy, then:
I took you for that cunning whore of Venice
That married with Othello.
[*Raising his voice*]
You, mistress,
That have the office opposite to Saint Peter,[18]
And keep the gate of hell!
[*Re-enter* EMILIA]
You, you, ay, you!
We have done our course; there's money for your pains:
I pray you, turn the key and keep our counsel.
[*Exit* OTHELLO]

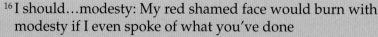

---

[16] I should…modesty: My red shamed face would burn with
modesty if I even spoke of what you've done

[17] vessel: body

[18] In the Bible, Jesus gave Peter 'the keys of the kingdom of heaven'.
In popular culture he is seen as permitting or denying entrance to
heaven.

Exploring *Othello*, Act 4, Scene 2

1. **(a)** What does Othello question Emilia about?
   (b) Do you think Othello believes her answers? Why/why not?
2. Do you feel that Emilia is a loyal servant to Desdemona? Explain your answer.
3. Describe the character of Othello as he is presented in this scene.
4. **(a)** Imagine you are the director of this play. Write down the instructions and advice you would give the actor who plays Othello for his performance in this scene.
   (b) Costumes can suggest aspects of a character's personality. Describe the costumes you would dress Othello and Desdemona in. Explain your choices.
5. Rewrite the following lines from the play in your own words:
   (a) DESDEMONA: I understand a fury in your words. / But not the words.
   (b) OTHELLO: Had it pleased heaven / To try me with affliction; had they rained / All kinds of sores and shames on my bare head... I should have found in some place of my soul / A drop of patience: but, alas, to make me / A fixed figure for the time of scorn / To point his slow unmoving finger at!
   (c) OTHELLO: I should make very forges of my cheeks, / That would to cinders burn up modesty, / Did I but speak thy deeds.
6. What do you think is going to happen at the end of this play?

Imagine you are one of the characters from this scene. Write a diary entry based on the events of this extract.

Tim Blake Nelson's film *O* is a modern remake of *Othello*. The film brings this tragic story to an American high school setting and provides an interesting comparison to the play.

Internal Conflict
We have already seen how conflict between characters makes for good drama. However, a character who is troubled, confused, uncertain or guilty also makes for fascinating drama. This type of conflict is called 'internal conflict'.

In the extract above, we see how Othello is deeply conflicted. On the one hand he loves his wife Desdemona and seems deeply jealous, but he also appears disgusted by her supposed infidelity and fears that she is making a mockery of him. The scene shows a man torn between two extreme emotions and it is this psychological conflict that is captivating for an audience.

Drama Project

Project: A Trip to the Theatre

Task
- **As a class**, organise and attend a dramatic performance in a local theatre.
- Individually, write a report on the trip.

Trip Guidelines
- Consult your local theatre listings for a play that will appeal to your age group.
- Contact the theatre and see if there is a discount for school groups.
- Consult with your English teacher so that teacher supervision can be arranged.
- Organise a method of payment.
- Make travel arrangements.
- Arrange a meeting time.

Theatre Etiquette
A trip to the theatre is not the same as going to the cinema. Theatres expect the audience to behave in a certain way; this is known as 'theatre etiquette'.
- Ensure mobile phones are turned off.
- Do not talk during the performance – it can be very distracting for the actors otherwise.
- Most theatres don't allow eating or drinking during the performance, so check beforehand.
- Make sure you are on time. Once the performance has started, audience members will not be admitted.

Report Guidelines
- Review the play. You may wish to comment on the play itself, the interpretation the director made, the actors, the stage, the use of music and sound, the lighting.
- It may be helpful to buy a programme while at the theatre. This will provide the actors' names and information about the production and the play itself.

Mechanics
Apostrophes

Apostrophes are used in two instances: to replace **missing letters** and to indicate **possession**.

Missing Letters

Some words are formed by joining two words together and replacing the omitted letters with an apostrophe. For example:

could + not = couldn't

In this example the apostrophe has taken the place of the missing *o*.

it + is = it's

Here, the apostrophe has replaced the missing *i*.

Possession

Apostrophes are also used to show possession. A misplaced apostrophe can radically change the meaning of the sentence. Look at the following example:

The cakes over there are my sister's. → The cakes belong to my sister.

The cakes over there are my sisters'. → The cakes belong to several of my sisters.

The cakes over there are my sisters. → The cakes *are* my sisters.

Putting the apostrophe in the wrong place here could leave this family fighting over the cakes – leaving it out may send the brother to a padded cell!

Singular Possession

When the noun is singular (one owner) add 's to indicate possession:

> *Brian's computer, the woman's child, the bird's beak.*

Plural Possession

For plural nouns ending in s, add an apostrophe after the s:

> *The ladies' meeting, the boys' school, the cats' meals, the witches' brooms*

If the plural form of the noun does not end in s, add 's:

> *The children's father, the men's wages, the women's club*

Names ending in s

For modern names ending in s, add 's:

> *James's bicycle, Mr Jones's house, Agnes's best friend*

For classical names ending in s, just add an apostrophe:

> *Socrates' pupil, Pythagoras' theorem*

Its / It's

It's means *it is*. The apostrophe has replaced the missing *i*.

Its indicates possession. For example: *The cat licked its fur.*

Double possession

When more than one person owns something, the last person's name is given the apostrophe. If both names are given apostrophes, this indicates separate objects.

Jack and Jill's hill	→	The hill of Jack and Jill
Noah and Barry's contracts	→	The shared contracts of Noah and Barry
Noah's and Barry's contracts	→	The separate contracts of Noah and Barry

Practising Apostrophes

1. Missing Letters – Use apostrophes to form new words from the following:

   (a) do + not =   _____

   (b) should + not =   _____

   (c) I + am =   _____

   (d) could + have =   _____

   (e) is + not =   _____

   (f) you + are =   _____

   (g) they + will =   _____

   (h) she + is =   _____

2. Possession – Rewrite the following passages adding apostrophes appropriately.

The childrens toys littered the floor. Douglas picked his way through the mess and flopped onto the couch. He heard the boys shouting outside. 'I dont want to deal with this now,' he thought, 'I just cant.' The boys shouts got louder and Douglass conscience forced him up from the couchs soft comfort. 'I couldnt even get a moments peace could I?' he thought to himself.

   'Whats going on out here?' he yelled as he swung open the backdoor. The suns bright rays blinded him momentarily but his eyes soon adjusted to the light. 'Where are you guys?' he shouted, sounding a little less angry as he couldnt see his boys anywhere. 'Lads? Michael? John? Are you out here?'

   Douglass ears picked up a whimpering from the bushes. He rushed to the sounds source. On the ground he found Michael with tears in his eyes; blood dripped from a cut on his leg. 'He pushed me Dad. John pushed me.'

   Douglass youngest son, John stood close by. Johns eyes shone with a fierce determination. 'Thats what you get when you dont share.'

   On the ground Michael and Johns go-kart lay smashed against the foot of tree. Two of its wheels were strewn on the grass. 'Thats what you get,' John repeated, 'when you dont share.' Douglas stared at his youngest son in disbelief.

3. Its / It's – Rewrite the following sentences using *its* or *it's*.

   (a) The dog dropped _____ bone.

   (b) _____ been too long since we last saw you.

   (c) Cuba is in the Caribbean; _____ capital is Havana.

   (d) '_____ just around the corner,' said the man, 'but _____ closed for renovations.'

   (e) The birdwatcher stared as the eagle gripped _____ prey in _____ claws. 'Looks like _____ lunchtime,' said the birdwatcher darkly.

6 Film:
The Most Beautiful Fraud in the World

> Cinema is the most beautiful fraud in the world
>
> – Jean Luc-Godard, film director

At last, the movie goers were finally settled and relaxed. However, seconds later, Larry would realize the error of sitting between spooked buffalo and the exit door.

Film

Film Production

Although films usually take only about two hours to watch, it may take months or even years to create a film. There are three stages involved in film-making: (a) Pre-Production (b) Production (c) Post-Production.

(a) Pre-Production – In the film industry, pre-production begins once a project has been given the 'green light'. This means that financing of the film has been secured. In the pre-production phase the director and the crew are hired, the script is refined, actors are cast and locations are scouted (found). At this stage a storyboard is often drawn up by the director. This looks somewhat like a comic book. It shows how each scene will be shot and where each actor will be placed during each scene.

(b) Production – During this second phase, the film is shot. Directors often film a number of 'takes' or versions of scenes until they are happy with the actors' performances. Apparently, the director Stanley Kubrick often demanded hundreds of takes of individual scenes, much to the annoyance of some of his actors. While he was making *The Shining*, 1.3 million feet of film roll was used!

(c) Post-Production – In this final phase the film is edited. This means that the director and the post-production team select the best takes of each scene and put the film together. During this stage the soundtrack, sound effects and CGI (Computer Generated Imagery) are added.

The decisions of the editor and the director at this stage can sometimes cause controversy. While filming *American History X*, the director Tony Kaye's edit of the film was rejected by the studio. The lead actor, Edward Norton, then re-edited the film. As a result Kaye disassociated himself from the film and unsuccessfully tried to have his name removed from the credits. Despite these problems the film was very successful upon its release.

Film Genre

Tastes in films vary widely. Some people enjoy comedies, others prefer action films. These classifications are known as film genres. Film genre is a way of categorising films according to their plot, setting, characters, themes and style. Some of the most common film genre categories are: Drama, Comedy, Romance, Western, Science-Fiction, Horror, Action, Historical, Satire, Disaster, Teen, Rom-Com (Romantic Comedy), Thriller.

These classifications are often too simplistic. Many films are a blend of genres. For example, romcoms are a very popular genre but they can also be classified as comedy, romance or drama.

Exploring Film Genre

List at least five films in each of the following popular film genre categories:

(a) Rom-com
(b) Action
(c) Science-Fiction
(d) Western
(e) Teen
(f) Disaster
(g) Satire
(h) Thriller

Film Posters

Film posters are marketing tools that encourage the public to see a film. Film companies use posters and other types of advertisements to create a 'buzz' around a film.

When writing about film posters it is important to consider the following features:

▼ **Colour Scheme** – As with advertising, the visual impact of a poster often relies on the colour scheme used. Think about what the colour scheme suggests about the film. For example, the use of bright colours may attract the attention of a younger audience or may be fitting for a comedy.

▼ **Tagline** – Film studios often include a line that sums up the theme or plot of the film. For example, the poster for the film *Alien* used the tagline, In space no one can hear you scream. This suggested the terrifying nature of the film and also established the film's genre as science-fiction.

▼ **Key Words** – Some posters will include words such as Terrifying, Gripping, Laugh out loud or Tear jerker to entice potential viewers to see the film.

▼ **Images** – Film posters try to grab viewers' attention by using striking images. These may feature a scene from the film or emphasise the performance of a celebrity actor.

▼ **Target Audience** – Most mainstream films are aimed at a specific group or target audience. Film posters reflect this through the images and text used.

▼ **Release Date** – This explains when the film is due to be released.

▼ **Age Classification** – The Irish Film Classification Office (IFCO) classifies films according to their age suitability. For example, films rated 16 cannot be viewed by anybody under that age. Sometimes film studios limit the amount of violence, sexual content and profanity in a film in order to receive a classification for a younger audience.

A. SOME THING HAS FOUND US

CLOVERFIELD

01·18·08

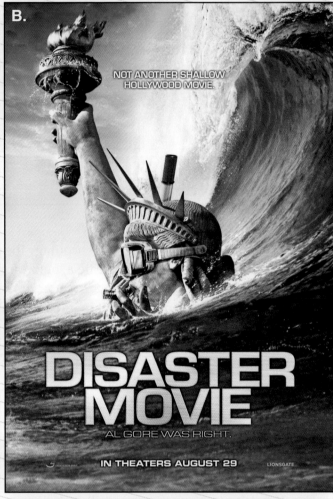

B. NOT ANOTHER SHALLOW HOLLYWOOD MOVIE.

DISASTER MOVIE

AL GORE WAS RIGHT.

IN THEATERS AUGUST 29   LIONSGATE

C. A NEW ROMANTIC COMEDY FROM THE MAKERS OF LOVE ACTUALLY AND BRIDGET JONES'S DIARY

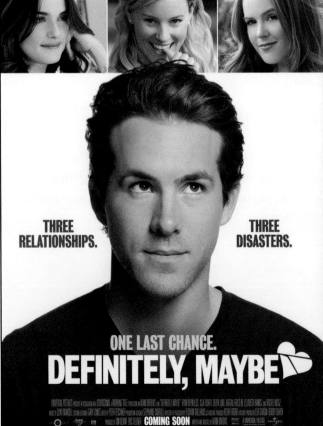

THREE RELATIONSHIPS.   THREE DISASTERS.

ONE LAST CHANCE.
DEFINITELY, MAYBE

COMING SOON

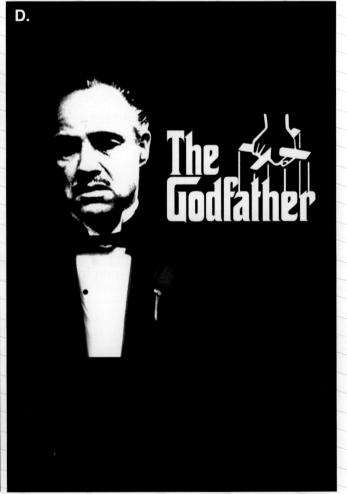

D. The Godfather

Questions

Exploring Film Posters

1. In which genre categories would you place the films advertised in posters A, B and C?
2. What is suggested by the image of the puppeteer's hand in poster D?
3. Poster A and poster B both contain a similar central image. In what way do the posters differ in their treatment of this image?
4. Which of the four posters do you feel makes the greatest visual impact? Explain your answer by referring to the posters.
5. In the case of each poster, state the target audience and how the poster appeals to its target group. Consider the images, colour scheme, tagline etc.
6. From looking at the posters, which film would you most like to see? Explain your answer by referring to the posters (not the films themselves).

Visual Response

Create a film poster for a movie of your choice. Find suitable images, choose a colour scheme and write a tagline for your poster. Keep in mind who your target audience is.

Film Reviews

Film posters and marketing campaigns inevitably present films in a positive light as they are created by the film studios. Film critics provide a balance to this as they attempt to assess a film fairly. Film reviews are published in newspapers, magazines and online and have great influence over the success or failure of a film at the box office.

When writing your own film reviews you should consider the following:
  ◆ The plot: was it enjoyable, interesting, believable etc? What was the film about?
  ◆ The actors' performances: who stood out? Who was disappointing?
  ◆ The film's soundtrack (or score): did it add or detract from the experience?
    The directing
  ◆ The film's target audience
  ◆ A star rating

The following is a review of *Hanna* starring Irish actress Saoirse Ronan.

Let's Hear it for the Girl

Hanna, a fairy-tale version of *Jason Bourne*, will touch your heart – and kick your ass, says Cosmo Landesman.

Once upon a time in films starring preteens, the lovable child would only break daddy's heart; nowadays, they'd slit his throat. Yes, killer kids are all the rage. Remember Mindy, that lovable bundle of blades and butchery from *Kick-Ass*? And let's not forget that blood-sucking sweetie Abby, from *Let Me In* – both played by Chloe Moretz. Now comes the latest and greatest of these girl assassins: Hanna (Saoirse Ronan), the 16-year-old heroine of the director Joe Wright's fairytale thriller.

A pale, albino-like blonde with riot-grrrl hair and blue eyes, Hanna lives in a snowy forest in Finland with her dad, Erik (Eric Bana), who teaches her the essential skills of survival: shooting, hunting, martial arts, throat-slitting and neck-breaking. Life with dad is like living with a drill sergeant at boot camp. 'Always think on your feet, even when you're asleep,' he tells his daughter.

In a film rooted in realism, we would regard Erik as a psychopath engaged in the emotional and psychological abuse of his daughter. He never gives her a hug or even a kind word. But this is a fairytale world where moral laws are suspended. Besides, Hanna's life is threatened by the film's very own wicked witch of the west, Marissa Wiegler (Cate Blanchett), who was Erik's CIA handler back in the days when he did dark and dirty things for the agency. Now Hanna is ready to leave the forest and make her way in the world. First, though she has to kill Wiegler, says Dad – or Wiegler will kill her.

Written by Seth Lochhead and David Farr, Hanna is a terrific film: Jason Bourne meets the Brothers Grimm. It's a thriller for people – like me – who are usually bored by thrillers. For, unlike so many so-called films of this name, it's actually thrilling, without resorting to car chases, shoot-outs, explosions and fast and furious editing. It's a chase film, with lots of running and fighting, and a pounding Chemical Brothers soundtrack – yet at the same time it manages to be still and quiet.

That's because Wright never loses sight of the human side of the story. He captures the essential childlike sweetness of Hanna without going soppy and sentimental. Here is a young girl who was never allowed to be a young girl; she wants to know what music sounds like and what it means to have a friend. Hanna is the open-hearted innocent, the noble savage, who looks at the modern world with a mix of wonder and bafflement. And she is as mystified as to who she really is as Jason Bourne. This, along with her hunger for life, gives her character a poignancy that you wouldn't expect to find in a fairytale figure.

Fairytales are allegories that teach children about the big bad world beyond their front door. The one weakness of the film is that it doesn't have anything to say to its adult audience about childhood or being a parent.

Every fairytale needs its baddies, and the best of the bunch are the camp, dyed-blond Isaacs (Tom Hollander) and his two skinhead henchmen, who exude menace like cheap aftershave. By contrast, Blanchett's performance, with its reliance on heavy make-up, a Texan accent and perfect hair, is overegged.

Yet the film belongs to Ronan. She has that rare gift of making the unbelievable seem real. She has brought to life a memorable character who can touch your heart – as well as kick your ass.

Hanna

15A, 111 mins

☆☆☆☆

- The Sunday Times, 8 May 2011 (adapted)

Questions

Exploring *Let's Hear it for the Girl*

1. Who is the director of *Hanna*?
2. Name two films Cosmo Landesman compares *Hanna* to in this review.
3. Describe the basic plot of the film as revealed by Landesman.
4. Basing your answer on this review, under which film genre would you classify *Hanna*? Explain your answer by referring to the text.
5. According to Landesman, who will this film appeal to?
6. **(a)** What is the reviewer's opinion of Saoirse Ronan's performance in the film?
   (b) What is his view of Cate Blanchett's performance?
7. Aside from some of the performances, what flaw does Landesman see in the film?
8. Would this review encourage or discourage you from seeing the film? Why/why not?

Writers' Workshop

Write a review of a film of your choice. You may wish to comment on the film's plot, characters, acting performances and soundtrack. Remember to give your film a star rating.

Wordsearch

Find the following 16 words hidden in this wordsearch:

ACTOR
AUDIENCE
CINEMA
COMEDY
DIRECTOR
FILM
GENRE
IMAGES
PLOT
PRODUCER
PRODUCTION
REVIEW
SCREEN
SOUNDTRACK
TAGLINE
WESTERN

P	I	H	V	A	N	L	A	Y	V	X	L	F	W	P
Y	S	V	V	P	O	H	D	V	D	K	Z	E	X	R
H	G	S	T	X	I	T	E	I	C	E	I	M	V	O
W	R	E	E	Y	T	E	G	A	R	V	M	I	E	D
S	D	G	R	N	C	S	R	A	E	E	J	O	P	U
F	L	A	Z	L	U	T	C	R	N	F	C	X	C	C
H	O	M	T	R	D	T	W	J	V	Z	T	T	O	E
X	A	I	X	N	O	N	R	E	T	S	E	W	O	R
Q	M	I	U	R	R	G	B	D	S	U	S	T	G	R
J	J	O	X	K	P	O	F	G	A	C	A	U	E	K
I	S	A	U	D	I	E	N	C	E	G	R	S	N	B
V	P	U	Q	T	W	N	E	G	L	I	L	E	R	O
M	L	I	F	T	O	Q	C	I	N	E	M	A	E	A
N	E	A	L	A	P	L	N	B	P	Z	T	R	Q	N
N	Q	C	R	R	D	E	P	Z	M	Y	Z	Z	B	Q

Cinematography

Cinematography is the art and technique of using a camera in film-making. It deals with all the visual elements of film, including the camera work, the lighting and the colouring of the film. It is usually the director and the cinematographer who plan how a camera will be used. Film-makers think about how a shot is framed, the distance of the camera and the camera angle. They also have to consider using lenses to colour the film and how to light the film. Theses decisions affect how the story is told. For example, if a camera is held low it may make a character seem more imposing; a high-angled shot will have the opposite effect.

Camera Shots

Extreme Long Shot – Extreme long shots require the camera to be placed very far away from the object that is being filmed. This type of shot is often used to establish the setting of the story. It may provide a bird's-eye view of a city or it may display the landscape from a distance.

Long Shot – A long shot shows a character visible from head to toe. It also provides information about the background.

Medium Shot – Medium shots present the viewer with an image of characters from the waist up. It is more intimate than the long shot but still displays the setting.

Close-Up – Directors may want to stress a character's emotions or add a sense of intensity. This can be achieved by zooming in on a character's face in a close-up. This encourages the audience to think about a character's emotional or psychological state.

Extreme Close-Up – An extreme close-up adds even greater intensity to the screen. A director may choose to intensely focus on a part of a character's face. This is often done during a key moment in a film.

Camera Angles

Straight-On – This is the most common camera angle. It is focused at eye-level.

High-Angle – Directors may wish to make a character look smaller or more vulnerable. This can be achieved by placing the camera above the character's head so the viewer feels that they are looking down on the subject.

Low-Angle – If a director wants to give the impression that a character is powerful, a low-angle shot may be used. This makes the viewer feel as if the character is towering above them.

Canted – To create a distorted feeling the camera can be tilted (or canted) to one side.

Camera Movement

Pan – In this movement the camera scans across the scene from one side to another.

Tilt – The camera can tilt up or down. This is like a panning shot except the camera moves up or down rather than from side-to-side.

Tracking Shot (or Dolly Shot) – This is when the camera is mounted on a wheeled base known as a camera dolly. The dolly then moves along a small set or rails as the camera is filming. This camera movement is an excellent way of following a character as they move across the screen.

Boom Shot – A boom shot allows the director to give the viewers an aerial view. To achieve this a crane is used to move a camera up or down above the scene.

Lighting and Colour

How a film-maker chooses to light the film is very important. Lighting can add atmosphere to a scene. For example a character who is partly shadowed may seem more mysterious or sinister.

Directors can change the colour of an image by using lenses and filters on the cameras. Colour can help to influence the emotions of the audience and communicate something about the characters and the setting. For example a blue tint may add a coldness to the scene, yellow may add more positive emotions.

The three film stills above show how lighting and colour can help a director to tell a story and add emotion to a scene.

Crossword

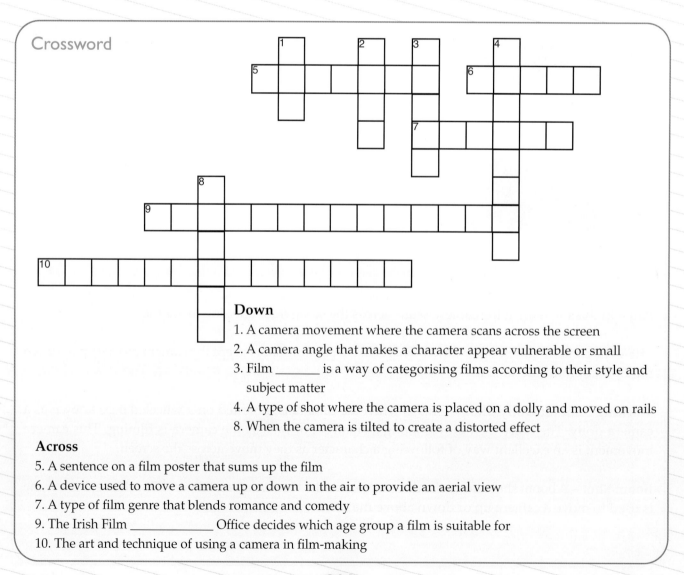

Down

1. A camera movement where the camera scans across the screen
2. A camera angle that makes a character appear vulnerable or small
3. Film _____ is a way of categorising films according to their style and subject matter
4. A type of shot where the camera is placed on a dolly and moved on rails
8. When the camera is tilted to create a distorted effect

Across

5. A sentence on a film poster that sums up the film
6. A device used to move a camera up or down in the air to provide an aerial view
7. A type of film genre that blends romance and comedy
9. The Irish Film _____ Office decides which age group a film is suitable for
10. The art and technique of using a camera in film-making

Project
Film Report

Task

❂ Write a report on a film you have studied independently.

Project Guidelines
Your report should contain all of the following information:

❂ **Cinematography** – Write about the cinematography used in the film. Think about the camera angles, camera movement, lighting and colour.

❂ **Soundtrack** – Write about the film's soundtrack. Was music used effectively in the film? Who wrote the music? Do you feel the soundtrack added to or detracted from your enjoyment of the film?

❂ **A character study** – Choose one character from the film that you found interesting. Write about the character's personality, outlook on life, attitude, ability to deal with problems and the degree of success they achieve in the story.

❂ **Key moments** – Choose two important episodes or moments from the film. For each key moment, describe what happened and explain why you felt this scene was important. An episode may be important because it is a turning point in the plot, reveals something about the characters, contributes to your understanding of the theme or is exciting or entertaining.

❂ **Theme** – Write about the theme of your film. Think about the message the author is trying to convey or the issue that is being explored.

❂ **Cultural Context/Social Setting** – Describe the world of the film. Is it a place where characters enjoy freedom or are there obstacles in their way? What are the values of the society in the film? Is the world portrayed in a positive or negative light? You may want to consider some of the following ideas about society: gender roles, religion, wealth/poverty, power, freedom, race.

❂ **Film Review** – Imagine you work for a youth magazine. Write a review of the film to be published in next month's edition of the magazine.

Mechanics

Revision of Punctuation and Capital Letters

The following extract is taken from *The Great Gatsby* by F. Scott Fitzgerald. The passage depicts an industrial dumping ground and the lives of an impoverished community. Fitzgerald then describes a billboard advertising an opticians: Dr T.J. Eckleburg. The eyes of the billboard seem to ominously survey the whole scene.

The passage is reproduced here without punctuation or capital letters. Rewrite it correctly.

about half way between west egg* and new york the motor road hastily joins the railroad and runs beside it for a quarter of a mile so as to shrink away from a certain desolate area of land this is a valley of ashes – a fantastic farm where ashes grow like wheat into ridges and hills and grotesque gardens where ashes take the forms of houses and chimneys and rising smoke and finally with a transcendent effort of men who move dimly and already crumbling through the powdery air occasionally a line of gray cars crawls along an invisible track gives out a ghastly creak and comes to rest and immediately the ash-gray men swarm up with leaden spades and stir up an impenetrable cloud which screens their obscure operations from your sight

but above the gray land and the spasms of bleak dust which drift endlessly over it you perceive after a moment the eyes of doctor tj eckleburg the eyes of doctor tj eckleburg are blue and gigantic – their irises are one yard high they look out of no face but instead from a pair of enormous yellow spectacles which pass over a nonexistent nose evidently some wild wag of an oculist set them there to fatten his practice in the borough of queens and then sank down himself into eternal blindness or forgot them and moved away but his eyes dimmed a little by many paintless days under sun and rain brood on over the solemn dumping ground

* West Egg is a fictional village in Long Island, New York.